THE COMPLETE SKI CROSS-COUNTRY

OTHER BOOKS BY MICHAEL BRADY

Nordic Touring and Cross-Country Skiing
Ski Nordique
Waxing for Cross-Country Skiing
Cross-Country Ski Gear
Citizen Racer

THE COMPLETE
SKI CROSS-COUNTRY:
The New Handbook
for Touring and Racing

by Michael Brady

The Dial Press
New York

Published by
The Dial Press
1 Dag Hammarskjold Plaza
New York, New York 10017
Manufactured in the United States of America
First printing
Book design by Margaret M. Wagner

Library of Congress Cataloging in Publication Data
Brady, M. Michael.
The complete ski cross country.
Bibliography: p. 262
Includes index.
1. Cross-country skiing. I. Title.
GV855.3.B7 1982   796.93   81-15131
ISBN 0-385-27450-5   AACR2
ISBN 0-385-27677-X (pbk.)

In memory of
CHARLES BREGY BOWDEN,
who personally shared
his joy of skiing
with so many

Contents

The first edition of this book was published in 1974. It was a translated, revised, and amended version of the Norwegian book *Langrennsboka* by Lorns Skjemstad and myself.

In the years after the books appeared, cross-country skiing in North America grew and changed. Fiberglass cross-country skis were mass-produced and skillfully marketed by major central-European ski makers. Factories were set up in Canada to meet the North American equipment demand, one of the largest in the world. A U.S. firm specializing in waxless cross-country skis grew to become a market leader, challenging the giants of the business. Magazines devoted to the sport were started. Cross-country ski racers from newer skiing countries broke the longtime Scandinavian dominance of the sport; Bill Koch won a silver medal in the 1976 Olympic 30-km race, the first for an American. Television brought cross-country skiing to a wider audience than ever. The 1980 Winter Olympics, held in Lake Placid, New York, brought top-level Nordic skiing to North America. Many urban and some rural Americans became ski commuters, and auto roof racks full of cross-country skis became common on major highways from coast to coast. Major cross-country ski centers were established throughout the continent, and citizens' racing, the on-snow equivalent of the marathons of running, grew to be a major activity. In some areas of the USA and in Canada, annual sales of cross-country skis frequently outstripped those of Alpine skis. Cross-country skiing had become part of the North American wintertime scene.

So when the time came to revise the books, it was clear that the information needs of Scandinavians and Americans had diverged. Therefore, Lorns Skjemstad, a Norwegian, assumed complete responsibility for the Norwegian book, and I, an American, assumed complete responsibility for this book. Skjemstad keyed his new book to the needs of the Norwegian skier in the 1980s: *Nye Langrennsboka* appeared under his name alone. Likewise, this is a totally new book, keyed to the needs of skiers here.

No such book can be the product of a single, unassisted hand, nor can a single person command all that is the sport today. So don't look for me in the photos of this book. Most coaches and instructors have some limitation, and one of mine is that my body proportions lend themselves poorly to photography. Therefore, persons more photogenic in skiing grace the pages of this book. One is Marianne Hadler, my wife, who also was my chief critic and supporter. Another is Otto Wiersholm, skilled in racing and blessed with an understanding of the technique of the sport. Finally, Dudley Rood's mastery of downhill technique added a finesse seldom seen on cross-country skis. Behind the camera for most of the photos was Fletcher Manley, a photographer whose cinema skills and special high-speed photo equipment are responsible for the precise technique-photo sequences. Ole Mosesen contributed time and enthusiasm for the effective staging of the on-flat and uphill technique photography done at the cross-country center he heads in Warren, Vermont. Expedition skier Ned Gillette's unique photos and frequent constructive comments have greatly contributed to the overall approach of the book.

Last but not least, I gratefully acknowledge the aid and unfailing interest of Dial Press editor Nancy van Itallie, who skillfully shepherded the book from its initial conception to final publication.

MICHAEL BRADY

THE COMPLETE SKI CROSS-COUNTRY

1
CROSS-COUNTRY TODAY
Old Yet New

Lapp on skis, woodcut from *The History of Lapland* by Johan Scheffer, published in 1674.

Cross-country can be solitude on a mountain plateau. *Michael Brady*

Skiing, all skiing, evolved from the utilitarian necessity of wintertime travel. The first skier left no record. Nobody knows how old skiing was when a pictograph of a skier was hewn on a rock wall in arctic Norway some 4,500 years ago. The work is unsigned. And nobody knows how many skis were made or how many people skied before the oldest known pair were discarded in a bog some 2,500 years ago. Skiing was already more than 4,000 years old when in 1674 Johan Scheffer related his travels among the Lapps of the north of Europe, describing their cross-country skiing in Latin and woodcuts like the one shown here.

Cross-country skiing on this continent is an anachronism, the oldest yet newest and now fastest-growing winter sport.

Perhaps the renaissance of the sport can be attributed to the widespread reawakening of interest in activity, in the joy of the harmonious union of mind and body—*mens sana in corpore sano* (a sound mind in a sound body), as the ancient saying goes.

The beauty of cross-country skiing is that it is not one activity, but many. There's something in it for everyone. It can be as totally private as a lone skier on a mountain plateau, or as sociable as a citizens' race where thousands sometimes ski together. It can be done in terrain as benign as a snow-covered city park or golf course, or it can be done in the heart of the most rugged mountain ranges of the world. It can be done in prepared, manicured tracks, made for rhythm and

Cross-country can also be sociable: start of the American Birkebeiner citizens' race. *Telemark*

speed, or in untracked snows wherever they may lie. It can be as flashy or as rustic as suits individual skier preference. It knows no limits of age, sex, income, or physical ability. It's what you make it.

There is only one thing truly difficult about cross-country skiing, and that is its name. It really should be just *skiing;* the term *cross-country* is only an accident of very recent history. Witness the description of the sport of skiing in the thirteenth edition of the *Encyclopaedia Britannica,* published in 1926:

SKI (pronounced "skee," Icel. *scidh,* snow-shoe, properly "piece of wood"), the wooden snowshoe on which the inhabitants of Scandinavia and neighbouring countries travel over the snow. Implements for this purpose were used by many nations of antiquity. . . . On level ground the skis are allowed to glide over the snow without being lifted from it, the heels being raised while the toes remain fast to the skis. At this gait very long steps can be taken. Climbing hills one must walk zigzag, or even directly sideways step by step. Gentle slopes can be ascended straight ahead by planting the skis obliquely. Downhill the skis become a sledge upon which great velocity is attained. . . . Skiing as a sport began about 1860 in the Norwegian district of Telemark and rapidly spread over all the Scandinavian peninsula. . . . The sport has been introduced into other countries where the winter is severe, and has become very popular in Switzerland and the United States, especially in Minnesota and the Rocky Mountain country.

It's where you find it, sometimes even in town.
Michael Brady

A SPORT OF MANY SPEEDS

You can ski as fast or as slowly as you wish when cross-country skiing. Discounting short bursts of speed, such as in racing sprints or downhills, even skilled skiers ski at varying speeds, depending on where and for what purpose they ski. For sustained skiing, the fastest cross-country skier on record is Bill Koch, an American. Early in the morning of March 26, 1981, Koch set out to ski ten laps on a carefully measured 5 km loop course on Marlborough Pond, near Putney, Vermont. Timed and checked by U.S. Ski Association officials, his goal was to ski 50 km in less than two hours. He succeeded by thirteen seconds. His time for the distance cannot be directly compared to the 28–30 min. slower best times for conventional 50 km races run on courses that have uphills and downhills, in addition to flats. But nonetheless, he set the unofficial world's cross-country skiing speed record of slightly over 25 km per hour, or 15.5 mph. The record for slow skiing by a recognized expert skier goes to expedition skier Ned Gillette. In the spring of 1977 Gillette headed across the pack ice between Ellesmere Island and Greenland towing a 220-pound sled, and in a full nine-hour day of effort, covered less than two miles. That's about

two tenths of a mile per hour; babies crawl faster. In more normal recreational and competitive cross-country skiing, speeds range from considerably more than Gillette's minimum record to less than Koch's maximum record. Cross-country race distances and distances along trails in many cross-country areas are stated in kilometers, so the speeds below are given in both kilometers and miles per hour.

SPEED IN KM/H	SPEED IN MPH	DONE BY/IN	EQUIVALENT TO
18–21	11–13	Top racers	fast running
13–16	8–10	Good racing, training	speedy run
10–12	6–7.5	Expert skiers	running
7–9	4.5–5	Skilled skiers	jogging
5–6.5	3–4	Ski walking, some glide	hike, walk
3–4.5	2–3	Slow skiing	stroll
2 or less	1.5 or less	Plod on skis	ambling

Cross-country has been around for a while, as this 1979 reenactment of 1870 skiing, using gear and clothing of that time, shows. *Jan Greve*

With some updating, that's a fair description of cross-country skiing, as it's now known.

Skiing might have remained the way it was described in that *Encyclopaedia Britannica* entry, were it not for two things that happened in the decade after it was published. First, skiing as a leisure activity spread rapidly through the Alps of Europe, in Switzerland, Austria, Italy, France, and Germany. Unlike the major mountain chains of North America, the Alps are relatively populated, with villages, towns, and even cities in the valleys below the peaks. As skiing caught on, it was seen, and then taken up by many who lived in the rugged Alpine terrain. The sport was to climb up, or sometimes take a train up, to a higher village, and whiz down. The appeal was a unidirectional thrill. Second, as more and more people took up the sport, devices were built to haul them uphill so they could pack more downhill runs into a day of skiing.

Lifts were also built in North America, as immigrants and returning tourists brought Alpine skiing from Europe. The sport evolved; more lifts and ski areas were built. The excitement of the downhill plunge on skis caught on, especially in the large cities of the Eastern part of the continent. Regular ski trains to the snow became part of the wintertime recreation scene by the late 1930s. Then, after World War II, the sport grew so rapidly that it eclipsed the parent sport of skiing. Its equipment was steadily refined for downhill skiing performance and ease—skis became broader, boots stiffer, and fixations between boot and ski more rigid. And because machines did the uphill work, lightness was no longer crucial, and gear became heavier. And somewhere along the line the description *Alpine* was

dropped: in the public consciousness the sport became just *skiing.* *

So when the original form of skiing reappeared, it was viewed as a totally different sport by the skiing community. By comparison the boots seemed too light, the bindings too flexible, and the skis too skinny for "skiing." Some of those notions persist: there are still Alpine skiers who believe that cross-country skis cannot be turned on downhills, and "skinny skis" is a frequent moniker for them.

Also, since the "new" sport differed from the "old," it needed a new name. Many were suggested and used.

Touring was one. But it ran afoul of *Alpine ski touring,* the sport of ascending peaks for the sake of a downhill run in places not served by lifts. *Langlauf* and *long run,* used mostly in racing, were also tried. Neither was completely correct. *Langlauf* is the German translation of the original Norwegian *langrenn,* meaning literally *long run.* In English this seemed a misnomer, so the name *cross-country* was borrowed from running to define a similar race on snow.

So that term, *cross-country,* came to denote all recreational and competitive activities in the sport; the racing variety is now burdened with the title *cross-country ski racing.* And *cross-country skiing* in general is classified as *Nordic skiing,* to differentiate it from *Alpine skiing.*

So Nordic and Alpine diverged, became different in purpose, practice, and popularity, switched names, and appeared then to be separate sports. As cross-country skiing enters the second decade of its

---

*It's just the opposite in Scandinavia, where the original meanings have been retained. If you want to look up the results of an Alpine slalom ski race in a Norwegian newspaper, you don't look under *ski,* because that's where you find the results of cross-country ski races. You look under *Alpin.*

Skiing is new to some. Here a Balti porter, from the village of Askole, Biafo Glacier, tries skis for the first time, with rubber walking shoes clamped into bindings. 1980 Karakorum traverse expedition.
Ned Gillette

renaissance, this is no longer so. Alpine and Nordic skiing now mix and overlap. Many Alpine skiers have discovered the joys of cross-country, and many diehard cross-country skiers have taken up Alpine skiing as a second sport. Surveys have shown that at least a quarter of the skiers in each group practice the other sport. Nordic skiers are rediscovering the joys of prelift Alpine skiing, as they ski downhill with equipment that may also be used uphill, reviving old turns like the Telemark. Alpine skiers now venture to places not served by lifts, and reski trails cut during the youth of their sport. The difference between the two forms of skiing is now more one of equipment and practice rather than basic philosophy.

Today *cross-country* describes a broad range of activities in *skiing*. These activities, and their associated skills, are what this book's about. Some chapters, like Chapter 3 on on-flat technique and Chapters 11, 12, and 13 on equipment and clothing, waxing, and gear care, focus on cross-country skiing only. Others, like Chapter 10 on backcountry skills and the downhill skiing portions of Chapter 4, are fundamental to all skiing.

It's not all here, nor should it be. Most of it's out on snow, both unique and universal. It's cross-country today.

SUIT YOURSELF
How to Start...

You can ski at cross-country centers where trails are well marked. *Michael Brady*

Cross-country skiing is perhaps the most varied of winter activities. The different ways to enjoy the sport, the spectrum of places to ski, the different terrains and conditions to ski in, and the varieties of equipment and clothing that can be used are endless. So you can suit yourself; the range of possibilities is unlimited. You can ski anywhere there is snow, from your own backyard to the fanciest of manicured resort-trail complexes. You can ski alone or in a crowd. You can use simple gear, or go for the ultimate incorporating space-age technology, sometimes at space-age prices. And behind it all is your technique, the way you do it. It, too, can and should be personal.

How to get started? It depends on your goals. If you want to become a highly skilled skier, there is only one known guaranteed way, and even that one doesn't work in all cases: get plunked onto skis before you can write or read books like this one, before you can tie your own shoes, and get shoved outside the door to play on the snow. Soon you'll manage, and then start playing with your playmates, forgetting that you have long objects on your feet. You'll run, turn, fall, get up, and run again. And then you can follow a parent around, skiing, going somewhere. It works. Or at least it has for almost every expert skier and top ski racer in the world today.

But if you are reading this book, you cannot take advantage of that method. Still, the principles will aid you. Just think of what you did as a kid, from your preschool days on. You probably spent endless hours in activities that to adults seemed pointless, and sometimes annoying. Perhaps you threw rocks, pounded mounds of sand, splashed in water, slid down slides, or tortured the family piano. And you did it again, again, and again.

These childhood activities are part of the background that enabled you to do other things later in life, from playing baseball to playing the piano. And if you found you were good at those activities, perhaps you were better in what you took up later on; you may even have been one of those described as a "born" this-or-that. The same general sequence of events that you might have followed had you been "born on skis" will speed your learning of cross-country skiing. All right, you don't have the limitless time available to a child, and you want to get on with it quicker. Just keep the principles in mind, as none are better.

First, focus on skiing, not on what it's done with or where you do it. If you are a technologist in your approach to all things, then by all means immerse yourself in ski gear. But otherwise, ignore it in the beginning. Just try to get some skiing in. A few hours on snow will do you far more good than plodding the aisles of ski and sports shops.

Think: would you buy a bowling ball before taking up bowling? A sailboat without ever having sailed? Most likely not. So start by renting or borrowing ski gear. Make *ski and see* your initial guiding motto.

When the first edition of this book was written, in the early 1970s, basic information on cross-country skiing was needed. So the equipment chapters came early in the book, much as descriptions of bowling alleys may have preceded descriptions of bowling in a book aimed at readers in a country where bowling was new. Now cross-country skiing is better known, so the equipment chapter is where it belongs: toward the end of the book. More information is also available, in the references listed in the back of this book.

Second, whatever maneuver you are

learning, be it your first time on skis or an advanced trick, start simple. Be a kid and take your time. If you swim fairly well, think of a parallel in that sport. More likely than not, many of your friends have admired your aquatic ability, decrying their own inability or their outright fear of water. In listening to them you probably recognize a common cause: some scary childhood experience, like falling out of a boat into deep water. So common are such happenings that we even have idioms using them to describe difficult situations, like "in deep water." The way to swim, we all know, is to start in shallow water, where we can stand and splash, but always touch the secure, solid bottom and get our head well above water.

The initial encounters with cross-country skiing would be far more enjoyable for many people if they would, so to speak, start shallow and put on their water wings before venturing into deep water. The sport might also be safer, as it should be. Surveys have shown that no sport, even Ping-Pong, is completely safe, and in cross-country skiing, as in other sports, beginners are the most frequently injured. The most common cause of beginning cross-country skier injury is skiing out of control on downhills, the skiing equivalent of deep water in the middle of the lake. Fatigue also plays a part, as it often does in many other types of accidents caused by human error. So to enjoy what you're doing and feel safe at it, stay out of deep water until you have enough experience in the shallow to face the deep with confidence.

Third, take lessons if you can. You will discover that even basic lessons accelerate your learning. No printed description, no article, no book can teach you flawless skiing. To see why this is so, think of anything else you do well, from typing to cooking, from driving a car to playing tennis. How much did you learn from books and how much did you learn from instruction? And in thinking of "instruction," include passive instruction, what you learned by watching others, seeing how skilled performers did it, and copying for your own improvement. You'll probably conclude that instruction was important, and that this book can only be a guideline, like the good school text that backs up a skilled teacher.

Instruction isn't just for beginners. It goes all the way. When outdoor clubs do it, they call it leading. When ski teams do it, they call it coaching. Everyone who skis can use a bit of it, not just to do better, but to enjoy skiing more.

But instruction can also be overdone, especially with kids. Instruction should add to your skiing experience, and not be an end in itself.

Picking a good instructor is getting easier, as more and more skilled instructors are working at cross-country centers in the USA and Canada. Ski instructor certification is an assurance of minimum capability, but, like all other professional registrations, does not automatically guarantee results for the client. The best guide is perhaps the reputation of the cross-country area or person involved. If many others are satisfied, chances are that you will be, too.

Group lessons are fine, be they in organized ski schools or informal ski tours. But nothing can beat the efficiency of a two-person, two-way exchange to improve your skiing: take a private lesson, ski with a skilled friend for an hour. You can pack a lot into that time, which gives you more time to do what really will make you a good skier: ski hour after hour after hour. Despite any preconceived doubts you may have, don't fear skiing with the ex-racer or the expert skier. Contrary to what you may think, these older dogs are still with the sport because they love it dearly. They are the ones who simplify, who draw on a large reservoir of experience to quickly analyze and aid your technique, the way you ski. It's often the young pups, the recent converts to the sport, who overcomplicate. There are teaching sequences in which the diagonal stride, the basic walklike maneuver of cross-country skiing, is broken down into as many as two dozen different submovements, a total perhaps useful for teaching centipedes to ski, but confusing to mere humans.

Fourth, think of "good technique" simply as a set of rules for efficient movement. Sports are like machines: as endurance requirements go up, economy of movement becomes more important. Endurance may not be your primary goal when you start skiing, but it's what enables you to enjoy an entire tour when you ski. If you can ride a bike, you can understand this process easily by remembering how you learned. At first you probably were stiff and afraid, and put a lot of muscle into keeping the bike upright. You were terribly inefficient, and if you didn't fall first, you tired quickly. The principle is simple: doing something poorly takes more muscle and therefore more energy. And the more energy you use for a given movement, the less efficient you are, the more you wear yourself out. The opposite, doing it well, puts you somewhat in the position of a musician getting on beat: body, mind, and execution of the maneuver come together in a unity strong enough to be felt. For those who have not felt it before, the effect may border on the mystical. Marathon runners and cross-country ski racers have

often reported visions, doubtless brought on by the sheer elation of doing the ultimate for which nature designed their bodies.

Fifth, be yourself. Imitate good skiing, but don't copy it exactly. Your skiing should be your way of doing it, keyed to your particular body build and personal capabilities. The "rules" for good skiing are somewhat like the "rules" for good walking, and include admonitions equivalent to standing fairly erect and not dragging your feet, the sorts of things your mother probably told you when you were a child. Trying to ski *exactly* like anyone else may force you to learn movements or habits unsuited to your body, which, as far as your body is concerned, are wasted. So trying to replicate a good skier's skiing may degrade yours.

If you seek someone to imitate, simply look for a graceful skier. Grace in repetitive movement, such as that of cross-country skiing, usually goes hand in hand with efficiency, and efficiency is your goal. If you ever doubt that this is so, go watch a race or jump in the track behind a racer and try to duplicate the movements yet maintain the speed of the person you follow. You'll quickly discover the rewards of efficient movement.

So important is grace, the beauty of movement, that it is the partial or whole goal in many sports. In competitive ski jumping, for instance, ski jumpers are judged equally for the lengths of their jumps and the technical grace with which they execute their flights and landings. Figure skaters are judged entirely on the technical perfection, difficulty, and grace of their maneuvers.

So important is the uncluttered, straightforward simplicity of graceful cross-country skiing, that only skiers epitomizing the grace of cross-country illus-

Cross-country skiers can make tracks where there are neither trails nor signs, as do skiers Alan Bard and Doug Wiens, carrying eighty-pound packs on the Ruth Glacier on the McKinley Circuit ski expedition. *Ned Gillette*

trate the technique maneuvers shown in this book. The principle is much the same as that of using good models for clothes:

in a well-posed clothing photo, the model wears the clothes so successfully and so naturally that your attention focuses on the garments, and only secondarily on the person wearing them. In good ski-technique photos, the maneuver done by the skier, not the skier, stands out.

Finally, start learning where it's easiest, on the flat, in a well-prepared track. You learn far more rapidly on a packed trail or area with set tracks than you do away from tracks. Tracks aid ski stability as you move, and they partially direct your movements, leaving you to concentrate on learning them properly. Tracks are usually fairly uniform over the stretches that you will use to learn the various cross-country ski strides; you can handle the surprises later, when your arsenal of technique capability is greater. Tracks allow you to ski more and faster in a given period of time. If "faster" seems scary, think of it as *more efficiently:* for the same effort you move more easily. If you ever doubt that skiing in tracks is faster than skiing out of them, watch what expert skiers and racers often do when they feel they are going too fast on downhills: they get out of the track to slow down.

All the stride-maneuver technique photos in this book show skiing in tracks, because tracks not only are easiest to ski, but allow the various details of skiing to be most easily seen. The principles of skiing you learn in a track can be applied out of tracks, so you've lost nothing by starting where it's easiest.

You don't have to cross-country ski long to discover that there's an ongoing controversy of in-track versus out-of-track skiing. Both forms of the sport have their attractions, and therefore often draw persons with differing goals in skiing.

Devotees of in-track skiing regard tracks as essential. Otherwise, they feel, it's like playing golf in an unmown pasture. Good kick and glide, the essential ingredients of the cross-country diagonal stride, are most easily attained and maintained in a track. Skiers learn and improve more quickly in tracks, and tracks are often available along with other facilities, such as warming huts, rental shops, parking lots, and other amenities that skiers use. They are, worldwide, as typical of cross-country skiing as tennis courts are of that sport. North American cross-country skiers have often been given the opposite impression, as ski photographers, usually with experience in photographing breathtaking Alpine skiing descents in powder snow, demand and produce the same in their cross-country shots. Those skiers you see charging through powder snow up to their knees, in beautiful strides with smiles affixed to their lips, probably collapsed just after the photos were taken. To see why this is so, try it on skis—it's like running in water halfway up to your knees: very exhausting. Real off-track skiing is slow. But it does have its advantages, its calling. It takes you away from others, off the beaten path. It lets you truly do your own thing, set your own direction and course. Most expert skiers ski both in tracks and out of tracks, and enjoy both forms of the total cross-country skiing experience. When they seek the elation of movement— skiing for the sheer pleasure of the art— they pick tracks. But with tracks come other skiers, some regulation, and a proximity to civilization. So for solitude, for adventure on skis, they go elsewhere, off tracks. Or, if they simply wish to ski where there are no tracks, they make their own.

If you're reading this book, chances are that you wish to be efficient in your *learning* of cross-country skiing, as well as in

Almost any snow-covered area can be a good cross-country ski center—here a summertime glider airport in its off-season is a haven for skiers.
Fletcher Manley

the skiing itself. There are no exact methods of learning that assure speed, as all of us differ in background, capability, and hence in the rapidity with which we can absorb and learn new maneuvers. Kids are the best, no doubt: some experts in biomechanics, the science of human

Track-setters, pulled by snowmobiles, put in tracks for skiers. *Michael Brady*

movement, say that once a child executes a movement properly, he or she can repeat it subsequently without error. Adults need more time. Yet they usually have less time than do children, and cannot indulge in learning by trial and error.

One of the best aids available is simu-lation, doing something that closely resembles something else that you already know how to do. Therefore I often refer to natural walking, and will assume that you have walked into a wind, can ride a bike, and have done a bit of hiking. Granted, you probably did not read a book or take instruction to learn to do these things, but the reactions you now have in practicing them, like leaning into the wind when walking, will aid you to learn cross-country skiing maneuvers.

Thinking of these simple maneuvers will also aid you in learning skiing. For instance, think of what you do when you walk. It may be difficult to picture yourself, so experiment a bit, in the privacy of your own home, if you wish. Walk toward a full-length mirror and observe your stride, starting as your feet pass one another. You push down on the floor with one foot, which pushes your body forward. As your body moves forward, your opposite leg swings forward, your opposite foot lands on the floor, and then the foot on which you started the sequence lifts off. Its leg swings forward as your body continues to move, and your feet pass one another, putting you in the equal but opposite position from where you started. This is one stride. You repeat it again and again to walk.

Now watch the center of your body, about your belly button, as you walk toward the mirror. If you are walking normally well at your normal speed, that part of your body seems to "hang" between your legs, and head straight toward the mirror as your feet alternately support you on the floor. Now, just as one foot passes the other, freeze, stop your forward motion, and watch your belly button in the mirror. What happens? If you're on your right foot, you must either touch your left foot to the floor to keep

ABOUT THAT WALK

Skiing originated in Norway, so much of the vernacular of the sport came to English directly from Norwegian, including the word *ski* itself. Strange, then, that modern Norwegian has no verb corresponding to *to ski*. The term, as used by most skiers in that country, is *gå på ski,* literally *walk on skis*. This idiom, plus articles in skiing magazines of the late 1960s, may be responsible for the often-quoted "If you can walk, you can ski" of the cross-country scene in North America.

Don't believe it completely. It is, as it first was, a truism with qualifications. Many of the natural human movements of walking transfer directly into cross-country skiing maneuvers. The diagonal stride of walking becomes the diagonal stride of skiing. The natural duckfooted position used to walk up a steep incline becomes the herringbone on skis. But the similarity has its limitations, as any beginning skier can attest. It might be best to qualify the original statement, to clarify its intent as was done in the articles where it appeared. "If you can walk well, you have the potential to apply that skill to learn to ski cross-country equally well." That's a mouthful, which is perhaps why the original has so often been misquoted.

Through the years skiers have experimented with many maneuvers to improve their strides, often incorporating movements foreign to on-foot movement. One old-timer of this type, which still is making the rounds, is *passgang,* or lateral stride, in which arm and leg on one side move in unison. The theory behind the stride was that the skier would slither along, rotating about the body's central vertical axis. It didn't work very well, just as it won't work for on-foot joggers or runners. Man, and most animals, moves with a diagonal gait. The camel is one of the few animals to naturally use the lateral gait, which is one of the things that makes that animal difficult to ride.

So the walk idea is still good, with its limitations. Often, skiers who seemingly cannot coordinate their skiing stride movements fail to do so because they do something on skis that they do not do on foot. Skiing evolved from walking and humans have not changed since the advent of skiing. So for stride-trouble cures, think about that walk.

---

your belly button centered on its track straight ahead toward the mirror, or you have to shift your hips a bit, moving your belly button to the right, to balance yourself without touching your left foot to the floor.

What's the difference? Why was it so natural, so easy, to keep your belly button headed directly toward the mirror when you were walking, while "freezing" your walk forced you to shift it to one side? The answer is that all motion, even your moderate walk toward the mirror, involves *dynamic (in-motion)* forces that allow you to assume positions that are not possible when those forces are absent, such as when you stand still. Dynamic forces are what keep a bicycle upright, allow a diver to flip in the air, and, for your simple walk, allow you to move without swaying like a belly dancer.

The term that describes what happens, what you do with your feet when you walk, is poor and somewhat misleading at best, but there's nothing we know that's better in any language. So here it is, for all its lacks: *weight shift,* or, in some cases, *weighting.*

What's wrong with those terms, so frequently used in sports? Just this, just what you saw when you froze your walk toward the mirror. In freezing your walk you tried to duplicate one phase of movement with a static, nonmoving position. And it didn't work, because when you stopped you removed those small dynamic forces that allowed you to assume that position when moving. Weight has true meaning only when you are standing still. Motion can either increase or decrease your weight. Enough motion can, in fact, make you "weightless" as it does astronauts in space flight.

When you walk, your foot puts a force on the floor that's greater than your weight. So you don't have to move your butt over your foot to "weight" it: the process happens automatically as you move: your foot gets your weight and some more force, too, as you move. Your speed determines the size of these extra forces. When you walk at a brisk pace or cross-country ski the diagonal stride well at the same stride speed, you "weight" each foot with a force of your body weight plus about 10% to 50% of your weight. If you run on foot or ski fast, you "weight" each foot with total forces greater than your body weight. Speedy runners or cross-country skiers apply forces of twice their body weight or more on the underlying surfaces.

You can see this effect clearly when you walk in moist sand that takes a clear footprint. When you jog you leave a deeper footprint than when you walk, and when you run, you leave a deeper footprint than when you jog. The deeper the footprint, the more force required to make it. You can also see the effect if you step quickly onto a rapid-reading scale: the indicator will usually swing up past your weight as you step on the scale, and then swing back down to your weight when you stand still. The upswing above your weight was caused by your motion.

You have probably also observed why weight alone is inadequate for determining motion. Think of any activity that you do well, and then look at some of the in-studio posed ads for clothing for that activity. Something is always wrong, not completely convincing. The tennis player looks off balance, the jogger strained, the skier in a peculiar stance. It's all because the models are standing still, and no static position can recreate a position that is part of a movement. No way. You saw it was so with your little experiment in walking toward the mirror.

So when you get on skis and hear of "weighting," or read of it in this book, don't think only of what you see on your bathroom scale. Think of those footprints in the sand. "Weighting" a ski means the same as "weighting" a foot in walking: the forces supporting your body are there.

Clear mental pictures, the way you lean into a wind, the way you "shift weight" when walking, aid your skiing. But if you do something incorrectly, your skiing suffers, and you generally cannot see it yourself—unless you are fortunate enough to see yourself on a videotape. Video, by the way, is a great aid in polishing technique for skiers who have been skiing long enough to see their own faults when they are displayed. When you think you've gotten to that stage, seek out a video camera and watch the playback. You may be in for more than one surprise. The most important part of learning any movement correctly involves being able to feel that it is correct. But often it's not possible to know or feel what is correct until you know or feel what is wrong—in the same way that meeting asphalt a few times when you were learning to ride a bike taught you that you need a little speed to stay upright. One trick that even expert skiers use to polish their technique is to overemphasize a wrong

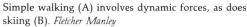

Simple walking (A) involves dynamic forces, as does
skiing (B). *Fletcher Manley*

move, to ski incorrectly in order to drill in
the feeling for what's not right. For instance, if your instructor tells you that
you are skiing *too* erect, too stiffly, you
might try skiing a bit as if a ramrod were
strapped the full length of your back.
You'll quickly find the position uncomfortable, and, in so doing, probably discover how to avoid it.

As you learn, keep skiing, both as your
goal and your means to attain that goal.
Remember, most of the world's best skiers never read a book on the subject and
have taken only a few lessons. They just
skied a lot, from the time they were very
small. That same recipe can work for you.
Take lessons and/or practice new maneuvers until you feel you have mastered
their rudiments, then go out and use
them. In Norway, where resort instruction
in skiing often is an all-day affair, instructors are admonished to keep their
students moving 80% of the time, and

use the remaining 20% for everything
else, including instruction. It works there
and it can work for you. Doing something
right many times, which you must if you
cover distance while skiing well, equips
you with the reactions of efficient movement and enables you to handle different
skiing situations well. It's like learning to
drive a car: at first your entire attention
was focused on the mechanics of controlling and steering the vehicle. Later, when
those chores became automated, you
could do other things as you drove, such
as carry on a conversation or hum a tune,
both impossible the first day behind the
wheel. So it is with skiing: increased skill
in the maneuver itself simplifies matters
and leaves you free to observe, to react to
things other than technique alone.

As you gain proficiency in one maneuver, add another. When you are fairly
pleased with your technique on the flat,
tackle hills, up and then down. That's

Cross-country can be an octaped activity if you wish. *Michael Brady*

how the instructional material in Chapters 3 and 4 is organized. Then try your skills in different terrains and snows, the subject of Chapter 5.

As you acquire skill, you'll ski faster, just as you once rode a bike faster after you mastered the basic balance of bike riding. Skiing faster puts your technique into focus: with less time to perform each movement of a maneuver, efficiency becomes increasingly important. So you become your own instructor, continuing the process you first started on the flat.

Some even do it on sand, as did expedition skier Ned Gillette on the beaches of Raratonga, Polynesia. *Jan Reynolds*

WHAT'S AN EXPERT?
AND WHY YOU SEE THEM IN
THIS BOOK

Expert skiers are not necessarily those with certificates or degrees to prove their competence. They are the skiers who execute the most skiing movements with clean efficiency, most of the time. They err, yes. But more often than not they seem to perform with ridiculous ease those feats which are struggles for others.

This is nothing peculiar to skiing; it applies to almost all human tasks which involve coordination and require learning. Think of any that you do well, from typing to playing racquet sports. What's the difference between your current level of ability and that of your initial attempts?

Practice, you might say. That's a contributing factor to skill. But accuracy and efficiency are the final products. In typing, say, the automatic finger reflexes instilled by practice enable you to hit a desired key accurately, without your finger wandering around, momentarily lost on the keyboard. Twenty-five words per minute may have seemed insurmountable when you started, but later it must have seemed slow. A skilled typist typing at that speed has time to do other things, as some indeed do—talk on the phone, glance around, smile at passersby.

It's much the same in cross-country skiing. Relatively speaking, time slows for the skilled skier: there's no haste when movements are performed with no waste. Waste movement wastes energy: in short, to do something poorly usually involves wasted movement, and thus more energy.

The technique of the expert skier is then elegant in its simplicity, stripped to the bare essentials of getting the job done as well as possible. This is why the technique illustrations of this book are of maneuvers as performed by expert skiers, some of them active, skilled racers. The way they do it is simple, not complex. You may have some difficulty learning to ski as they do, but in so doing, you will be learning to ski without difficulty. Isn't that the goal?

3
LEVEL BUSINESS
Technique for Skiing on the Flat

Togetherness takes timing—try it for fun
sometime; it will sharpen your technique.
Fletcher Manley

Technique in cross-country skiing is nothing more than a name for the collection of on-ski maneuvers you use to move around in snow-covered terrain. You can learn as few or as many of them as you please, to suit your actions to the skiing you intend to do.

Whenever you ski uphill or downhill in cross-country, you use maneuvers partially shared with snowshoers and Alpine skiers. But in moving on the flat, you are uniquely and unmistakably a cross-country skier. This is why the diagonal stride, with the skier gliding on one ski, arms and legs stretched out, has become the very symbol of cross-country skiing, used in everything connected with the sport, from ads to logos to signs.

If you are a newcomer to cross-country, don't be misled into believing that you will ski like that symbol your first time out. Initial steps in any new activity are almost always awkward, as you cannot "naturally" do a thing until you have done it a few times. The diagonal stride of cross-country skiing evolved from, and therefore was named after, the natural diagonal gait humans use in walking, jogging, and running. Opposite arm and leg move in unison, automatically. Knowing how to walk, jog, and run gives you an edge on learning the basics of the on-ski diagonal stride, as abilities in similar movements do transfer between differing activities. So the basic diagonal stride, the symbol of and the most frequently used maneuver in cross-country skiing, is where you should start.

What you do thereafter depends on your background, on how many spinoffs you can exploit to speed your learning of cross-country technique. If you're a skilled Alpine skier, hills are no problem and sliding over snow is old hat. So you'll want to concentrate on what's foreign to

your previous experience, self-propelled skiing on the flat. If you are a skater, sliding over flat surfaces is your forte, the skill you can use in cross-country skiing. You will probably quickly pick up on-flat cross-country ski technique as soon as you become accustomed to your "longer skates" and your poles, but be stymied by the inclines foreign to your skating experience. You will zip through the maneuvers of this chapter, and spend most of your learning time on the ups and downs of Chapter 4. If you are an average person with no single, strong specific skills from other sports, you'll quickly find what you manage well and what you manage with difficulty on skis.

EASY DOES IT

There are many ways to start learning cross-country skiing on the flat. You can simply find a level, snow-covered surface—a field, golf course, parking lot, or your own backyard—and start. In so doing you'll probably start with a cumbersome waddle as you gingerly shove one foot forward, and then the other, supporting yourself with your ski poles on the disconcertingly slippery surface beneath your feet. This is the equivalent of crawling before you can walk.

Better yet is to set things up to your best advantage, so you may bypass the crawling stage and utilize some of your capability as a walker, jogger, or runner. Build on what you can do, to your advantage. The exact sequence of your learning activities is unimportant. But making things easy for yourself is important. Here are some guidelines on which almost all instructors and expert skiers will agree:

START WITH GOOD EQUIPMENT: "Good" doesn't mean expensive or advanced. It simply means equipment in good repair that fits you. If you start on waxable skis, they should be waxed for good grip, and not slip or stick. If you start on waxless skis, they should grip well on the snow where you ski. Grip is the traction that allows you to move forward. Slipping is like spinning the wheels of a car: it gets you nowhere and wastes energy.

DRESS FOR THE WEATHER: Dress warmly, especially in your legs. You'll be surprised how a little chill there can detract from your ability to learn. If in doubt, put on several layers, which can be peeled off if you are too warm.

SKI WITH AN INSTRUCTOR OR A SKILLED SKIER: Mimic what you see. Think of anything else you do well, and how much instruction aided that skill. It's the same way in skiing: a little feedback from another person goes a long way.

START IN TRACKS: In tracks you can concentrate on the movement of skiing, and not be bothered with plowing your way through untracked snow. Starting to ski in tracks is the equivalent of learning to drive on a deserted road. Removing external problems allows you to concentrate on mastering the rudiments.

STOP WHEN YOU TIRE: In your initial encounters with skiing, you'll probably discover muscles you never knew you had. Just maintaining your balance on skis may tire you, just as did your first efforts at balancing on a bicycle. Take a break, then go back.

FEAR NOT FALLING: Falling isn't failing. Quite the contrary. In fact, if you get

---

THE JARGON

Cross-country skiing has its own vocabulary, its own jargon. Here are the terms that apply to skiing on the flat, the subject of this chapter:

DIAGONAL STRIDE. Gait on skis in which opposite arm and leg move in unison, as in walking, jogging, and running on foot.

POLING. The pole movements of the various strides.

POLE PLANT. The act of sticking a pole into the snow.

GRIP. Purchase on the snow that gives you traction to move forward.

GLIDE. Slide on snow, on one or both skis.

DOUBLE POLING. Both arms and poles move in unison; poles are planted to provide forward power.

DOUBLE-POLE STRIDE. Double poling, with a leg stride providing additional forward power.

KICK. Downward-and-backward-weighted foot movement that provides forward power.

WEIGHTING. Placing force on a pole or on a ski. The total force involved may be larger than body weight, such as during a well-executed kick.

---

through your first day on skis without falling, you probably have failed to push yourself enough. But most adults fear falling, often because they fear the potential injury that may result, but even more often because they fear the scorn of others leveled at those too clumsy to stand

upright. If you fear falling for these or other reasons, try it on snow a few times before you start skiing. Sit down in the snow; you'll probably find it soft and cooling. Get up again. And do it over. You'll lose your fear quickly. Many instructors start their beginners' classes with falling, as they know that taking falls well and getting up from them are skills that skiers use as long as they ski. If you think that taking spills is the stigma of the new skier, stick around a popular ski area for a while and watch the experts. They fall less frequently than do less skilled skiers, but when they do, it can be a bailout equaled only by comic-strip mishaps.

DO IT AGAIN, AND AGAIN: In almost all physical activities, the body is smarter than the mind. Once you master the basics of a new movement, doing it over and over and over again will make you skilled in it far more quickly than any amount of time spent analyzing or thinking of how you might do it better.

YOUR STRIDE COLLECTION

There are no hard and fast rules as to where and when you should use one par-

ticular cross-country ski stride, and when you should shift to another. Terrain, snow, tracks, weather, wind, and your own abilities all count in determining what stride is best for each stretch of snow you ski.

Think of it as being remotely similar to driving a manual-shift car. When the weather and visibility are good, you can zip along the interstate at the legal 55 mph. in top gear. Blow a bit of fog onto the highway, and you automatically slow down to suit the restricted visibility. Turn off the interstate onto a snow-covered side road, and you may slow down even more. If you do that often, you'll want snow tires for that road, or even chains if it gets steep and icy during the winter. Come spring, driving a muddy gravel road will become an exercise in seeing how slowly you can ease over bumps while still maintaining some speed.

In a similar fashion, on skis you suit your strides to the prevailing conditions. When the track is fast, you may be able to swoop down it with effortless strides. But if it gets choppy, you must shorten your strides to suit the bumps. If it gets downright bad, such as the glazed, slithering mess that tracks sometimes become in the spring, you may automatically elect to double-pole, simply because you feel

GETTING UP FROM A FALL
Skier sprawled on snow (A) starts getting up by placing skis parallel (B), and then shifts weight over skis (C). Pushing up onto one knee (D) starts the rise to a full standing position (E). *Fletcher Manley*

more stable gliding on two feet than on one at a time.

The strides on the following pages are shown on a flat, good track, where they are most easily learned. But where you will finally use them is up to you and depends on your skiing. Add them to your stride collection and use them on tours. That's the way to find what they can do for you.

WALK FIRST

The best way to learn the basics of cross-country skiing is to use the same method you probably would use were you too young to read this book. Start by walking on skis, then embellish the basic maneuver as you progress. It's a safe, sure method, and there's an immense amount of living proof that it works.

Start, in tracks with your skis on, and just walk straight ahead, letting the tracks guide your skis. In only a few steps you will discover the essential difference between walking on foot and walking on skis: when you bring a foot forward and down on a ski, it doesn't stay put, as in walking, but continues to move forward. This is ski glide, a very useful part of your technique. If you are a skater or an

HOW TO HOLD A POLE

Grasp your pole grips by putting your hands *up* through the pole straps and then down onto the grip, so the strap circles the back of your hand and fits against the grip, under your palm. This fitting causes the pole to roll into your hand in the cross-country poling maneuvers, assuring you of poling ease.

Cross-country strides require you to push and pull on your poles in several different directions. Therefore poles are not gripped as are bicycle handlegrips or Alpine ski poles, but rather are held with a varying grasp. The grip on a pole planted in front of the body is closed, yet relaxed. As the pole and arm swing past the body, as in the diagonal stride or in double poling, the grip on the pole loosens. When the arm is behind the body, the hand is open, so the pole shaft and the arm are in a straight line. Some skiers prefer to snug their pole straps so they can open their hands completely at the end of a poling movement, while others prefer to ski with slightly looser straps, and hold the pole grip between thumb and forefinger at the end of the poling movement. This relaxed grip sequence gives you the necessary pole power without the tenseness of a constant grip, which can quickly tire your arms. A fixed grip pits muscle against muscle, and should be avoided.

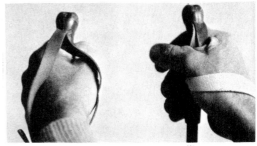

Wrong   Right

HOW TO HOLD A POLE
Grasp a pole grip by placing your hand *up* through the loop of the wrist strap and *down* around the grip, *not* by grasping the grip straight on, through the wrist loop to the grip. *Fletcher Manley*

The movements of an ordinary on-foot walk (upper sequence) can be done on skis (middle sequence). Leaning a bit more forward as if facing a breeze, and kicking a bit more emphatically, just as the feet pass each other, turns the walk on skis into the basic diagonal ski stride (bottom sequence). *Fletcher Manley*

Alpine skier, you already know the feeling. If not, it may take you a while to become accustomed to it, not to clutch up as you might do when a foot slips while you're walking on foot.

As soon as you get the feel of your skis sliding down the track, lean forward slightly, as if into a wind, and push off harder with each foot, as if you were starting to jog or run. You'll probably find that in doing so you cover the same distance in fewer strides than you would by walking. If so, you're already getting the idea; you're already starting to ski.

Your push-offs on alternate feet, or *kicks,* are your motive power. A good kick puts pressure down on a ski, and, as your leg extends, launches you forward over onto your other ski. Just as in walking, you alternately "weight" your feet to propel yourself forward, as your body "hangs" midway between your legs.

What happened to your arms as you bent forward and kicked harder to increase your glide? You probably swung them, each in unison with the opposite leg, as you strode down the track. Just like a child discovering the same thing for the first time, you found that swinging arms aid your stride, just as a sprinter's swinging arms contribute to forward running speed.

Put it together, make it rhythmic, and keep moving. Look at the illustrations shown here, and try to imitate them. Hum a waltz if it helps, kicking on each downbeat.

Thus far you've been skiing without your poles. Without them you have had one less thing to think about, and have been able to concentrate on doing what comes naturally, using your natural diagonal walking movements in a new situation. Most people need no more than half

DIAGONAL STRIDE

Shown here is one complete phase of the diagonal stride, starting with the skier gliding on the left ski, with no weight on the right ski or on either pole (A). As the right leg swings forward, the right pole is planted in the snow opposite the left foot (B). The right pole then pushes (C) and, as the legs pass, the

A good pole starts with the hand holding the pole firmly but not tightly when the hand is in front of the body (A), continues with the hand loosening its grip as the arm passes the body (B), and finishes with an open hand when the arm is in back of the body (C). *Fletcher Manley*

an hour or so of poleless skiing to catch the basic idea, to get into the rhythm of the basic ski stride.

Now put on your poles, and repeat with them what you just did without them. Start by walking slowly, swinging your arms, and holding the poles loosely. Don't bother planting their tips in the snow; just let them drag if it's easier. Continue your former sequence: kick more emphatically, lean farther forward, and seek glide on your forward ski. Now make use of your poles. When an arm is ahead, plant its pole tip in the snow. Pull

downward and backward on the grip until your hand passes your body, and then push in back on the pole until wrist, elbow, shoulder, and pole are in one straight line. Your arm movement should be almost identical to the one you had when you skied without poles, a free and easy swing, forward and back.

TROUBLES?

Got it all together, or are there a few rough spots in your diagonal stride? If, on

kick starts on the left foot just as the right hand passes the body (D). The left kick and right pole-push finish in unison (E), which then puts the skier into a glide on the right ski, with neither pole touching the snow (F). *Fletcher Manley*

GET ARMS AND KNEES TOGETHER WITH THIS EXERCISE. Stand erect, on skis or on foot, and swing your arms in diagonal rhythm (A) forward and back, bending down and then up in the knees as arms pass (B) the body, then swing up (C). *Fletcher Manley*

your first time out, you ski like the expert skiers you may see, stop reading now. You are one of those rare, gifted "natural" athletes.

If, on the other hand, you are a mere human, reflect that those expert skiers you see also had their first times on skis, whenever that may have been for them. Your diagonal stride may look more like a cakewalk than a rhythmic, flowing ski stride. Rest assured, the experts ski well by virtue of having done so for a long time, and by virtue of having polished off the rough edges of their techniques.

So here are a few tricks to help you cure the most common difficulties with the diagonal stride:

THE OUTRIGGER OBSESSION: On foot on a slippery surface, your natural reaction to maintain balance is to seek support with your hands—putting them out, for instance, to break a fall. So the unfamiliar slip of skis may cause you to spread-eagle your arms, sticking your poles into the snow like canes, and leaning on these outriggers for support. This position is inefficient: it slows you down and shortens

THE OUTRIGGER
Some skiers err in using their poles as outrigger
canes, which robs them of forward push.
Fletcher Manley

your glide. The secret of a good stride is complete arm movements matched to your leg movements. To master correct poling technique, start each poling movement with a decisive downward and backward pull just after you've planted the pole. Be emphatic, and your arm will follow through naturally. With a little practice you'll find that your balance is better than when you used your poles as outriggers. If you still have difficulty, try going back to poleless skiing. If you don't have outriggers, you can't lean on them. Ski poleless awhile, get your balance, and then put on your poles anew.

THE STILT STEP: If you have not yet become accustomed to the glide on skis, you may be cutting it short because it feels unsteady. One major cause of this uneasy feeling is that you may be skiing with rigid legs, as if they were stilts. This position is not only inefficient; it is tiring. Just as nature abhors a vacuum, the body abhors rigidity at places where it is intended to flex. Skiing stiff-legged takes more energy than skiing with your leg joints—

hip, knee, and ankle—suitably flexed. The secret of attaining such a "stay loose" position starts down at the snow. Begin by concentrating on bending your ankles. You will find that you cannot flex your ankles without flexing your knees, and you cannot flex your knees without bending at the hip. Overdo it a bit to get the feeling. Then do the opposite: deliberately stiffen your legs, pretending they actually are stilts affixed to your body at the hip. Try to ski that way, and you'll probably discover what's right by trying to do it wrong. Then go back to a more flexed-joint leg.

THE SKI SLAP: Do you kick and glide well, but find that your trailing ski slaps down in the track after you have completed each kick? Slapping of the trailing ski in the diagonal stride indicates that your kicking leg comes down weighted on the snow before your legs pass each other. The slap is heard when the ski hits the snow as it is brought forward for the glide. It happens because your weight is slightly backward rather than completely over your gliding ski during a glide. The cure is to get your weight farther forward. To do so, practice leaning, as if into a wind, when you glide. Another trick is to focus on your glide rather than your kick. Keep your tempo—the rapidity with which you stride—and strive for as much

SOME TROUBLES
Common errors are a stiff grip on the poles (A) and a squat (B), which puts weight back so the skier glides on two skis instead of one. *Fletcher Manley*

glide as you can, pressing forward onto your gliding ski after each kick. The kick will then follow naturally.

THE CAMEL WALK, OR CHOP: Do you feel that you have a comfortable and efficient diagonal stride, marred by jerky poling? Most likely your leg movements and arm movements are each done well, but they are not done together, are not as coordinated as they should be. There are two successive cures for this difficulty. First, go back to skiing without poles. Synchronize your arm swings with your leg kicks, so an arm is extended in front when the opposite leg is behind you, after its kick has finished. Speed up a bit: jog on your skis. In doing it quickly, you'll find that your arms and legs must be synchronized, or else you cannot jog. Then put your poles on again. Now, as you ski, glance downward toward the tip of your forward ski: watch each tip as it comes forward and back, in and out of your field of vision. Then try to "hide" it with the opposing hand as it swings forward. Block out your right ski tip with your left hand as both swing forward into your field of vision, and vice versa. In so doing you "tie" your hands and forward swinging arms to the opposing ski tips. This will coordinate your arm and leg movements, and smooth your stride.

THE POLE PAIN: Many newer cross-country skiers, particularly those experienced in Alpine downhill skiing, find that they have a good diagonal stride, but can't seem to get their poling together: it's jerky and tiring, grinding and uncomfortable. This is usually because they hold their poles with a single, fixed grasp, as do Alpine skiers. In cross-country such a fixed grip restricts arm movement and forces the upper body into uncomfortable, tiring positions. Smooth poling starts with the hands. The grip on the pole should be firm when the pole is in front of your body, and should loosen as the hand passes the body; at the end of the stroke the hand should be open. If you fear losing your poles, tighten the wrist straps until the pole grips fit snugly in your hands when your fingers are relaxed and your hands are partially open. Practice skiing with your hands open, relying on the pole straps to transfer power when you plant your poles. Follow through on each poling movement, letting the straps pull the poles into your relaxed hands. Got the feeling? Then ski normally, starting each pole movement with the hand firmly, but not tightly, around the pole grip.

THE TIPTOE STRIDE: Do you ski rhythmically, yet feel that your glide and each stride are short? If so you are probably standing

When you ski the diagonal stride, think of this view from above: note all movement parallel to the track, the direction the skier is going. *Fletcher Manley*

too erect, like a silent-movie character tiptoeing onto the scene. This is a natural on-foot walking stance, easily identified by the legs not being very far apart, a stance necessary for balance when you walk on your toes. But on skis you glide and can go faster, so you should lean further forward. A forward lean allows maximum arm and leg freedom, which makes for easier striding. Practice the upper-body forward lean by deliberately overdoing it, leaning forward as if you were starting a sprint. See how it lengthens your stride and makes skiing more restful.

THE LATE KICK: Even many proficient skiers could improve their diagonal strides by coordinating their movements better. The most common and most serious coordination or timing error among more advanced skiers is the late kick. "Late" means late in relation to the correct timing in the stride: the kick starts well after the feet have passed each other. A late kick is inefficient because it has less distance to act on the snow and because it starts behind the body, when you've already started your glide on the opposite ski.

Correctly timed, a kick should start just as the feet pass each other, when the body is over the kicking foot; this maximizes forward power. The correctly timed kick can be short and rapid, yet still allow

the leg a greater swing area than a kick which is initiated later.

Excessively long strides are the most common cause of a late kick: skiers who overemphasize the extent of their reach may actually end up shortening instead of lengthening their glide.

The first step in correcting a late kick is to feel that you are more over your feet when you kick and less stretched out when you glide. Practice by increasing your tempo (the number of strides you take per minute). Make each kick emphatic and short. With a little practice you'll find that long glides will come automatically.

TIRED POLING: Do you ever feel that you ski more efficiently when you're a bit tired than when you start on a tour? If so you probably are overdoing some movements, most likely in poling.

The most common excess pole movement is a side-to-side swing, where arms swing inward in front of the body and toward the outside in back of the body, a rhythm similar to that used by skaters to pick up speed. The inward-outward swing contributes nothing to forward poling power, and therefore is wasted movement. And wasted movements mean stride inefficiency, which tires you more quickly.

To eliminate wasted arm motion, take a

cue from the poling you do toward the end of a tour when you're too tired to overdo.

Watch your hands in front. Do they cross over in front of your body? Do you feel that your poles whip inward? If so, correct your poling by practicing a slower stride, concentrating on arm swings parallel to your skis. Remember that all stride movements should be as parallel to the track as possible, because that's the direction that you're going.

THE CONTINUAL SLIP: Do you seem to slip more than others, lacking their grip for efficient diagonal striding? There are several causes of continual backslip, some having to do with your technique, and others with your gear:

· You may be dragging your feet, and not shifting weight from one ski to the other. With no weight shift your skis may not grip well enough to give you traction. Check, and correct if necessary, your kick and glide.

· The "scooter kick": Some skiers envision cross-country ski kicks as similar to those done on a scooter, where weight rests on the foot that is on the scooter, and forward power comes from the other foot kicking backward on the underlying sur-

face. Kicking only backward robs you of power, as it gives you no traction. Cure the scooter kick by jogging a bit on skis, using the same stride as if you were jogging on foot. A downward punch with each kick will give you the traction that prevents backslip.

· An ultralate kick, done when there is little weight on the kicking foot, also robs you of traction. Go through the cure for the late kick.

· Skis far too stiff for your weight and skiing ability: If you cannot press the center sections of your skis down flat on the snow with each kick, you can't get grip, and you'll slip. It's the center of your ski bottoms that does most of the grabbing on the snow to give you traction, so check ski stiffness first if you suspect your skis are at fault. If in doubt, have an expert check your skis for you, or, if you want to do it yourself, see how in Chapter 11.

· Ineffective waxless section of waxless skis, or incorrectly waxed waxable skis. If your waxless skis don't grip, you might consider returning them, as gripping is what they are intended to do best. If your waxable skis are waxed incorrectly, change your wax for more grip. How to do this is also described in Chapter 13.

DOUBLE POLING

Shown here is one complete double-pole movement, starting with the skier's arms extended forward, planting the poles, with pole shafts angled just slightly back (A). Bending over the poles the skier sinks upper body downward for power (B), and the arms follow through when the body is at its lowest

·Impossible snow conditions: Sometimes other skiers may have just the thing for prevailing difficult snow conditions, whereas you are not so fortunately shod underfoot. In troublesome transition snows a skier with waxless skis may zip by you as you struggle along with an imperfect wax job. On the other hand, skiing with some waxless skis in ultralight powder may leave you behind skiers whose well-waxed skis suit the snow exactly. Under these conditions it's best to stop for lunch, gaze at the scenery, or retreat to the lodge. Nothing in this world, including skiing, is 100% certain.

SKIING CRAMPS: Do you find that you feel cramped and tired after a relatively short cross-country ski tour, even though you can easily walk or hike for the same period of time? If so, your fatigue may result from an unnatural, tiring body position. As in many other sports, the head and hands lead the body in cross-country skiing, so the difficulty most likely is in the way you hold your head. Chances are that you're watching your skis, craned over with your head hanging down, a po-

sition that can cramp and tire. To relax, hold your head up as you would when walking normally, focusing your eyes 30 to 40 feet ahead. Glance at your skis occasionally if you must, but make "heads up" your posture maxim. It's easier on your shoulders and back.

THE BACKACHE AND THE WIGGLE: If you are healthy and have had no previous back problems, yet find that you have lower-back pains during and after skiing, it's probably because you unknowingly load your back in ways nature is not prepared to cope with. Both twisting and bobbing in the upper body place undue loads on the upper and lower back and result in inefficient striding. Rid yourself of these unnecessary motions and you can ski with less effort and less discomfort. The best trick is to pretend that you are wearing a small backpack as you ski, and in that pack are several bottles and glasses of something you want to drink later on, all without tops, all open. Ski so you don't spill a drop. This will make your back "neutral" and steady, a comfortable, efficient position.

stance (C). The arms pass the body, finishing the pole push (D), and the skier rises to a more erect

stance (E), and swings poles forward in unison for the next pole plant (F). *Fletcher Manley*

DOUBLE POLING

Double poling means that both arms work in unison, much as in the natural movements you perform in jumping or diving. In skiing you use double poling to vary your flat-track technique, or to speed up on the flat or on slight downhills. Double poling may be done with or without leg kicks, or strides.

In its simplest form double poling requires only arm and upper-body movement to provide forward power. Start double poling by setting both pole tips in the snow, shafts vertical or nearly vertical, at arm's length ahead of your body. Now, as you glide forward toward the planted poles, bend at your waist and knees, and let the weight of your torso and upper body "sink" over the poles. In this maneuver you should definitely feel that it's the sinking of your upper body weight, and not your arms, that pushes you forward. If it helps, pretend that there's a ring in your nose, and a weight gets dropped on that ring each time you initiate a double-poling movement. Drop,

then push is the rule. Arms bend as you drop.

When your upper body is at its deepest bend, straighten your arms to push on your poles. The pole push finishes with shoulder, arm, wrist, and pole in one straight line. The hands grip the poles as in the diagonal stride: firm but loose in front, loosening and opening continually through the end of the pole push.

Rise to a more erect stance after each pole push. Then glide forward, with your weight equally on both skis. Swing your arms forward, with your hands open and relaxed. Some find this movement difficult; even top racers sometimes finish the pole push and swing their poles forward with the poles gripped slightly between thumb and forefinger.

DOUBLE-POLE STRIDE

The double-pole stride combines the leg kick of the diagonal stride with the arm movements of double poling. The maneuver is best understood by thinking of it as starting in the same position as the finish

DOUBLE-POLE STRIDE
Preparing to kick, the skier sinks in the knees (A), and then starts a kick, here on the right leg, as the arms continue to swing forward (B). When the kick is completed, the skier glides on one ski, with both poles off the snow (C), and then, as poles are planted in unison for double poling, the right leg

of a double poling, when you're gliding forward on both skis, arms swinging forward and body rising to a more erect stance.

Now, as your arms swing forward to plant both poles for the next double-poling, kick with one leg, as in the diagonal stride. Then, as you glide on one ski, plant your poles in the snow. As you sink down over your poles, as in ordinary double poling, the kicking leg swings forward again, coming alongside the other leg as the poling movement finishes behind you.

Practice the basics of the double-pole stride by alternating kicking legs, and by changing to and from ordinary double poling, to suit your own skiing style. If you have difficulty at first, start practice in a track that slopes slightly downhill. Get up speed in the diagonal stride, shift to ordinary double poling, and then try a few double-pole strides. Then change back to the diagonal stride, and repeat the process.

TROUBLES?

Double poling is more stable than the diagonal stride, because you usually have two skis underfoot, not just one. But success in double poling depends on strength—it's just your upper body and arms that provide your motive power— and, for the double-pole stride, on balance. Skilled, strong skiers can literally throw themselves over their poles for amazingly effective thrusts, and assume with ease the somewhat unnatural position of gliding on one ski with both arms forward.

But you may have difficulty with the maneuver. Here are the most common troubles, and how they may be cured:

THE SIT: If you feel that you expend tremendous effort in your double poling, yet get nowhere, perhaps your body position is at fault. Most likely you squat, instead of bending at the waist, to throw your weight over your poles. It's an easy habit to get into, especially if you have done a lot of diagonal-stride skiing and little double-poling.

The secret of good double-poling is to let your upper-body weight, not your arms, do most of the work. Practice by starting your double-poling arm movement with your arms extended far forward as you plant your poles. Keep your arms relatively straight as you let your weight "fall" onto your poles, and then "give way" at the elbows as your hands sweep past your legs, at or below knee level. This will both speed and ease your double poling.

THE POLE STOP: Many skiers cheat themselves in double poling by chopping off

starts to swing forward (D). As in straight double-poling, the body bends over the poles for push (E) as the leg comes forward. The maneuver

finishes with a glide on two skis when the pole push is over (F). *Fletcher Manley*

DOUBLE-POLE TROUBLES
Here's a typical pole plant problem (A) that ends the skier up in a sitting position (B), poor for forward power. *Fletcher Manley*

their pole movements as soon as their arms come back alongside their bodies. They don't follow through, and hence lose the power in the final pole push. This usually happens because they fail to bend at the waist, and try to use only arm power to execute their double polings.

To cure this habit if you have it, try double poling in a good track on a slight downhill. Deliberately stand erect, plant your poles firmly in the snow as you glide forward, and keep the pole tips in the snow as long as possible, letting the poles pull your arms backward. You'll probably find the pull uncomfortable as your arms pass your body, unless, of course, you bend at the waist to let your

arms swing further back. But that's what you're trying to learn to do—so just start it earlier, and you will have improved your double poling.

THE SHAKY SLAP: Gliding on one ski with both arms raised and ahead of the body requires practice to do well. If you have difficulty with the maneuver, if your kicking ski slaps down early or if you shake on the gliding ski, practice the position when standing still, on foot, off your skis. Stand on one foot, with your hands clasped together behind your neck. Bend at the waist, letting one leg swing back as in the kick on skis. Rise to an erect position, and repeat the maneuver, changing to standing on the other foot.

CHANGE FROM DIAGONAL STRIDE TO DOUBLE POLING

Change from the diagonal stride to double poling by maintaining your leg stride rhythm and letting your arms do the changing. Here, for instance, the skier is in the diagonal stride, gliding on the right ski (A); holding the left arm forward as the left leg and right arm swing forward (B) accomplishes the change. As

Do it several times, until you become accustomed to balancing on one foot at a time. Then try your newly found balance on skis.

CHANGING STRIDES

In skiing you'll want to change between the diagonal stride and double poling, and back again, to suit your speed and the varying snow conditions and terrains you encounter. There is no one way to change between strides, as skilled skiers match the technique of a change to the prevailing conditions so they don't lose forward speed.

One method of changing from the diagonal stride to double poling is to drop one poling movement, keeping that arm forward instead of swinging it back. When the opposite arm swings forward, both arms are forward, and you're in position to start a double poling. Some skiers do the opposite, and hold one arm back, waiting for the other arm to come back before swinging both forward in unison for a double-pole stride that follows the rhythm of the diagonal stride they have been doing.

You can do the opposite to switch from double poling to the diagonal stride. Here the most commonly used trick is to take one double-pole stride. As the poling movement finishes, swing one, not two, arms forward as you kick, and you're back in the diagonal stride rhythm.

STRIDES ARE INDIVIDUAL THINGS

The more skilled you become in the various cross-country strides, the more you acquire individual stride traits that set you as much apart from others as does your natural gait on foot. Don't view them as incorrect, as they are what distinguishes you, a human, from a skiing robot. If you stick to the basic rule of directing as much of your energy as possible directly parallel to the track, forward, as that is where you are going, then you will ski with maximum economy. And aside from maximum economy, there is no other simple description of "good" cross-country ski technique.

Some skiers, skilled in other sports requiring arm strength and coordination, have particularly powerful arm movements. Others may "kick like a horse" or "flow along the track" depending on their particular skills. Still others may have slight abnormalities or old injuries, such as restricted motion in a joint once broken or a lower back stiffened by impaired discs, and will therefore not be able to ski as "perfectly" as they otherwise might have. Just as where you go in cross-country is an individual thing, the way you get there is individual.

the legs pass (C), the kick starts and both arms swing forward in unison as the right leg kicks (D), to put the skier into a glide on the left ski (E). Then both poles are planted in unison (F), which finally puts the skier in the double-pole stride rhythm.
Fletcher Manley

VARIATION IS THE SPICE

Almost all cross-country strides and other maneuvers can be varied to produce different strides and maneuvers. Just as walking is the most commonly varied human movement—you can stroll, walk briskly, skip, jog, run, dance, and so on—the diagonal stride on skis is the most commonly varied cross-country skiing maneuver. Some cross-country ski instructors, and, in fact some books on the subject, dwell on these variations as

KNEE DRIVE AND HIP BLOCK

Knee drive and *hip block* are not, as they may sound, skiing versions of defensive football lineman tactics, but rather descriptive terms applying to facets of the diagonal stride. *Knee drive* is a term describing a forward motion that brings the knee ahead of the ankle on a gliding ski. *Hip block* describes a lack of the rotating hip motion seen from the rear as an alternating right-left movement of the buttocks.

There's an ongoing discussion among instructors and coaches on these two maneuvers, mostly on how to obtain the first, held to be good, and how to avoid the second, felt to be bad.

The recent upswing in the scientific analysis of cross-country ski technique, prompted in most skiing countries by increasingly keen international racing competition, has contributed new understanding and negated much old misunderstanding. Two older concepts now questioned, if not found outright lacking, are knee drive and hip block.

Starting in the mid 1970s many top international coaches and their scientific attachés noticed that knees actually didn't lead ankles in the glides of the diagonal strides of top racers. In fact, among the very best racers, knees were often behind ankles on the gliding ski. Some felt that this represented a change from the previous skiing style and others questioned whether the so-called previous style had ever existed in the first place. It's the body, not the knee, that should be forward, over the ski.

As Russian racers continued their medal march in the late 1970s and early 1980s, their technique was examined by their rivals, to see what it was they did to ski so fast. One discovery was that the Russians skied with blocked hips! Glory be!

Guess I won't mention those two things any more in this book. . . .

different techniques in themselves. But most of them don't have to be learned; you'll probably invent some of your own as you ski along.

Only a few of the major variations have ever been classified. Swedish and German skiers speak of variations in terms of rhythmical "beats," or number of kick steps executed for one complete set (one right, one left) of poling movement. Thus the ordinary diagonal stride, with two kicks per set of arm-pole movements, is the "two-beat diagonal" or "two-step diagonal." Variations on the "two-beat" or "two-step" are called the "multiple-beat" or "multiple-step," with the most common being the three- and four-beat, or step strides. The three-step involves "missing" a single arm-pole movement, while the four-step involves dropping one complete set of arm-pole movements. Try them. They're fun to do. And you might be doing them already, if you have ever scratched your nose or adjusted your glasses or cap while skiing the diagonal stride. They're great for breaking up the monotony of diagonal striding on a long, flat track.

TURNING

There are many ways to turn on skis on the flat, and if you have skied a bit, you've probably discovered some of your own accord, without instruction or prior knowledge. Just as is the case for walking on foot, turn technique depends on how much you wish to change your direction and on whether or not you are moving. So turns are classified as *stationary* (done when you're standing still) or *moving,* and *partial* (slight change of direction) or *complete* (reversal of direction).

STAR TURN
Here the skier starts a star turn to the right by resting all weight on the left ski, and taking a step out to the right on the right ski (A). When the right ski comes down on the snow, it is weighted (B) and the left ski is brought around parallel (C). Repeating the process (D) completes the turn to the new direction (E). *Fletcher Manley*

SKATING TURN

Approaching a turn, here to the right, in the diagonal stride, the skier times strides to approach the new track gliding on the outside (left) ski (A). As the left ski crosses the new track, the skier picks up the inside (right) ski and angles it in the new direction (B), swinging both arms forward in unison. Arm swing continues as the right ski comes down in the new track (C). Then the skier pushes off on the left ski (D) and brings it around parallel to the right (E) as arms continue their forward swing for a double-pole plant (F) in the new set of tracks.
Fletcher Manley

The easiest turn to perform is the stationary STAR TURN, named for the pattern the skis make in the snow. It's probably the first turn you discovered by yourself on skis. You simply lift one ski, angle it out slightly in the new direction, and then bring the other ski in parallel, repeating the process as many times as necessary to change direction.

Done in motion, the star turn becomes the STEP TURN. Practice the step turn on a slight downhill slope. While gliding on parallel skis, step one ski out, weight it, and then step the other ski around in the new direction. Repeat as many times as necessary to complete the turn. Although the step turn is usually the first moving turn learned, it's seldom forgotten, as even expert skiers find it useful in deep or soft snow.

The SKATING TURN is named after its basic movement, which resembles ice skating. Instead of just stepping as in the step turn, you push off on one ski to land on the other, pointed in the new direction. This movement combines well with the rhythm of the diagonal stride or double poling, and therefore is often used in tracks, to negotiate sharper turns.

KICK TURN—STANDARD OUTSIDE SWING

The skier starts the kick turn, here to the left, with skis parallel (A). Placing the left pole behind (B) for stability, the skier then kicks the inside (left) ski up (C) and around and down in the new direction, which puts the feet in what's called the *fourth position* in classical ballet (D). Moving the right pole around and planting it in the snow in line with the left (E), the right ski is brought up, around (F), and down (G) in the snow to complete the turn. *Fletcher Manley*

KICK TURN—INSIDE, OR "TWIST" VERSION

This version of the kick turn starts like the standard kick turn, with the left pole behind, for stability and to allow clearance for the kicking ski. But here the outside (right) ski starts the turn (A), by crossing the left ski, and being placed on the snow in the new direction (B). The right pole is then planted in the snow level with the left, and the left ski is kicked up (C), twisted around (D), and brought down parallel to the right (E) to finish the turn. *Fletcher Manley*

As you gain cross-country skiing skill, you probably will want to go faster, to do all maneuvers more rapidly. The KICK TURN is a rapid way of turning completely around while standing on the flat or on a hill. Executed like a military march *about-face* maneuver, it requires your legs to assume a yogalike position, and therefore should be attempted only after you have become skilled in the more elementary skiing maneuvers.

There are many ways to do a kick turn, but all have in common the initial *kick*, in which one ski is picked up off the snow, and turned completely around to face in the opposite direction. Chances are you'll only see the two varieties shown here, the *outside swing kick*, and the *inside swing kick*,

named after the direction the kicking ski first takes, to the outside or inside of the turn. But there are others. Should you ever ski in Asia, you may routinely see skiers there kick turning with what seems exactly the reverse of the procedures shown here—kicking ski tails, not tips, around first, and then turning by crossing and untwisting the legs. If you think it sounds difficult when described in words, watch it closely should you ever see it done. It's a spectacle, performable perhaps only by persons whose genetic heritage has endowed them with suitable hip structures.

From the steepest uphills to the fastest downhills,
there are techniques for all slopes. *Fletcher Manley*

4

UP AND DOWN
Technique for Skiing Up and Down Hills

The ability to ski both up *and* down hills is what sets cross-country skiers apart from all other skiers. Ski jumpers walk up stairs or ride elevators for their return, downhill flights. Alpine skiers use an awesome array of mechanical contrivances, from tows to gondola lifts to helicopters, to hoist them up for their unidirectional downhill runs, and to be complete and include all activities under the name of "skiing," water skiers ski only on a flat surface, using a motorboat for motive power. The cross-country skier is the only skier free to go in all terrains, powered only by a human Calorie engine.

It is understandable, then, that hills require the most of the skier. They are both the nemesis of the neophyte and the ultimate challenge to the racer, as it is still correctly said that cross-country ski races are won on the uphills.

Uphill skiing is not particularly difficult, and downhill skiing is not inherently dangerous. But to a somewhat lesser degree than activities in water, hills in skiing are unforgiving of carelessness or incapacity. This is why you should attack them seriously only after you have gained confidence in your cross-country ski technique on the flat, the subject of the previous chapter.

GOING UP

In going uphill on skis, you use exactly the same principles that you might use in ascending the same hill on foot.

Just as you may walk straight up moderate hills, you ski straight up a hill using the *uphill diagonal stride,* which is nothing more than the ordinary diagonal stride with movements shortened to accommodate the incline.

As the hill gets steeper, you may slide

backward using the uphill diagonal stride. Then it's time to alter your technique. First, you can effectively reduce the slope and stick to your uphill diagonal stride by not going straight up the hill, but rather up at an angle, on a traverse. You then zigzag up the hill, much as a hiking trail, road, or railroad zigzags with switchbacks on a hill too steep to handle straight on. Second, if you don't have far to go or otherwise want to keep going straight up the hill, as might be necessary for you to stay on the trail, then you can *herringbone.* The herringbone is a maneuver similar to what you might naturally do on foot on a steep hill: you walk duckfooted, and your skis leave a herringbone pattern in the snow, tips out in a V, tails together.

Finally, if the hill is too steep to herringbone or traverse upward, you may *sidestep,* which is walking uphill sideways with your skis perpendicular to the fall line (the imaginary line running straight downhill, the path a freely rolling snowball would take), much as you might do on foot carrying furniture up stairs.

UPHILL DIAGONAL STRIDE
Weight forward, over your feet, is the rule for a good uphill diagonal stride. Because of the slope, there isn't enough glide or speed for a complete arm-push and backward swing, as in the diagonal stride on the flat, shown on pages 28–29, which gives the uphill stride an appearance of jogging.
Fletcher Manley

UPHILL DIAGONAL STRIDE

If you have a good diagonal stride on the flat, there's little you need to do to use it up hills. This is because the uphill diagonal stride is nothing more than a minor adjustment of the on-flat diagonal stride. The adjustments are similar to those you might make in your natural, on-flat walk to ascend a hill: because of the incline, arms and legs bend more and move less. Forward glide is shortened or disappears completely as the incline becomes steeper. The kick that provides your forward power comes more from the toe than from the foot rolling over onto its toe. These differences give the uphill diagonal stride its characteristic jogging look.

But just as walking uphill takes more energy than walking on the flat, skiing uphill requires more work than skiing on the flat. Your arms must supply more power, especially if your skis don't grip quite as well as they should. Your legs must supply more power to maintain your forward speed. Hills place a premium on the efficiency of your technique.

There are no fixed rules for skiing uphill, as tracks, snow conditions, your speed at the bottom of the hill, the length of the hill, and the slope of the hill all influence how you can ski it best. However, here are a few tricks that apply to skiing all uphills:

· Direct all your energies forward, up the hill. Side-sway or up-down bobbing, the most common unnecessary movements done on uphills, rob you of the energy that you can better use to ascend the hill. Keep your arms moving straight, parallel to the direction you're headed. Pick a spot up the hill and focus on it to keep your head and upper body steady.

· Shorten your stride before the incline demands that you must do so. "Shift gears," so to speak, in anticipation of the slope.

· After you have "shifted gears" and get into the slope, drop slightly in your knees, as if you were jogging up the hill on foot. Angle your poles farther back, and keep your hands low in front: this maximizes your forward poling power.

· Shorten your poling movements to match your shortened leg strides. Do so by angling your poles more toward the back when they are planted, rather than by

IT'S WRONG TO SIT
Weight back will put you back down the hill.
Fletcher Manley

THE STRUGGLE
Trying to pull yourself uphill with your poles might
end you up with your nose in the snow.
Fletcher Manley

chopping off your poling before you've completed your pole push.

· On uphills you should feel that you press down on the heel of your forward foot to initiate the kick. This is what places your body in the correct position for secure uphill skiing.

· Begin practicing uphill technique on short, gentle grades. Start from the flat with a good diagonal stride, and shift to a more rapid tempo with a shorter stride as you start up the hill. Shift weight completely and feel your heel as you start the kick from each forward foot. As you gain proficiency, try a longer hill of the same grade, and then shift to a steeper hill.

TROUBLES?

Working too hard and/or slipping backward are the most common difficulties skiers experience on hills, when they otherwise ski well on the flat.

THE SIT: Dropping in your knees by sitting backward rather than leaning a bit forward puts your weight back, in an excellent position to slide downhill. Cure the sit by maintaining your slight forward lean from your flat-track diagonal stride, and flexing your *ankles* as you start up the incline. It's impossible to flex your ankles

without flexing your knees and yet remain upright.

THE STRUGGLE: Just as some car drivers fail to shift gears on steep hills and therefore lug their engines until they vibrate, shake, and sometimes stop, some skiers grind up even moderate hills with incredible displays of wasted energy. Usually they violate almost all the basic principles of good uphill technique: they bend at the waist, which puts weight downhill, great for descending, but poor for ascending; they ski stiff-legged with almost no knee bend, or their legs, trailing their bodies, churn a rearward jog as if they functioned like an outboard motor on a boat, both of which errors prevent efficient weight transfer; and they plant their poles straight, thus robbing themselves of most of their potential poling power. If you ski hills this way, give up. Start over again, on the flat. Ski well on the flat, and then up a very gentle incline. Select successively steeper inclines until you feel comfortable and natural on hills.

THE SLIP: If you slip on hills when your skis seem to grip well in your diagonal stride on the flat, several things may be wrong. Here's what you might try to correct them. First, try "punching" your leading ski down with more exaggerated force. This will flatten the ski out more

HERRINGBONE
The herringbone is done in the diagonal rhythm, one stride on the left shown here from ahead (A, B) and behind (C, D). *Fletcher Manley*

on the snow for better traction. Second, try going out of the track into the area alongside, where poles normally are planted. The looser snow here may make your skis grip better. Finally, if you have waxable skis, your wax may be too smooth for hills. Thicken the wax or extend it farther forward of the heel. If you have waxless skis, maybe they are too stiff to allow the waxless sections to grip; you need "softer" skis for the hills you ski.

HERRINGBONE

When nothing you can do prevents backslip down a hill, or when the incline is simply too steep for you to ski straight up, break into a herringbone for more climbing power. Spread your ski tips apart, keeping your ski tails together, to form a wedge, or V, pointing downhill. Roll your knees inward to bite the inside edges of both skis (left edge on your right ski, right edge on your left ski) into the snow. Now you're secure. Walk straight up the hill in this duckfooted position, using your normal diagonal stride rhythm, moving your right pole with your left leg and your left pole with your right leg. For greater grip, spread your skis into a broader wedge and roll your knees inward more for more edge bite. For greater speed uphill, bring your ski tips closer together, for a smaller wedge, and flex your knees slightly more outward, to lessen edge bite. Practice the uphill herringbone by skiing in the diagonal stride up a hill of increasing steepness. When you get to the point where you start to slip backward, spread your skis in the herringbone position and continue up the hill. When you reach the top of the hill, bring your ski tips together, and continue in your normal skisparallel diagonal stride, trying not to break your rhythm. In so doing you are learning to handle terrain variations.

If your herringbone feels inefficient or

SIDESTEP

SIDESTEP
Here the skier stands across the hill, with uphill to the left and downhill to the right. Each sidestep stride starts with stepping an unweighted left ski upward (A), bringing it down, weighted in the snow (B) and repeating the stride (C) as many times as needed. Poles can move in unison, as shown here, or in a staggered rhythm of left pole, left ski, right ski, right pole, as suits the skier. *Fletcher Manley*

clumsy, you probably are sitting too far back, as in the incorrect "sit" position of the uphill diagonal stride. To cure the sit, stop, stand fairly upright, secure on your skis, and then start uphill again. The herringbone takes a bit of practice to do right: in your initial attempts you may find that you step on your own skis, or get your poles mixed up with your skis. If so, try taking larger uphill steps and try carrying your arms a bit wider, planting your poles further out, away from your skis. But do not despair: even racers sometimes foul up a herringbone or two, as their speed overpowers their care in executing the maneuver efficiently.

SIDESTEP

The sidestep is the last resort for ascending a hill with skis on your feet. Beyond it you'll need something else on your feet, like mountaineer's crampons or a ladder.

Start the sidestep with both skis parallel, across the slope, perpendicular to the fall line. You should feel that you can stand in this position without sliding either forward or backward. Flex your knees toward the hill, in the uphill direction. This bites your uphill ski edges into the snow, giving you a secure platform underfoot. The steeper the hill, the more you must roll your knees inward; but do *not* lean your body into the hill; doing so may push your skis sideways, starting them sideslipping downhill. "Rump out" is the rule for stability. Plant both poles for stability. Then step the ski furthest up the hill a bit upward, and bring the other ski up and parallel to it. You can move your poles in unison as you step sideways up the hill, or you can do a sequence of uphill pole first, then uphill ski, then downhill ski, and finally downhill pole, as suits your feeling for the stability of the situation.

The uphill tacking turn connects two uphill traverses in the diagonal stride rhythm. Here the skier turns left, starting from a diagonal stride when weight is on the forward, right ski (A). The left ski is unweighted (B) and swung around and down on the snow in the new direction, then weighted (C) as the right ski and pole are brought around. Weight on the right ski and a right pole put the skier back in the diagonal stride rhythm (D); only one pole plant has been lost in the diagonal rhythm through the entire turn. *Fletcher Manley*

UPHILL TRAVERSING

You can effectively lessen the slope of a hill by skiing up at an angle to a slope. Like a trail or road winding up a hill, this lengthens the distance you must cover to get up the hill, but it's often easier and quicker than bulling your way up an extreme slope. In traversing upward, you can use your flat-terrain diagonal stride, modified for the slope of the path you follow. You'll find that you must ski a bit lopsided to suit the slope, shortening your uphill poling movements, and lengthening your downhill poling movements.

You can connect your uphill traverses, at the ends of your zigzags, with a variety of turns. The simplest turn is the kick turn. Stop, kick your downhill ski around first, complete the turn, and proceed in the new direction. You can also connect uphill traverses with an in-motion turn, done in diagonal stride rhythm. This is the *tacking turn*, named after the *tack* of sailing.

UPHILL TACKING TURN

The tacking turn is most used to connect two uphill traverses, skied with the uphill diagonal stride. In appearance it's an uphill version of the flat-terrain skating turn. It starts with one ski angled out in the new direction, and finishes when the other ski is brought around. As the sequence illustrations here show, it can be done completely in the diagonal rhythm, missing only half of one stride.

DOWNHILL

In all cross-country skiing you propel yourself and change direction through reaction with the underlying snow surface. Most of the forces that act upon you are generated through and limited by the friction of your skis, and sometimes your poles, on snow. Your traction, direction stability, and control depend on how well you direct that friction. This is especially true in downhill skiing, where your manipulation of ski-to-snow contact is the essence of what is called downhill technique.

But the skills required for that manipulation, the movements of downhill skiing, are those that break most radically with any former experience you may have on foot. This is why the downhill-skiing part of cross-country often takes awhile to learn well enough to inspire self-confidence.

If you are a skilled Alpine skier, you may be surprised upon first trying your downhill skills on cross-country skis. Cross-country gear is lighter, smaller, and less rigid than its Alpine counterpart, and therefore is less solid underfoot. This is why many Alpine skiers contend that cross-country skis cannot be turned because the skis usually have no metal edges and boot heels are free to lift off skis. This observation, which you may have heard or even seen in print, is a quarter-truth at best. Cross-country gear is simply less forgiving than its Alpine counterpart: you must ski downhill correctly to manage at all; there's no room for cheating as there is with Alpine equipment. Executing downhill turns on cross-country skis brings you back to the basics, and requires you to muster all your skills to ski well. It's good practice.

There are also many other compensations, as cross-country skiers can attest. You can pick a small hill, scamper up it, and ski down it, and in so doing practice more downhill turns in a day than you could if you were dependent on waiting in a lift line to get uphill on a bunny slope, as are neophyte Alpine skiers.

Cross-country skiing has, in fact, spawned an offspring sport, a throwback to the early days of Alpine skiing in North America, the skiing of the 1930s. Known by several names, *cross-country downhilling, Telemarking,* or *Norpine* (from *Nordic-Alpine*), it's simply the sport of skiing downhill using cross-country ski boots, bindings, and skis. But for the clothing and quality of the photos of it, pictures of the sport look amazingly like those of pre–World War II skiing. The good old days seem to be back again for those skiers. But it's a separate sport, falling somewhere between cross-country and Alpine skiing, as its practitioners often ride lifts.

STABLE DOES IT

The basic rules for skiing downhill are few. If observed, they will minimize the surprises that tracks and terrain can deal out, and maximize your confidence.

· Ski "wide-track," with your skis one or two boot widths or more apart. Except when initiating some turns, weight your two skis equally.

· Feel that your weight is distributed over your whole foot, pressing down on the centers of your skis. If you err slightly, it's better to be a bit back than a bit forward. Skiing with your weight too far forward may end you on your nose, if your skis suddenly slow down.

WHAT ELSE IS NEW?

Browsing through old ski magazines can provide an economic laugh or two, as well as bringing to attention forgotten aspects of the sport. Two generations ago ski-association certification of proficiency by test was popular with skiers. Here are the highlights of the proficiency tests administered by the U.S. Eastern Amateur Ski Association, as described in *Ski News* for January 17, 1941:

FOURTH-CLASS TEST
1. A candidate must demonstrate ability to ski correctly on the level with both the one-step and the two-step and demonstrate the proper use of poles.
2. Demonstrate kick turn left and right on the level.
3. Demonstrate side step on a steep slope.
4. Herringbone 50' up a 10° slope.
5. Traverse up a slope of 100' using a kick turn between traverses.
6. Breaking speed—50' on 15° slope with a double stem from a standing start.
7. Demonstrate connected snowplow turns.
8. Straight running in downhill position for not less than 50' on 10° slope.

Upon successful completion of the fourth-class test, the skier was awarded "an attractive white button bearing the Roman numeral 4, U.S.E.A.S.A., which will designate him or her as one step on the road to being an expert."

The third- and second-class tests comprised executions of various downhill skiing maneuvers, and allowed the skier some freedom of choice in selecting both slopes and turns. The third-class test required, for instance, that a skier be able to execute "four continuous stem turns on hard snow, on a slope of not less than a fifteen-degree gradient." In the second-class test the skier could choose between "(a) Four linked jump turns, on a fifteen degree slope, or (b) Four linked Telemark turns in soft snow, on a slope of approximately twenty-five degrees." Upon successful completion of these tests skiers would "upon payment of fifty cents, be given an attractive bronze or silver pin showing further progress on the way to developing an all-round ski technique which will enable them to run any slope or trail in perfect safety and control."

Those were the days when there was only one kind of skiing, what is now called cross-country skiing, as the boom in uphill transportation that made modern unidirectional Alpine skiing was yet to come. No wonder, then, that as ski instructor and ski explorer Ned Gillette observes: "By looking at some of the photographs of skiers in the 1930s—their low, stable stance utilizing extreme edging—we get a good image of the technique that a cross-country skier needs for skiing down hills."

• In downhill skiing as in many other sports requiring whole-body coordinated movement, it's the hands that lead. So keep your hands low and out in front, as if you were holding the handlebars of an ordinary bicycle. If a hand gets behind your body as you ski forward, straight, or in a turn, it pulls your arm back, which pulls your shoulder back, which may unbalance your body and upset you. Hands in front for control and stability is the rule.

• Except when planting your poles to aid a turn, keep your poles angled back, tips and baskets off the snow, close in so as not to snag on anything on the side of the trail or strike skiers you may pass.

• Retain, and exaggerate, your forward, relaxed lean from your on-flat diagonal

ERECT   CROUCH   EGG

The erect stance allows maximum readiness, but also
has maximum wind resistance. The crouch is good
for speed and is a restful stance. The egg is for
all-out downhill speed. *Fletcher Manley*

stride. Bend at your knees and hips, and
lean your upper body slightly forward. In
this position your legs act as shock absorbers, and your feet can go up or down
without upsetting your balance. It is the
position of readiness.

· Bend your ankles. Flex at your ankle joint
lets your legs go either way, affording
you maximum stability and control. If
you ski with unflexed ankles, your legs
can bend only one way relative to your
feet: forward. So every upward movement
of your ski tips, such as a bump in a
downhill track, will tend to upset your
balance, and throw you backward. Backward falls are embarrassing and can hurt.
So flex your ankles for downhill ease. If
you find it difficult to tell when your ankles are flexed as you ski, press forward
until you can feel your boot laces.

STRAIGHT DOWNHILL

Ski downhill with a stance that suits the
conditions, you, and your desired speed.
If you're apprehensive about speed, think
of it as ease: the faster you glide in a
downhill track, the farther you coast out
onto the following flat or up the following hill without expending stride effort.

The faster you want to go, the lower

you must squat. If you doubt that this is
so in cross-country skiing, think of how
difficult it is to ride a bike against even a
moderate breeze. Just as hunching over
your handlebars cuts your wind resistance
and makes pedaling a bike against the
wind easier, crouching down on skis cuts
wind resistance and increases downhill
speed.

The more stable you wish to be, the
more erect you should stand, in a position
of readiness to react to track and terrain
variations. So your choice of a downhill
position is always a compromise between
maximum readiness on one end and maximum speed at the other end.

The *natural stance* is the most frequently
used, easiest, and most erect body position for downhill skiing. It offers the most
wind resistance, and therefore is slower
than the lower stances. But it puts you in
a position of maximum readiness, so you
may quickly negotiate track or terrain
variations.

The *crouch* is a medium-speed downhill
stance. Some skiers use it as a rest stance,
resting their arms on their thighs. Others
merely squat low, as if they were ready to
receive a tennis serve. Both positions are
stable.

The *egg* is a position used by expert
skiers and racers for all-out downhill
speed. There are several varieties, all in-

tended to minimize wind resistance. Some have actually been proven to do so by wind-tunnel tests conducted by major ski teams. The egg places a high static load on the legs, and therefore requires well-developed thigh muscles to maintain on longer downhills. It's the least stable of the downhill positions, and therefore is recommended only for skiing downhill in good tracks.

THE UNIVERSAL SNOWPLOW

The *snowplow* is the easiest way to slow down or stop on downhills or on the flat. It is named for the V-wedge of the skis, which plows up snow and leaves a wake behind you, much as does a V-plow on a snowplow vehicle plowing a road.

With knees and ankles bent and weight even on both skis, form the snowplow by pressing your heels out until your skis assume the wedge, tips together in the reverse of the uphill herringbone position. Bend your knees forward and roll them slightly inward to edge your skis. The wider the wedge and the more you edge, the more snow you plow up, and the greater the braking effect to slow your speed.

Practice the snowplow by starting directly down a moderate, packed hill, in the erect downhill stance. When you have picked up a little speed, spread your skis into the snowplow, widening the wedge and increasing the edge until you stop.

If your snowplow fails to brake on the snow and slow you down, two things may be wrong. First, if you are heading straight down the hill but not braking enough, it's probably because you are not edging your skis, or rolling them onto their edges on the inside of the snowplow V. Practice this maneuver standing still on

SNOWPLOW
From a plow position (A) the skier spreads the skis to a wider wedge (B) rolling inside edges in to plow to a stop (C). *Fletcher Manley*

the flat: press your knees forward and slightly inward to roll your skis onto their edges, then try the maneuver on a gentle downhill. Second, if one ski seems to head straight downhill of its own accord, you probably have a lopsided snowplow: your leg over the straight-running ski is

SNOWPLOW TURN
Snowplowing on a downhill traverse (A), the skier weights the outside (right) ski to initiate the turn (B), which starts the skis turning (C), through the fall line (D), to finish the turn in the new direction (E). *Fletcher Manley*

probably stiff and weighted, while the other leg, on the correctly plowed-out ski, is virtually unweighted. If you weight only one ski, it will go where it is pointed. So you need to practice equal weighting of your snowplowed skis. Do so by starting straight down a gentle hill that you can ski without fear and without having to slow down. Then use the snowplow to slow down, spreading out your skis, and then closing them again to the parallel position. Do this several times: spread out to slow, close in to glide ahead, and spread out again. Hum a tune to yourself if it helps, and do the exercise in rhythm. Soon you'll automate the

spreading and weighting of your skis, and will have mastered the correct snowplow ski weighting.

THE SNOWPLOW TURN

The snowplow turn is the simplest and one of the most reliable of downhill ski turns. Master it, and you'll have the basics necessary for learning more advanced turns.

The principle is simple. If you weight one ski more than the other in the snowplow position, you will turn in the direction that ski is pointing. So you initiate and execute a snowplow turn by weighting the ski that points where you want to go: left ski for a right turn, and right ski for a left turn.

Weight the desired ski by leaning out over it. If you have difficulty feeling where you lean, try skiing the snowplow

Linking snowplow turns gives you rhythm for downhill skiing. *Fletcher Manley*

with both hands resting lightly on your knees. Press down on the right knee to weight the right ski, and down on the left knee to weight the left ski.

Weight the decisive ski until you have finished the turn and are headed in the new direction. Then resume your stance between the skis, weighting both skis equally. Throughout the turn, keep your hands low, and poles pointed backward.

Start practicing the snowplow turn on the same gentle, packed slope where you practiced the snowplow to a stop. Here you have mastered the slope and are therefore able to focus your attention on learning the turn, rather than on negotiating the hill. Start with a snowplow straight down the hill, and alternately make right and left turns to a complete stop. In so doing you have found a way of stopping which is faster than the straight downhill snowplow. Next narrow down your snowplow V, forming your skis to a smaller wedge, and ski down the same hill, alternately weighting left and right skis to make right and left turns. Don't execute these turns to a stop; make them small. Just after you have started one turn and are heading in the new direction, stand erect, between your skis, and then weight the opposite ski to initiate a turn in the opposite direction. This is what is called making linked turns.

EDGING

In both the snowplow and the snowplow turn, you made use of *edging,* so you already have capability in this maneuver, a vital part of the turns to follow. Getting a feel for your ski edges, as if they were extensions of your feet, will greatly aid your turn technique. Here are a few tricks to get that feel.

· Stand on a packed, flat snow surface, in the snowplow position. Bend your knees forward and inward to roll your skis on their inside edges, as you did in snowplowing downhill. You are edging the right edge of the left ski and the left edge of the right ski. Edging differs for other turns. So:

· Stand in the same place, with your skis parallel, about one or two boot widths apart. Start with your skis flat on the snow. Then bend both knees forward and slightly to the left. This will roll your skis onto their left edges. Repeat to the right, rolling your skis onto their right edges. Got the feeling?

· Now go up on a slope, preferably packed and smooth. Stand with your skis across the hill, perpendicular to the fall line, the same position you used to start sidestepping uphill. Roll your knees *into* the

Roll knees into the hill to edge skis. *Fletcher Manley*

hill: to the left if uphill is to your left and downhill to your right, and to the right if you are standing the other way. You are rolling your skis onto their *uphill* edges. Now roll your knees the opposite way, to flatten your skis on the snow. They'll probably start to slip sideways down the hill. You can stop that sideslipping by rolling your knees back into the hill to edge again. But get the feel of the motion, as *sideslip* is part of many turns. Alternate edging and sideslipping until you feel comfortable on the slope, facing in both directions.

STEPPING AND SKATING TURNS

Like the snowplow, stepping and skating turns work in an obvious way: to go a new direction, you point a ski that way, then weight it. They are simply downhill versions of the same turns done on the flat. They are useful in almost any type of snow conditions, and are really the only turns you can always rely upon to get

STEPPING TURN
Here the skier starts a turn to the left from a traverse (A) by stepping out the left ski (B). A pole plant sometimes helps to time this maneuver. With weight on the left ski (C), the right is brought around (D), and the step repeated (E,F,G) to complete the turn. *Fletcher Manley*

you out of a fast downhill track, or to turn when you ski deep, heavy snow that otherwise tends to lock your skis onto course like fresh-poured concrete.

If you quickly got the feel for hills, you may be able to step and skate down them, simply by adapting your flat-terrain step and skate-turn techniques. There are only a few tricks required to adapt:

· Ride the *inside* edge of the *outside ski,* the one you step or skate *from* in a turn—your left ski in a right turn, your right ski in a

left turn. This gives you a sturdy foundation for the turn.

· When you have shifted to the other ski in the new direction, edge it into the hill for stability, weighting it only after you have edged.

· It's better to take more, smaller steps or skates, rather than committing yourself to one giant step or skate that can unbalance you on a hill. Many smaller transfers of weight will get you around more securely than one giant thump on the snow.

Here the skier starts a turn to the right, with weight
mostly on the downhill (right) ski in a traverse (A).
A sink in the knees to weight the right ski
completely (B), and then a right pole plant to aid
unweighting allow the left ski to be stemmed out, in
a half-wedge (C). The stemmed (left) ski is then
weighted (D), and the skis are brought parallel (E) as
they cross the fall line. A sink in the knees
completes the turn with the skis parallel in the new
direction (F). *Fletcher Manley*

THE STEM CHRISTIE

The *stem christie* is a manner of making
downhill turns that don't slow you down.
In principle it combines aspects of the
snowplow turn, edging and sideslipping,
and the step turn.

Begin a stem christie by skiing comfortably downhill, at an angle. Push or step
the *uphill* ski tail out to form half a snowplow. This is your wedge, or *stem.* Your
stemmed ski now points in the direction
you want to turn, more down the hill.
Now, shift your weight to that ski by
leaning out and over it. This weight shift
is what provides the power to initiate
your turn, much as weight shift powered
your snowplow turns. Keep your weight
on that ski as it turns. As you turn, bring
the other, unweighted ski in parallel to
the stemmed, turning ski, finishing the
turn with your skis completely parallel.
You are now in a position to execute a
turn in the opposite direction.

Practice the stem christie on a packed
hill, perhaps a bit steeper than the one
where you first practiced snowplow turns.
Ski down once or twice, making linked
snowplow turns. Then start anew, skiing
down with your skis at an angle to the
hill, widening them out into a snowplow,
making a snowplow turn, and then bringing your skis parallel again in the new direction. Link several of these turns. Now
that you can "handle" the hill with parallel runs linked by snowplow turns, ski it
again, with narrower and narrower
wedges in your snowplows. Soon you'll
be able to cut out half of each snowplow,
and start your stem christie turns down
the hill.

PARALLEL TURNS

Parallel turns are downhill turns done with the skis parallel throughout the turn. Just as the limbs-stretched phase of the diagonal stride has become the very symbol of cross-country skiing, the parallel turn is the symbol of downhill skiing, the goal for which many skiers strive.

But you need not strive if you don't feel the call to do so, as you can both enjoy and master cross-country skiing without ever doing a parallel turn. On the other hand, well-executed parallel turns are both fun to do and beautiful to watch. If you want to learn them, you can, by building on your stem christie technique.

With few modifications, a parallel turn is nothing more than a stem christie turn

PARALLEL TURN
Here the skier starts a turn to the right from a traverse (A) by planting the right pole (B) to unweight and start the skis turning as weight comes onto the left ski (C), powering the skis around (D) through the fall line, into the new direction (E).
Fletcher Manley

without the stem. You may already have done a few in practicing your stem turns. What gets you around in a parallel turn is weight shift, as in the stem turn, and sideslipping, instead of the stem of the stem turn.

Start a parallel turn as you did the stem turn, by skiing with skis parallel, down at an angle to the hill. To initiate the turn, edge both skis sharply into the hill by flexing your knees forward and into the hill. This gives you a "platform" from which you then spring up to initiate the turn. This upward motion unweights both skis, freeing them to slip sideways in the direction you push them.

As you unweight, push both heels uphill, and come down on a weighted uphill ski. This little twist is what provides the power to initiate the turn, allowing you to change direction. As your skis turn through the fall line, press your knees forward and inward toward the hill, keeping your weight on the outside ski. Your inside ski carries little or no weight as you turn.

Poling aids parallel turning; you actually turn around your inside pole, the left pole for a left turn, the right pole for a right turn. Plant the inside pole in the snow, angled forward and slightly to the side just as you hop slightly upward to

Linking parallel turns is one of the thrills of skiing downhill. *Fletcher Manley*

unweight your skis. The poling motion aids your ski unweighting. As your skis start to turn, pull the pole from the snow, and press your heels outward and knees inward to apply your turning power.

Keep your body "square," that is, directly over your skis throughout the turn, and let your knees do the directing. Keep your hands in front, as you did when skiing straight downhill. When you plant a pole to aid unweighting and initiate a turn, pull it out of the snow before you ski far enough past it to pull your arm backward. This keeps your weight where it should be, forward, on your skis.

There must be almost as many ways of learning parallel turns as there are ski instructors or ski schools. How you can combine the components of your previous skiing capabilities into a parallel turn depends on your skill and experience, the hill, the snow conditions, and, to some extent, on your equipment. Your greatest difficulty in learning the parallel turn probably will be in learning the parts of it that differ from components of the other downhill turns. Here's a couple of exercises to aid your learning:

THE SMALLER STEM: Successively ski stem christies with smaller and smaller initial stems, and then see how far you get in turns by adding a poling movement to aid unweighting. You may simply slide into parallel turning, presto!

POLE RHYTHM: Ski straight down a packed slope in a snowplow position, making small, linked snowplow turns. Then ski the same turns, poling for each transfer of weight: plant your left pole as you shift your weight to your right ski, and your right pole as you shift your weight to your left ski to turn. Practice until you feel that the poling aids your weight shift;

then ski with a smaller V-wedge in the snowplow, and a more emphatic pole plant and weight shift. Ski with progressively shallower snowplows as you gain skill in coordinating poling and unweighting.

THE TELEMARK TURN

The Telemark turn is the oldest downhill turn known. It was first done more than a century ago, when it was made possible by the first bindings and boots to afford a measure of ski control. Earlier skiers had not been able to turn their skis on downhills, as boots mated to skis simply by being stuck under loose straps on the skis.

As skis, bindings, and boots developed, other turns became possible, and the older Telemark turn was seldom seen outside of jumping hills, where ski jumpers still used to steer their long, heavy skis after landing.

But just as the older waltz can still hold its own on dance floors throughout the world, the Telemark has a grace all its own. No matter how many other turns you master, doing a few Telemark turns will add a flair to your skiing that you get in no other way. And with modern gear, the Telemark is the only turn that cannot be done on Alpine skis. This may be why the Telemark turn is now enjoying its renaissance, and why there is now even special gear available to let you enjoy, in modern clothes, Alpine skiing as it once was.

The basic Telemark turn is a steered turn. Unlike other downhill turns in which ski tips are roughly level throughout a turn, one ski trails the other in a Telemark turn.

The trailing ski is angled to the leading ski, with its tip about level with the boot on the leading ski. When viewed from above, the two skis form sort of a long, shallow boomerang, curved in the direction of the turn. The principle is simple: when moving, a curved object tends to follow a curved path.

You can start a Telemark turn just as you do a snowplow or a stem turn, by weighting the ski that points in the new direction. This weighting provides the turning power to get you around. Bend your opposite, inside foot, and let the inside ski trail behind, weighted just enough to keep it in place, slightly angled to the leading ski. You can even edge it slightly on its inside edge, which helps carve your Telemark turn in the snow.

The Telemark position, with one knee bent at an extreme and one ski trailing, is very stable in the fore-aft direction. This is why it is used by ski jumpers upon landing. But as you are stretched out in the direction of motion, the position is less stable laterally. So skiers hold their arms up for balance, much as you might instinctively do on foot in trying to walk on a thin board.

TELEMARK TURN
Here the skier starts a turn to the right from a traverse (A) by planting the right pole, and allowing the right ski to slide backward, bending at the right ankle and knee (B), to attain the Telemark position, with the right ski tip almost at the left boot (C). Steering through the fall line (D) and following through (E) completes the turn to the new direction (F). *Fletcher Manley*

The current craze for *Norpine* or *Tele-marking,* with slalom races on packed hills skied using Telemark turns, has obscured one of the original, and perhaps the greatest, utility of the turn. The Telemark turn is a great turn for heavy, untracked snow. If you've ever skied with a heavy pack, you know that step and skate turns are an effort and parallel turns are sometimes impossible in such snows. It's then that the Telemark turn comes into its own.

ABOUT THAT T AND HOW IT CAME TO BE

Telemark turns seem strongly in vogue in the U.S. cross-country ski scene of the 1980s. So much so, in fact, that they seem to have spawned a separate subsport within skiing, with their own devotees, books, and jargon, and a new name, *Telemarking,* or, in some circles, *Norpine.*

But as with all fads that leap quickly to prominence, error abounds as fact and fancy are hastily mixed. It need not be so, as no mystery is involved.

First, *Telemark* can be correctly written *only* with a capital *T.* To do otherwise would be like writing *florida oranges.* Telemark is an existing geographic region, one of the eighteen provinces in Norway, the equivalent of states in the U.S.A. It's relatively small, about the size of Rhode Island and Connecticut put together, and has but three major cities, but since 1783 can claim tourism as a major industry. So Telemarkings, as its residents are called in Norwegian, have long been accustomed to travelers, and to traveling themselves, including on skis.

Perhaps the most famous skiing Telemarking was Sondre Norheim. Like other skiers of his time he was also a ski maker, as then, more than a century ago, ski gear was not available in shops. Norheim was innovative, continually improving his gear, and in the course of doing so, invented sidecut on skis and modern ski bindings. These improvements afforded him greater ski control, enabling him to actually turn his skis, maneuvers previously not possible with feet simply stuck into loose straps on the skis.

Norheim's two daring turns, one a steered turn characterized by a trailing ski and one bent knee and the other characterized by parallel skis, were quickly adopted by ski jumpers, to turn to a stop after landing. By 1901, when the first ski jumping rules committee met, these two stopping turns were well-established maneuvers. The committee, meeting in the capital Oslo, then called Christiania, worked out the first guidelines for judging ski jumping. At that time jumps were smaller and shorter, and judges evaluated a jumper's entire performance, from the start at the top of the jump, down the inrun, in the air, landing, and to a complete stop on the outrun. So the two turns originated by Norheim thirty years earlier needed names. Both had come to jumping from Telemark. The bent-knee, trailing-ski, steered turn was the easier to perform on the gear of the day and had therefore been the more frequently copied when the Telemarkings had wowed the capital with their skiing skills eleven years earlier. So the committee let current jargon stand on that one, dubbing it the "Telemark turn," and selecting the name of the capital for the other: the "Christiania turn."

The Christiania turn went on to become the bastion of flamboyant Alpine skiing, developing into the *christie* of that sport. As gear improved, the christie became easier for more skiers, and spread with the sport, leaving the Telemark where it had started, on the jumping-hill outrun.

The Telemark turn has now been revived, and is most useful in the snows for which Sondre Norheim invented it in the 1860s: deep, untracked, and sometimes wooded and tricky. And with modern gear it has flash impossible in Norheim's time, as skiers can now control their edges, tightening and linking their turns in a fashion beyond the capability of Norheim's skis.

STEEP HILL

Always expect the unexpected. *Michael Brady*

UPHILL BUMPS IN TRACKS
Approach a bump in the diagonal stride (A), timing the kick (B) so the feet close (C) to start the kick on the down side of the bump (D), which pushes you forward, as from a starting block in running, onward in the track (F). *Fletcher Manley*

One of the greater pleasures of cross-country skiing is to master snow, to ski it well where you want to go, whatever condition it is in, wherever it lies.

SNOWS AND TERRAINS DICTATE

Skill in the skiing techniques described in the previous two chapters will equip you to ski cross-country almost anywhere you might wish. The skier who skis all terrains and snows well, continually selects from this basic bag of tricks, modifying technique as needed, and continuously changing techniques to suit conditions. Just when to modify and just when to change are impossible to describe in a book. There's no way to predict here, in print, the techniques and maneuvers that will best suit the various terrains and snows you may encounter in skiing.

However, there are a few accessory techniques which, when added to your main repertoire, will enable you to handle a wide range of conditions. In learning them, and in gaining experience through skiing, you'll probably invent minor tricks of your own. That, in fact, is how ski techniques come to be: someone finds a new maneuver, a new trick that works better than the old ones, and skis that way. Others observe and copy, and it

spreads. So fear not the experiment. Strike out on your own if you wish; you may leave more than a ski track behind.

WHAT'S COMING?

The golden rule in dealing with the unexpected is to expect it. Find out as much as you can about it and watch for it.

This means you should know something of the present and immediately past weather where you intend to ski. Has there been any new snow? If so, you may encounter deep stuff. Did it rain yesterday, and then freeze last night? If so, you may ski into a few icy spots. Is it springtime and the sun high? Slush is the order of the day. And so on.

As you ski, look ahead and see what's coming, both close up and far ahead. Watching your skis may continually assure you that they're still there, but it won't warn you of surprises in store ahead of you.

WASHBOARD

Varying snow depths, wind, and skiers sometimes produce bumps and dips, or *washboard,* in a snow surface, just as cars often make washboard out of dirt roads.

You can ski these irregularities without losing speed or stride rhythm.

Most bumps and dips, especially those that form in tracks, are best skied using the diagonal stride or double poling. There is a variety of ways to kick and plant poles, but there are no set maneuvers, simply because there are no set types of bumps and dips. Following any set pattern is equivalent to trying to force the terrain to suit your skiing. You're no bulldozer; trying to be one will only roughen your skiing. So learn a few timing tricks, and suit them to the bumps and dips you encounter.

Most bumps on the flat and up hills can be skied with the diagonal stride. Diagonal striding through bumps is smoothest when you kick just after the middle of the kicking ski, just under the foot, has passed the top of a bump. Let your ski ride up the bump, and then, as it slides off the back side, kick, using the bump as you would a sprinter's starting block.

Bumps seldom suit your diagonal stride rhythm, so you'll have to adjust, continually changing your stride tempo and length to suit the conditions. Kicks not off the back sides of bumps should be weaker.

You should avoid kicking in a dip, especially if it is short and deep. Kicking here will plow your ski straight into the next bump, hardly what you want to do to

get over it. Worse yet, if your ski bridges between two adjacent bumps, kicking in the dip between them can damage the ski if done frequently. This is less of a danger with modern fiberglass skis than with wood skis, but most delaminations at the centers of skis in cold weather are caused by this type of ski misuse. You can kick in the bottom of a dip if the dip is shallow, and if the kick is necessary to maintain your diagonal stride rhythm and speed.

Skiing the same bumps and dips in the opposite, downhill direction can be a chattering experience if you try to diagonal-stride through them. Best to double-pole, timing your double polings on the tops of bumps, and riding out the dips with your legs acting like the shock absorbers on a car.

This "shock absorber" technique is also a happy way to handle bumps and dips when skiing downhill on more open slopes. When you see a bump coming, rise to a more erect position, and absorb the bump by bending your ankles and knees. Do the opposite if you see a dip coming, making the sequence bend, stretch, bend. In both these maneuvers you can keep your head and upper body level by focusing on a point ahead of you on the hill.

You can use bumps on hills to your advantage in turning. Ride up on a bump,

shift weight and swivel on its top, and sideslip down its back side to complete your turn.

Sometimes you may encounter waves, or "bicycle bumps," in tracks, particularly if you ski downhill in a track that has been made by skiers plodding upward in soft snow. Here there's a dip in the left track when there's a bump in the right track, and vice versa. If you're skiing downhill or gliding fast when you meet such a mess, just ride it out, letting your legs absorb the shocks of the bumps, flexing up and down as if you were pedaling a bicycle. If you encounter the mess skiing uphill, forget it. Get out of the track and make a new, smoother track yourself.

TURNS IN TRACKS

ON THE FLAT you can turn in tracks by:

• Step turning or skate turning, from the outside ski onto the inside ski, aimed into the track at the end of the track's turn.

• Double-pole striding through the turn, kicking only from the inside ski of the turn. Kick just as you enter the turn, so through the turn your inside ski is unweighting. With less total ski area on the snow, you can follow the turn more easily.

• Double poling before the turn, and riding it out on equally weighted skis. Here you rely on the track to guide your skis, a trick useful for gentle, but not sharp, turns.

ON DOWNHILLS, or when you are gliding fast on the flat, you can turn in tracks by:

• Step turning or skate turning, from the outside ski onto the inside ski, in one or two strides.

• By gliding through the turn with most of your weight on the outside ski, and with the inside ski trailing as in the Telemark turn. Here, as in the Telemark turn, you form your skis into a single, long curve, to match the curve in the track.

• For faster, sharper turns, ride around and steer with your knees as if you were doing a parallel turn.

STOPPING IN TRACKS

There is only one sure way to stop in tracks: get partway or all the way out. For moderate braking, lift one ski out of the track and fan it out into a half snowplow, keeping your weight mostly on the ski remaining in the track. Edge the snowplowed ski, and gradually weight it to slow down. If that doesn't work, weight it completely for just a moment so you can get the other ski out of the track, and go into a full snowplow.

DOWNHILL BUMPS IN TRACKS
Approach a bump in a glide, preparing for a double-pole stride (A) to kick (B) in time to plant poles on top of the bump (C), and glide (D) on both skis on the down side of the bump, through the following dip (E), and over the next bump (F). *Fletcher Manley*

Kicking on the inside ski when the track turns (A) speeds glide and adds stability on the outside ski (B). *Fletcher Manley*

Trailing the inside ski on a downhill turn in tracks adds stability. *Fletcher Manley*

Changing tracks, such as you might do in passing another skier, starts with a double-pole stride's glide (A). Here the skier changes to the tracks to the right by angling the right ski out when poles are planted (B), pushing on the poles and bringing the right ski down at an outward angle (C), and kicking with the

CHANGING TRACKS

If you're skiing in one set of tracks in a parallel set of two or more, you may sometimes wish to change tracks, to take advantage of a better set of tracks or to pass another skier. You can change tracks with three rapid movements, keeping your rhythm. First, take one skating step out at an angle and across both tracks of the other set. Bring your inside ski, the one closest to your old set of tracks, around, down, and into the inside track of the new set. Then pick up the ski you skated over on, and drop it into its track. Start and finish the maneuver with a double poling or two, and you'll find that you can change tracks without losing speed.

TRACK VARIATIONS

Even tracks set by machines are not always the same. They vary according to the underlying snow when they were set, the weather conditions and snowfall since they were set, how much they have been skied, and myriad other factors, including how much dirt, pine needles, and whatnot has fallen into them.

HARD, COLD tracks in granular snow or very hard-packed powder snow are fast. In skiing them you may feel like a train on its tracks. The best way to handle them is to be a locomotive: kick hard and glide long. Double-pole whenever you have the chance, to get extra distance from track speed.

WET TRACKS can be hard or soft, but they are almost always slow. Here your glide will be minimal, and you'll have to maintain forward speed by literally jogging, increasing your tempo.

SOFT OR MUSHY TRACKS can give way if you kick hard, so treat them with careful respect. Easy does it, both in kicking and poling. Here is where top technique pays off, where your feel for what's underfoot will speed you more than the power you may muster.

WOBBLY TRACKS: Sometimes new snow at freezing temperatures compacts with a glazed surface to produce rounded bottoms and sides in tracks that seemingly afford no decent surface for ski grip or glide. Kicks produce little forward glide, and glides slow quickly. Balance is difficult as skis wobble from side to side on the uneven, rounded surface underneath.

left ski (D). The left ski is then brought up, parallel to the new track as the right ski crosses the new tracks (E), and dropped down into the new track, weighted, as the right ski is unweighted, and then swung parallel to the left (F) to complete the maneuver. *Fletcher Manley*

Here, again, delicate skiing is the order of the day, and double poling, without kicks, is one of your better maneuvers. But endless double poling can tire, unless you are blessed with Herculean arms. So you might find it easier to hop out of the tracks and ski alongside, making your own, and getting back into the set tracks in stretches where they look good.

TRANSITIONS IN TRACKS: The snow in tracks can change, sometimes rapidly, such as when you ski in or out of a shady section of track on a sunny day. In midwinter, sections of a track exposed to the sun usually are faster, because the surface snow is slightly warmer, with more surface moisture. In the spring the opposite is usually true: sun-warmed snow can be wet and sticky, while that in the shade can be icy and horribly fast. If the track goes under pine trees, still another problem can arise: spring winds can blow needles from the trees down into the track. Few things are slower under skis than pine needles, especially if you ski into them with a good glide after a downhill. Whenever temperatures rise and the sun comes out after a wet snowfall, tracks under any trees may give staccato skiing. Sun-warmed snow, falling from tree branches down into a colder track, can brake as well as strips of sand strewn on an icy sidewalk.

TRACKS ENDING in deeper snow pose a problem only if you are skiing downhill fast, out of the track into the deep snow. This occurs often in touring, if you ski downhill using the track made by a skier skiing uphill. At some point the track may take a sharp ninety-degree bend, where the uphill skier changed direction with a kick turn. But skiing down you can't negotiate so sharp a turn, so there you are, whizzing out into the deep stuff. Simply sit back a bit, flex your knees, and let the tips of your skis ride up as you ski into the deeper snow. Then as you slow down, press more forward and keep going.

You can use the same trick to avoid upsets whenever you ski from fast snow into slower snow: sit back and flex to absorb the shock. Do the opposite—flex and move forward—to ski from slow to faster snow or terrain.

SKIING CHUTES

Chutes are trails on hillsides where snow gets packed by skiers into a rounded profile, lowest in the center and sloping up toward both edges of the chute. They are most common in, but not restricted to, the ski trails of the East, Midwest, and Far West, where trees restrict open-slope skiing.

UPHILL IN CHUTES: Chutes seldom have tracks, as they usually are formed by skiers sideslipping and plowing in the downhill direction. Tracks set in them are quickly obliterated. The snow in them is often loose, for the same reason. This is why it is often difficult to do the uphill diagonal stride in a chute: with no tracks and loose snow, grip is often poor. Sometimes the chutes are too narrow to allow use of the herringbone, and, besides, herringboning up a long chute can be exhausting. There are alternatives.

First, try your uphill diagonal stride, keeping it going as long as you comfortably can. When you start to lose grip and slip, stem out one ski in a half herringbone. Maintain your diagonal stride rhythm, one ski straight up the chute and one in the herringbone. When you feel the maneuver getting lopsided, shift over: herringbone the other ski out by itself and go ahead. Sometimes the chute may be too steep or narrow for the half herringbone to work well, or you may not have it to yourself, as other skiers whiz by downhill. Then stick to the sides of the chute.

On the side of the chute, with your skis angled uphill and inward toward the chute center, walk uphill with a stride halfway between the sidestep and the uphill diagonal stride. Use the diagonal

In tracks, half a herringbone will sometimes do. It's also faster than a full herringbone. *Fletcher Manley*

rhythm and balance, but lift your skis successively upward and forward at an angle to climb the chute wall.

DOWNHILL IN CHUTES: If the chute is short and you can see a clear runout and feel confident, then ski it straight down, if you wish. But if it's long and twisting and/or if you cannot see far ahead, you'll probably have to snowplow a bit. In wider chutes the standard snowplow works fine. In longer chutes, break up your snowplowing sessions with straight runs: it's both good practice and great fun to whiz along a bit.

But sometimes chutes are too narrow for you to plow both skis out enough to brake adequately. Then you can ride the sides of the chute. Start on one side, snowplow down and up the other side, turn slightly, and snowplow down in the

Pigeon-toe in, crossing your skis, to scrape base of one against top side edge of other, or ski slowly across another skier's edged skis to scrape over two top edges. *Fletcher Manley*

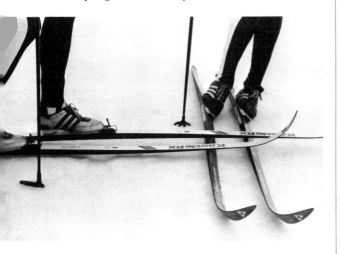

other direction across the chute. If you feel confident enough in your stem christies or parallel turns, you can also use the same zigzag, linked-turn pattern to ski faster down the chute. But before you do so, be sure that there are no obstructions, stumps, trees, rocks, or other skiers in your intended path.

Fast corners in chutes can be as much fun as riding a roller coaster if you ski them right. One trick is to ride the outside bank, with your outside ski in a stem, weighting it as you go through the turn. In this type of turn be sure to lead with your hands in front of you. When you are off the horizontal, skiing like a small bobsled, a hand behind can land you on your behind.

UNRULY SNOWS

Cross-country skiers ski more different terrains and places than do any other skiers. So they encounter and must contend with an extremely broad range of snow conditions and combinations of conditions, some of them downright unruly. But they all can be dealt with.

ICING: All skis, both waxable and waxless, both wood and fiberglass, can ice up, if the conditions are, so to speak, wrong enough. One of the more common causes of icing is when very cold skis get dipped into water. This can happen when you ski over a snow-covered, frozen lake. The snow insulates the ice surface, which can be slushy or wet from previous thaws. As you ski through new, cold snow your skis sink down into the wet slush, and in a flash you're iced up. You can encounter the same problem skiing in cold conditions in the woods, when sun-warmed snow on tree branches drips water into the track. The only practical solution to these two icing problems is to keep your skis solidly in the wet, and don't expose them to cold air. Double-pole through the wet stretches and into the drier stretches of track, where the drier snow will probably wipe the moisture off your skis.

If your skis have iced up, you can first try to stomp the ice off by standing in place and kicking your skis downward and forward and backward in the snow, to wipe the ice off. Another trick is to use someone else's skis as a scraper: have them turn their skis on edge in the snow, and ski slowly over the exposed edges of their skis to wipe off ice. If all these measures fail, there's nothing else to do but stop, take out a scraper, and get to work with your hands.

DIRT: Klister is notorious for picking up all manner of dirt from ski tracks, from all types of soot to pine needles or anything else lying around. The only sensible solution is to stop, scrape off the mess, and rewax. Waxless skis are seldom better under such conditions. If they are used in tracks where others have skied with klister on their waxable skis, then the waxable hair sections or patterns become clogged with klister picked up from the track, creating a truly unbeatable mess. The only solution is to keep your waxless skis meticulously clean. New or newly cleaned ski bases shed both water and dirt well. But even slightly dirty bases will collect more dirt quickly.

DOWNHILL DIFFICULTIES

When you stray from smaller, packed slopes onto bigger hills, you can expect a variety of snow conditions to add to the challenge of the hills themselves.

POWDER: The definition of powder snow varies depending on where you ski and with whom you speak. But from the standpoint of executing turns in it, it may be defined as relatively light, new snow where your skis sink in so far that you cannot see your feet. You can ski almost any turn in powder that you can on a packed slope, once you become accustomed to its resistance and to the loss of visual contact with your feet. Keep your weight more evenly on both skis than

you would in turns on a hard-packed slope, and weight your skis slightly farther back to bring your ski tips up and around in a turn. The faster you ski, the easier it will be, as your skis climb up and plane on the snow. If you can do a Telemark, try it in powder: that's the snow for which it was devised a century ago.

ICE AND HARD PACK: These are seldom natural conditions, but are often encountered where skiers or machines or both have packed snow. Here you may find that you've lost the edge control you had on softer snows. To compensate you must edge more and be emphatic in every weighting and edging move. You'll probably slide and slip more than on softer snow, but if it gets unnerving or out of hand, turn to a stop and then start again, skiing more slowly.

WIND-DRIFTED SNOW AND SKARE

Wind-drifted snow and skare can be produced by natural phenomena alone. *Wind drift,* as its name indicates, is snow that is packed by wind into a dense mass. Abrasion in the process rounds the snow crystals slightly, giving wind drift far different characteristics from surrounding, undrifted snow of the same age and temperature. *Skare* is a Norwegian word, now part of the international vocabulary of terms describing snow. It defines all types of crust produced on top of a snow layer, by the various combinations of the effects of wind and sun on snow. It's slicker than any other snow surface going, and therefore there's even a special klister for use on it, skareklister.

Crust and wind-drifted snow are fine as

long as you can stay on the top surface and manage to edge and control your skis. The real problem arises if you either break through the surface crust, or ski into a patch of the stuff from more benign snow. If you cannot get up on top again or if the crust cannot support your weight, then step turns are usually your best bet. As a last resort, ski slowly on slight downhill traverses, and link your traverses with kick turns until you are out of the crusted section. Some gifted, strong skiers can pull off successful Telemark turns or parallel turns in breakable crust, while some of the wilder acrobats of Nordic downhill can leap through the stuff using jump turns reminiscent of those normally done only for show on packed slopes.

A trail cabin or mountain lodge, goals for a day's
tour. *Michael Brady*

6
ALL IN A DAY'S SKIING
Day Tours and Longer Trips

A day on cross-country skis can be anything you wish to make it. It can be a shorter outdoor stint in your own backyard or neighborhood park. It can be an all-day trip at a cross-country ski center. Or it can be a day- or multiday wilderness trip. No description of any one skiing day matches any other one, for all are different, as individual as skiers themselves. But just as there are ways of skiing, called technique, and paraphernalia to ski with, called equipment and clothing, there are approaches to a day's skiing, that skiers have evolved through the years in enjoying their sport.

PICKING A TOUR

A day's tour can be a few miles, or it can be as much as eighty kilometers or more, if you are a speedy skier burning up the tracks. The only guideline as to how far you should ski is set by your own abilities. In general you should ski at a pace and for a distance that you normally can maintain in similar terrain on foot. This is where most errors of overestimation are made: unprepared skiers, who seldom walk in their daily lives, attempt a ski tour that many others apparently achieve with ease. They are surprised to find that they tire rapidly, sometimes in less than an hour on skis. No small wonder, if they haven't ever walked for an hour. There are ways of preparing for skiing, for increasing your capability to cover distance; see Chapter 8.

Select a tour that matches or maybe even challenges, but does not exceed your skiing skills, or those of any other persons you ski with. If, for instance, you want to ski into a trail cabin at a cross-country ski center, but are not strong on the uphills or are a bit shaky on the downhills, forego

those slopes, and select the longer, more gentle route. In so doing you may see things never seen by the mass of skiers taking the most direct route to the cabin.

You can ski alone if you wish, but should only do so if you are familiar with the area where you're skiing and underski your ability for the day, to leave a margin of reserve capability for emergencies—which can be as simple as breaking a ski pole or rubbing off all your wax on an icy stretch of trail. Mountaineers and skilled outdoorsmen generally agree that three is the minimum for a backcountry party, while ten is getting to be a cumbersome crowd.

Skiing in a group can be one of the greater pleasures of cross-country skiing, as there's always something in the experience that brings out the unexpected in people. The serious executive jokes continually, the shy child darts here and there, looking at animal tracks. People, it is said, are different on skis. Find out for yourself: mix ages, sexes, backgrounds, in a ski party and ski for the fun of it.

A group should pace itself so the slowest skier can easily manage to keep up. Fatigue can be disheartening or even dangerous when you're outdoors: more than three quarters of all skiing accidents happen to skiers who are fatigued and have skied more than they should for the day. On skis, return is not retreat.

KNOW WHERE YOU GO

It's not only enjoyable to know the goal of your tour and how to get there, ticking off the "milestones" on the way, it's the practical way to pace yourself and the safe way to ski. If you always know where you are, how you got there, and where you're headed, then you can make sensible decisions whenever something unexpected happens, as it usually does on a tour. If the weather changes for the worse, should you return to your starting point or push on? What's closer, your car or the cabin ahead? In skiing at a cross-country area you rub a blister on one foot with your new boots, and want to return to your car for a little preventative first aid. What's the shortest route, the short-cut back? You are enjoying the day's skiing, and are lying in the sun after lunch. Suddenly you realize that the bus will leave in forty-five minutes, without you if you aren't there. What's the fastest way back? Knowing where you are is not just a precaution to take for unexpected emergencies; it's also a great convenience for any day's skiing.

Most cross-country centers' trail complexes are marked, with some coding of trail or trail intersection names or numbers on a center *sketch map.* Some of these maps are detailed and accurate, while others only show you the general trail layout. Look them over carefully before you go out on the trails, and if there's anything you don't understand, ask the staff of the center. Carry the map with you if you can as you ski, and note trail intersections or terrain features as you ski by them.

In finding your way using a cross-country ski-center map, you are practicing *orientation,* the art of using a map to keep from getting lost. Skilled orientation requires experience, as you probably know simply from reading road or city maps. So exacting can the skills required be, that a whole sport, *orienteering,* has been built up around map reading. Fortunately for almost all skiing purposes, map use is simpler, involving compass-guided orientation using Forest Service maps, pictorial relief maps, or topographic maps. If you want

to know more about these skills, read one of the references listed in the back of this book.

In using a simple trail sketch map, it helps to have a fixed point of reference in the terrain and on the map. A nearby lake or peak that you ski toward or away from, a valley that you ski along or across, all help you know where you are on the map. If you have a compass, use it to orient the map to north. If you don't have a compass and the sun is shining, you can get a rough check on direction from its position. For most of the wintertime in the snow belt in North America, the sun rises about in the southeast and sets about in the southwest. As you face south, it goes from left to right. If you have difficulty remembering this, picture yourself as standing, facing south, at Chicago on a large map of the USA. The sun rises from the direction of Florida and sets somewhere around Arizona. At midday it's directly south of you.

SKIING WEATHER

One facet of *past* weather—whether or not it has resulted in snow on the ground—determines whether or not you can ski. *Current* weather, and your willingness to take account of it or cope with it, also affects your skiing.

Weather conditions like snowfall, rain, wind, and temperature affect waxing (Chapter 13), the performance of some skis (Chapter 11), and your choice of clothing (Chapter 12). Some knowledge of past and current weather is one of the best safety measures whenever you travel in terrain where avalanches can occur (Chapter 10).

Weather affects your most prudent choice of routes to ski. When it's windy,

All strides are possible, even with a larger pack,
provided it fits and rides well as you ski.
Fletcher Manley

trails in the woods offer more protection than exposed trails in the open. But in the woods strong winds can be dangerous, as they can blow dead branches off trees or blow trees over onto skiers.

In conditions of poor visibility—"whiteouts," where snow and fog blend into one—finding your way can be difficult, even on marked trails. Heavy snowfalls blown by wind can also blot out terrain features, trail signs, and ski tracks, making even finding your way back to where you started difficult.

Fortunately for most skiers skiing in

cross-country ski areas, the weather is not as unpredictable as it once was. Satellite photos, computers, and other modern methods have made forecasts surprisingly accurate. Check and heed forecasts, and always ski prepared for the worst they offer.

ON-TRAIL NOURISHMENT

The only rule about eating when skiing is don't go hungry when you're miles away from your food. And as skiing cross-country burns Calories at rates probably far higher than customary for your other activities, you should plan on eating well. From then on it's all individual, and can be anything from frequent snacks from pocket caches, to full-blown gourmet feasts in cabins.

Most important are liquids. When skiing you not only lose liquid through perspiration, as you do when jogging or running, but you can also lose through the exhalation of moisture, as winter air is often very dry. The total loss and your resultant thirst can come as a shock if you've not experienced it previously. So replenish liquids: you'll find it almost impossible to drink too much when exercising in cold weather. Any slightly sweet drink will do: many skiers carry tea with a bit of honey, a "runner's drink" such as ERG or Gatorade, or fruit juice thinned with water. Drink temperature should be just body temperature or warmer. Out on the trail, cold drinks can cool your stomach, which is not what you want when skiing. Wait until you get inside for the cold ones.

CROSS-COUNTRY WISE

Few laws or regulations apply to cross-country skiing, but the FIS—the International Ski Federation—and various major skiing organizations have recommended codes of skiing ethics and rules of conduct for skiers. These "rules of the road" are designed to promote safe, enjoyable skiing for all cross-country skiers.

CHECK YOUR GEAR. Even if you rent equipment, check it before you ski. Look for damage that could weaken skis, boots, bindings, or poles. Make sure that you have a good boot-to-binding fit. If you have waxless skis, be sure that they are in good repair and work on the snow involved. If you have waxable skis, see that they are waxed for the day's conditions.

LEAVE PETS AT HOME. Don't let your dog walk on a ski trail. Dog tracks can punch holes in even the best of prepared trails, not to mention what dog droppings can do to ski tracks. Dogs can collide with skiers, causing injury. If you must go on a trail with a dog, keep it on a leash and stay to the side, well away from the ski tracks.

Leave pets home.
Bob Bugg

KNOW WHERE YOU'RE GOING. Learn your route and your destination, however short your tour. Take advantage of all posted maps or information at ski centers, and read trail signs as you ski. Plan the length and speed of your tour to be within your ability.

PAY TRAIL FEES. The fees cross-country ski areas charge, even those posted as "voluntary," pay for trail maintenance, marking, and preparation, and for the salaries of ski patrols.

SKI SAFELY. Always ski within your ability. Adjust your speed to terrain, snow conditions, and visibility ahead, especially on downhills. If you truly doubt you can handle a downhill, sidestep down, at the edge of the trail. Keep a safe distance from other skiers. When skiing uphill, watch for skiers skiing toward you, down the hill. They are moving faster than you are, and have less control; give them the right-of-way, even if you have to get off the trail.

SLOW DOWN. Slow down at all blind trail intersections and curves, especially if you are skiing fast downhill. Avoid collisions by seeing other skiers before they see you.

Ski in control.
Bob Bugg

WARN OTHERS. Shout warnings only when absolutely necessary and only to caution others. When overtaking a slower skier on a downhill, for instance, use the standard warnings, "track left'' or ''track right,'' to indicate the side on which you will pass.

RESPECT OTHERS. Ski so that you do not endanger or offend fellow skiers. Don't hog a trail.

KEEP RIGHT. If there is more than one track on the trail, ski to the right. Groups should always ski in single file, on the right. Don't ski side by side unless there are more than two tracks, or adequate room for other skiers to pass in either direction.

Stay right. *Bob Bugg*

PASS CAREFULLY. You may pass another skier on either side, in any free track or outside the tracks. Always allow a faster skier to pass, but you don't have to get out of a track for an overtaking skier, except when racing.

Pass carefully. *Bob Bugg*

KEEP POLES IN. Don't swing your poles wide to the side; keep them close in to your body. This is also good ski technique.

Keep poles in. *Bob Bugg*

KEEP TRAILS CLEAR. If you stop, get out of the track. If you're on a busy trail, leave the trail. If you fall, get up and out of the track quickly.

Keep trails clear. *Bob Bugg*

AID OTHERS. Be helpful whenever you can. Your offering wax or giving directions or advice can make the day for another skier. At the scene of an accident identify yourself whether you're involved or not, and give aid if you can. Summon the ski patrol if necessary. Cold is especially dangerous to injured persons, so if you have extra garments, offer them.

REPORT IF NEEDED. Report trail washouts, creek overflow, fallen branches or trees, or other obstructions to the staff of a cross-country ski center. Always report accidents, avalanches, or major damage to ski center staff, rangers, or whoever administers the area where you ski.

DON'T TRESPASS. Request permission before skiing on private land. Check with ski center operators before skiing away from their marked trails, as often they do not own all the land on which their trails run, and have permission for skiers to cross property belonging to others only on marked trails.

RESPECT PROPERTY. If you open a gate, close it. If you remove a fence rail, replace it. If you use an unattended trail cabin, try to leave it in the same condition that you found it in, or better.

DON'T LITTER. Carry out everything that you carry in. If you must answer a call of nature away from indoor plumbing or outhouses, ski off the trail, dig a "potty" in the snow, and cover what you leave, like a cat.

Don't litter. *Bob Bugg*

DON'T PLAY WITH FIRE. Snow does not prevent forest fires. Check with ski center operators or rangers before you camp, use stoves, or build fires. If you smoke or use a waxing torch on the trail, don't discard the matches.

OBEY SIGNS. Respect all trail markings and information signs. Ski only in the marked direction on one-way trails.

Obey signs. *Bob Bugg*

NOTIFY OTHERS. Before leaving on longer point-to-point tours or any tour in an unpatrolled area, leave notice of your route and your estimated time of arrival at your home or lodge. If you ski from your parked car, leave a note on the dashboard, visible from outside, describing your route and anticipated time of return to the car. Always check back wherever you've left such notes, to be certain that it's understood that you have returned. It's embarrassing and often expensive to be the object of a search when you're safely home.

EXPECT THE UNEXPECTED. Always be prepared for poor weather and for unexpected delays. Wind can be a hazard on any ski trip, so take along windproof garments. Gloves and caps can be lost, so take spares. A bit of food taken along can be a valuable emergency ration if needed.

ABOUT ALCOHOL: Imbibe if you wish, but only after skiing, when you are back inside. Alcohol is a depressant, hardly the sort of thing you want to consume when outside in cold weather. Remember, alcohol is only a couple of atoms different from ether, and was, in fact, used as anesthetic until ether was discovered. Above all, *never* give alcohol to a person suffering from cold, no matter whether he or she just feels chilled or is suffering from frostbite or hypothermia. A nip out in the cold may put the person out cold.

BE WARY, CLOTHE AND CARRY

You don't have to ski very long to have seen the two extremes of preparedness in cross-country skiers, and to understand that they both are equally undesirable.

At the heavy extreme is the *catalog-syndrome skier.* This poor soul appears at a trailhead outfitted for a modest day's skiing with gear that would do for crossing a major mountain range, and usually carrying a pack of the type otherwise used on extended ski expeditions. You'll meet this mule of the ski trails again, a few hundred yards up the trail, wet with sweat, peeling off clothing, and stuffing it into an apparently full pack. And later you may hear or meet the mule-skier again, chilled by sweat-wet clothes, stopped by the track, putting garments on again. The process repeats itself several times during the day, as the mule plods on. Poor mule. It really wasn't necessary to carry *all* that stuff.

At the feather-light extreme is the *racer image* skier. You'll generally meet this skier inside in a warming hut or cabin, close to a stove, shivering and complain-

NO-BOOZE BERNARDS

Many skiers imbibe on the trail, taking swigs from wineskins, pocket flasks, and bottles. Often they feel they have extra good reason to do so. After all, there were those St. Bernard dogs that carried brandy in small casks tied around their necks to save snowbound travelers in the Alps. The monks who sent the dogs out certainly must have known what they were doing.

It's a good story, part of the common legend of snow sports. Its only shortcoming is that it is fiction, not fact. Nobody knows how the myth started. The basic story must have been well established when cartoons depicting a St. Bernard dog carrying a whiskey or brandy cask to save marooned traveler(s) first appeared in the early 1930s, in *The New Yorker* and other magazines. There's no count of the appearances of similar cartoons or drawings that have been published since worldwide, but there obviously have been so many that the situation depicted is presumed by many to be founded in fact.

The keepers of the hospice of the 8110-foot-high Grand Saint Bernard Pass connecting Switzerland and Italy were, indeed, the original breeders of the first St. Bernard dogs, and did send the dogs out to rescue travelers lost in the snows of the pass—with blankets tied around their necks. From Charlemagne on, St. Bernard Pass travelers had better sense than to imbibe while out in the snows.

ing of the cold. Lightly clad in clothing suitable for a racer moving fast, this skier is simply underdressed for the conditions and his/her skiing.

Both the catalog-syndrome skier and the racer image skier get cold, and end up not enjoying their skiing. They've arrived at the same degree of misery from opposite causes.

The principles of sensible clothing for cross-country skiing are simple and straightforward (Chapters 9 and 12). Applying them to suit your skiing and the prevailing weather is the only secret to feeling comfortable on a cross-country ski tour. Sitting inside, you may find it difficult to judge just how much to put on to keep yourself warm while moving at subfreezing temperatures outside. One trick some skiers use is to dress warmly enough to feel comfortable while sitting in a cool room, 18°C. (65°F.) or so; the same clothing will be about right for recreational skiing at outdoor temperatures a few degrees below freezing. Another trick is to see how you feel the first few minutes when you step outdoors: if you're just slightly too chilly, then you're probably dressed about right to ski at that temperature. In all attire take the possibility of wind chill (see box, p. 194) into account. A useful trick for avoiding chill when skiing is to pace yourself fast enough to keep warm, but not so fast that you perspire unduly. Your body heat can then evaporate the perspiration in your garments and you'll stay warm, without being chilled by wetness against your skin. The risk of chill due to your own perspiration is greatest when you *stop* skiing, when your body no longer produces enough heat to evaporate the moisture. That's the time to change clothes.

If you plan to ski for several hours, take a few extra items along—a spare cap and/or headband, mittens, dry socks. Having extra items along not only prepares you for weather changes, but allows you flexibility as you ski and stop to eat lunch or view the scenery.

Carry a small pack if you wish. If you ski in a group, especially with kids, a pack is indispensable. Its contents vary according to the length of your tour, the weather, and your own personal tastes. After a few trips you'll learn what to carry. But here's a checklist of the more frequently forgotten items that should go along on all tours of a few hours or more:

- pocket knife (a "Swiss army knife" is one favorite)
- small flashlight or skier's headlamp (if a mishap delays you, you'll have some light as it gets dark)
- roll of cloth-backed adhesive tape (for repairing gear and skiers)
- spare plastic ski tip (for tip breaks, the most common. Also useful for digging snow, scraping skis, and so on)
- if you're on waxable skis, the next softest and next hardest wax to the one you've used
- scraper-cork (even if you're on waxless skis, a useful item to have)
- screwdriver that fits your binding screws, or one blade on your pocket knife that will do the job
- sunglasses
- map of area, and a compass if you're on a longer tour
- food, in small plastic portion bags (for convenience, and protection against melted snow)
- money (if you ski to an attended cabin where drinks and food are sold)
- toilet paper (never count on outhouses having enough, and there's never any along the trail; also useful for drying skis, blowing noses)
- adhesive bandages
- sun-protection oil or cream, "frost cream," or Vaseline, as needed

Summer hiking can prepare you for winter skiing.
Michael Brady

·spare clothing as needed, windproof over-suit as indicated by terrain and weather forecast (always along on longer tours)

The gear for extended overnight trips, ski mountaineering, or wilderness skiing is a subject in itself, too comprehensive to be included here. There are many excellent, authoritative books on the subject; a few of the better-known ones are listed in the reference section of this book.

OBSTACLES AND THE UNEXPECTED

Even shorter ski tours away from the maintained trails of a cross-country center may be full of small surprises, obstacles not easily overcome with ordinary cross-country ski technique. Even tours in city parks or snow-covered golf courses can toss a few unexpected difficulties in your path. Here are a few of the more common ones, and tricks for negotiating them with proper skiing aplomb:

CREEKS, BROOKS, AND SMALL TRAIL WASHOUTS: Stop. Sidestep over, for you don't want to risk dirt either in your wax or clogged in the waxless section of your skis. Don't try to ski straight over, as this may "bridge" your skis across the gap between the snow on either side, straining the ski laminations unduly, causing damage.

ROAD CROSSINGS: If the snow is fresh and new and neither plows nor sanding/salting trucks have been by, look out for passing vehicles, and when the road is clear, ski right across. But don't trust any road surface that's been plowed or driven on to any extent, as few things destroy ski bases more quickly than sand and road salt. Take off your skis and walk across.

FENCES: Vaulting over, as you may have seen in photos of hotshots doing it, can offer more surprises than running hurdles if you've not done it before. The safest way over depends on the fence height and what's on top. For sturdy wood or stone fences, you can kick-turn over or sit on top and swing one leg over at a time. Barbed wire is worse. Take off your skis and have someone else either part wires so you can creep through, or hold the top wire down so you can kick-turn over.

ICY, ROCKY, DOWNHILL CHUTES: No way to ski safely. Take your skis off and walk down, until you can see a good stretch of snow with a reasonable outrun.

7

RACING
There Are Many Ways to Compete

Classified races have individual starts—here Raisa Smetanina starts in the 1980 Winter Olympic 5-km race, which she won. *Galen Rowell*

Cross-country ski racing is a calling all its own within the sport. Like mountaineering, it is a way of life for its practitioners, often incomprehensible to outsiders. Many skiers know enough about the call of racing to want to give it a try, yet feel reluctant to start.

One reason may be that common skiing myth surrounds the racer with extrahuman powers, with a glowing nimbus of capability to which normal skiing mortals cannot aspire. Nothing could be further from the truth. To get started or to participate in racing, you don't need a background of super training, a lifetime of skiing, or flawless technique. Granted, in this competitive age, superiority in racing requires both extraordinary ability and genetic gifts, but the other component, the bulk of a racer's capability, from citizen racers to Olympic medalists, lies in evaluation of one's own abilities, some planning, and lots of just plugging away at it. A race is really nothing more than a long, fast ski tour, run on a schedule, over a specified track.

THE SPECTRUM OF RACING

As in running, there are two major forms of cross-country ski racing. *Classified,* or *sanctioned, races* correspond to track events in running. *Citizens' races* correspond to the fun runs, road races, and marathons of jogging and running.

CLASSIFIED OR SANCTIONED cross-country races are the highly organized skiing equivalent of summertime track events. Like track meets, they are a part of club and university athletics, and are the events of the sport incorporated in World Ski Championships and Winter Olympic Games. Entry in these events is restricted to competitors classified by national ski associations, such as the USSA—the United States Ski Association—or the CSA—the Canadian Ski Association. The skiing distances, like the various distances in track, from the sprints to the long-distance events, were originally intended to be so different from one another as to challenge a range of athletic capabilities. This is why there are four international-standard distance events each for men and women: 15-, 30-, and 50-km individual events and a four-man, 40-km relay for men, and 5-, 10-, and 20-km individual events and a four-woman, 20-km relay for women. In the individual events racers start one at a time, usually at 30-second intervals, and they race against the clock. The final outcome of such a race is decided only after the last racer has finished. Relays, like relays in track, are mass-start events: the first team to put their last racer over the finish line wins.

The men's 15-km and women's 5-km events were originally envisioned as the "sprints," suited to younger, faster racers, while the longest events would be mastered by the seasoned veterans of the cross-country ski tracks. The relays should reflect a country's depth of racing talent.

Though simple in original concept, this picture is no longer valid. Individual racers now can, and often do, win at all distances. Norwegian Berit Aunli won three Gold Medals and one Silver Medal in the four women's cross-country events of the 1982 Nordic World Ski Championships in Oslo. Before Aunli, Russian super skier Galina Kulakova twice swept the field, winning all women's events at a Nordic World Ski Championships or Winter Olympics. In the 1980 Winter Olympic Games in Lake Placid, New York, Kulakova's teammate Nikolai Zimjatov

INTERNATIONAL RACE REGULATIONS

Virtually all classified, or sanctioned, races are organized following the established international rulings of the FIS, the International Ski Federation. Maximum height differences (between lowest and highest points on a course), maximum height difference of a single climb, and total elevation gained in all the climbs of a course are specified to assure uniformity in racing. The maximum allowable elevation of an internationally sanctioned course is 1,650 meters (5,412 feet) above sea level. The courses in Lake Placid, used in the 1980 Winter Olympics, are well below this level, being no more than slightly over 760 meters (2,493 feet) above sea level at maximum elevation.

Racing bib colors and/or start numbers usually agree with course marking colors, so if you see a color photo of a racer taken in an international race, you can identify the event. For relays, all members of the same team wear the same number, with colors for the first through fourth laps being in sequence red, green, yellow, and blue.

COURSE	REGULATION COURSE MARKING COLOR	Total climb of course REGULATION METERS	TYPICAL COURSES: 1980 LAKE PLACID WINTER OLYMPICS METERS	FEET
JUNIOR				
girls 5 km		150–200		
boys 10 km		250–400		
boys 15 km		300–450		
WOMEN				
5 km	blue	150–200	154	505
10 km	violet	250–300	282	925
20 km	violet/red	400–500	*	*
4 × 5 km relay	red/blue	150–200	162	531
MEN				
15 km	red	450–600	477	1565
15 km combined	green	400–500	463	1519
30 km	red/green	750–1000		
50 km	orange	1000–1500	1448	4750
4 × 10 km relay	green/orange	300–450	315	1033

*20 km not Winter Olympic event in 1980; will first be so in 1984.

won the 30-km and 50-km races, was on the gold-medal Russian relay team, and placed fourth, by just five seconds, in the 15-km race. Even in the increasingly keen competitive environment of the past two decades, the super skier is no new phenomenon: Norwegian Gjermund Eggen won three of the four men's events in the 1966 FIS Nordic World Ski Championships. And in terms of the character of the sport today, that was long ago, in the days of wood skis with tarred wood bases, tonkin bamboo ski poles, leather boots with leather soles, two-piece racing

THE CLOSENESS OF CROSS-COUNTRY

That a single individual can dominate all international cross-country ski racing distances may be ascribed to modern knowledge and practice of effective training, aimed to equip racers with the physiological machinery to win. It also means that classified races are now run flat out: there is little, if any, slowing down over the longer distances. Different cross-country ski races are run on different tracks, with varying proportions of uphills, downhills, and flats, and snow conditions are seldom the same from race to race. This means that times cannot be compared directly, as they can be in track. There are no "world's records" for times for cross-country ski races.

Nonetheless trends are evident. For instance, in the 1980 Winter Olympic Games held in Lake Placid, the women's 10 km was won in just 17.7 seconds more than twice the 5 km winning time. The men's 50 km was won in just 2 min. 20 seconds more than 1 2/3 times the 30 km winning time.

The differences between the events involve tactics: pacing for judicious use of energies is more important in a 50-km race lasting about 2½ hours than it is in a 15-km event lasting less than 45 minutes. But modern, year-round training also has made the converse true: racers lacking the tactical ability to do well in a 20-km or a 50-km race, have small chances of winning a 5-km or a 15-km race.

Similar observations may, of course, be made of the Alpine skiing events, more commonly felt to be events of speed and frequent photo-finishes. From Jean-Claude Killy's legendary sweeps of the field, to Ingemar Stenmark's multiple wins, to Hanni Wenzel's two golds and one silver in the 1980 Winter Olympic Games Alpine skiing events, the

Thomas Wassberg in 1980 Winter Olympic 15 km.
Galen Rowell

international Alpine racing scene is often dominated by super skiers. But one of the lesser-known aspects of cross-country ski racing is that it is as close as and often closer than Alpine, both on relative and absolute scales.

Ingemar Stenmark won the 1980 Winter

Olympic Games' slalom by half a second, barely ahead of American Phil Mahre, a very close finish in that event. Yet Stenmark's Swedish ski teammate Thomas Wassberg won the 15-km cross-country race in the same Olympics by one hundredth of a second, ahead of Finn Juha Mieto. What makes Wassberg's win even more astounding is that it was in an event that lasted almost 42 minutes, while each of Stenmark's two runs lasted less than a minute. Stenmark effectively won by a couple of ski lengths; Wassberg won by less than the length of one of the small toeclip bindings on his skis. Beating the season's cross-country world cup winner isn't easy, but Wassberg had done it once before—in the 1979 Holmenkollen 15-km race the year before; he won in a time of 44.40.7, just one tenth of a second ahead of Norwegian Oddvar Braa, winner of the 1979 cross-country world cup. In the 1980 cross-country world cup standings, Wassberg ended up second, 12 points behind Mieto.

This keen competition is no recent development. Looking back a few Olympiads, to those held before the current renaissance of cross-country skiing, the competition was just as tough. In the 1968 Winter Olympic Games in Grenoble, France, French super Alpine ski racer Jean-Claude Killy skied on home snows to win the downhill in 1.59.85, just eight hundredths of a second ahead of teammate Guy Perrialt, a sensationally small margin. But in the same Games, Norwegian Harald Grönningen won the 15-km cross-country ski race in 47.54.2, just 1.9 seconds ahead of Finn Eero Mäntyranta, exactly the same margin as Killy's win in terms of percentages. Cross-country ski racing at the international level always has been close, and now it's closer than ever.

suits with wool knee socks, and foot-tramped, skied-in tracks on race courses.

CITIZENS' RACING may sound like a socialistic form of regulated recreation, but it's far from that. Citizens' races are the equivalent of the fun runs and marathons of the jogging-running world, where the joy of participation is primary. The term "citizen," which works in most languages of the skiing world, simply means that the races are open to all, not just a qualified few, as are the classified events.

In mass-start citizens' races, or *touring races* as they sometimes are called, the first skier across the finish line wins. But that skier is simply declared the overall winner, or, as it's usually a man, the overall men's winner. Therefore there's usually also an overall women's winner, the first lady to finish. And there are also many other winners, as the skiers race together, but in terms of results are separated into classes by age and sex in the result lists. There can be as many as twelve classes by age, from *under 13* to *over 60*. Therefore, in addition to the two overall winners, there can be as many as twenty-four individual class winners in a citizens' race, and as the first three places in a class are often awarded medals or trophies, a total of seventy-four "medalists" in a single race. There are more than three chances to place well in a citizens' race.

Race lengths range from 5 to 100 km, with most races being in the 5-to-15 km and 40-to-60 km ranges. Many of the larger races feature half-length events, run simultaneously, for juniors and older racers who don't wish to go the full distance. Usually the only restraints imposed are that younger racers are limited to distances of 25 km and down.

The first citizens' races in North America were held in the early 1960s, and now

Racing can be scenic. *Michael Brady*

Citizens' races have more social starts—this is the start of the American Birkebeiner in Cable, Wisconsin. *Telemark*

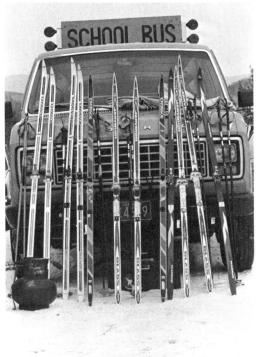

Present and future racers abound. *Michael Brady*

there are hundreds held each winter. They range from low-key local events, where you may enter the day of the race, to major meets that attract skiers from all over the continent and some from abroad, for which many skiers register months in advance. There is even an international league for citizens' racers, the *World Loppet League,* a series of ten races in ten countries. Some skiers have raced all the World Loppet races in a single season, while others are content to race once or twice a season, at party races, where the get-together after the race is the day's main attraction. Above all, citizens' racing is what you want to make it. You can be as serious or as loose as you wish, and enjoy it in your own way.

SUPER SKIERS

In all sports, there's an ongoing discussion of just who are the greats, the stars, the best practitioners. The measures differ, from numbers of knockouts for boxers to numbers of cups won for tennis players. For ski racers, and other winter sports athletes competing in individual sports, the ranking is by number of medals won in World Championship skiing. And here cross-country wins hands down, far ahead of all other skiing disciplines.

Including the Winter Olympic Games, which also count as World Ski Championships, it's a toss-up between Swede Sixten Jernberg and Russian Galina Kulakova as to who is the all-time superstar of the sport. From 1954 through 1964 Jernberg amassed a total of fourteen World Ski Championship medals, half of them gold. From 1968 through 1980 Kulakova collected fifteen World Ski Championships medals, ten of them gold. Kulakova was a threat in all women's cross-country ski events, having taken gold medals in all three events in both the 1972 Winter Olympics and the 1974 FIS Nordic World Ski Championships, a feat unequaled by any other racer. The superstar of skiing is a cross-country skier and a woman.

Galina Kulakova in 1978 FIS Nordic World Ski Championships 5 km. *Michael Brady*

THINK AHEAD, JUDGE YOURSELF

There are no set rules for evaluating your ability to race. But most racers and coaches agree on three general guidelines for participation in racing, be it citizens' racing or classified racing.

First, and most obvious, you must be healthy enough and fit enough to race. If you are in doubt, consult your physician.

Never too late to start racing: E. Rutledge Gish, a doctor from Fulton, Missouri, was 73 and had been racing in citizens' races for three years when this photo was taken at a 25-km race in 1981.
Michael Brady

Some races require that you have a medical checkup the same season that you intend to race. In any case, if you are not an experienced competitor, it is advisable to have a medical examination before taking up a competitive sport of any sort.

Second, you should be skilled enough to race at the level at which you intend to participate. Skill is perhaps the most difficult capability to assess, but common sense dictates that it may be evaluated in terms of speed. Just as it makes little sense to "run" a marathon at a walking pace of five miles per hour, it is inadvisable to race unless you can ski at reasonable speed. In most citizens' races, the winning time plus 20 percent to 30 percent is regarded as good, and is often recognized by the award of a certificate or a pin. Double the winning time of any one age/sex class in a race is slow skiing. In terms of present racing times for able persons, this means that you should be able to ski a course similar to the one you intend to race at a speed of 9 to 11 kilometers per hour or faster.

Third, you should be able to race the distance involved, to your own satisfaction. Here is where you are most on your own, as nothing but personal experience will tell you how long you can maintain your desired speed in a race. As a general rule you should be experienced in skiing over a distance before you attempt to race that distance. But even so obvious a rule has its exceptions: for the ultralong events, such as some of the 80-km-plus citizens' races, practicing over the full race distance is impractical, even for full-time athletes. So an even more general rule is that you should be able to move fast, jog on foot or ski fast, for a time equal to or greater than the time you need to finish a race.

HOW TO START

Getting started in citizens' racing often is easier than it seems. All you have to do is to find out where the races are, enter and pay your entry fee, show up at the right time, and ski the race. It's that simple.

Even if you are an athlete bent on "serious" racing, citizens' racing may be a good start, to see if you take to the sport. Classified racing has its own well-organized hierarchy of clubs, school and college teams, coaches, training camps, and association divisions. For further information contact the United States Ski Association in the USA or the Canadian Ski Association in Canada; addresses are listed in the back of this book.

Local ski shops, cross-country and touring ski centers, ski clubs, and ski magazines and newspapers all carry information on and ads for citizens' races. Entries, postmarked at least a week before the race and accompanied by the entry fee (from a few dollars for local races up to forty or more for major meets), are usually made on special forms for each race. If you don't have a form, send the information you know is needed: your name and address, birth date and age as of January 1 of the year of the race, sex, racing class if you know it, and ski association membership number if you are a member. Many races require you to sign a waiver stating that you race at your own risk, which is usually done on the application form. If you send in your own entry without the official application form, you may be required to sign a waiver before you pick up your start-number bib.

A RACE DAY

The first rule for successful racing is to get to the race early. If you're half an hour early, you are at least half an hour late. You will be surprised how fast an hour or two can go when you have to get your start-number bib, check your equipment and clothing, wax your skis, and ski a bit of the course, all of which you should do before the start gun goes off.

If the snow conditions for the day are tricky and you are on waxable skis (still the best performers for citizens' racing—see Chapter 11), plan to carry a bit of wax, a scraper, and a cork along. Some skiers use pockets for this purpose, while others favor small fanny packs. In any case, take only what you think you will need. Some seasoned citizens' racers minimize weight and bulk of items carried by taking only half-full tubes of klister or half cans of wax, compact scraper-corks, or a klister-spreader paddle for a scraper and part of a waxing cork that has been cut into halves or thirds for the purpose.

Check your gear and clothing well before the start. Do you have enough clothes on? Experienced racers swear by transport-type underwear, even for warmer skiing conditions. They find it better to stay dry and warm than wet and chilly. Do your boots and bindings mate well and function as they should? Are your pole straps adjusted to fit your hands with the gloves or mittens that you intend to wear in the race? The time to do all these things is when you don't have to do them fast.

If possible, ski a part of the course, or, for shorter multiloop courses, the whole thing if you wish. Knowing where you are going, what to expect, always helps. Look for steep uphills or fast downhills,

Feeding stations are the pit stops of cross-country ski racing. *Michael Brady*

turns, long tracks, wind-exposed stretches, different snow conditions, such as patches exposed to strong sunlight, and any other course peculiarities that will affect your skiing. Plan for them when racing.

Drink a bit half an hour or more before the start; stock up on liquids. Half a cup or so of a slightly sweet drink, such as tea with a little sugar or a runner's drink, such as ERG or Gatorade, is all that most skiers need. During the race, drink at the "feeding stations." Don't pass them up, as in so doing you may suffer a slowdown later; liquid loss debilitates. Slow down at the stations, so the drink gets into your mouth and down your throat, not all over your face and down onto your bib. Avoid solid food, except the orange slices offered at some feeding stations. Racing and digestion don't go well together, and if you eat you may soon suffer discomfort or worse as you race along.

Get to the start early and stake out your place. Mass starts can be mob scenes reminiscent of movie scenes of medieval battles, so pick a good spot to defend your skills. If you are a fast starter and feel you have a chance to win, get up front: that's where you belong. If you're average, get somewhere in the middle, to avoid being run over by those behind. If you are among the more leisurely racers, the rear is best: let the others charge ahead, and ski the race at your own pace.

There are several ways to stay warm as you wait for a start. One is to jog in place and swing your arms. Some races provide numbered plastic bags in which to stow your outer clothing before a start, so you can overdress until the last few minutes before the starting gun goes off. At races not offering such a convenience or where it's too far back to your belongings to return outer garments there, improvise temporary outer layers if you feel chilled when standing still. Some racers use garbage bags for warm-ups. Cut openings for your neck and arms in the bottom of a

SKILLED SKIER

RACER

DIAGONAL STRIDE

Racers ski faster because they kick more vigorously, and exploit all maneuvers more completely than do skilled recreational skiers. Here the track is marked off into six-foot intervals with flags in the snow.

The skilled skier covers a lot of track with a single stride, 6 feet. In the seven tenths of a second elapsed between the first and last photos of the above sequences, that amounts to a speed of 5.8

large plastic garbage bag, and put it on. It's windproof and will trap enough still air to keep you warm. Discard it just before the start, preferably at the side of the start area, in a refuse container, so it won't get in the way of other skiers and won't litter the course.

Ration your resources as you ski the race. A fast start may look impressive, but it's the start-to-finish time that counts. You may find that during a race you pass others who sprinted away from you at the start. Think through each stretch as you ski it. You can afford an all-out sprint up a hill if a downhill follows so you can rest. But if another hill follows, take it easy, so you get to the top smoothly. Ski behind someone who is skiing well and at about your speed, and you'll be "drawn" along, cruising behind

easily. But pull out and pass if you feel the pace too slow.

After a race the first thing on your mind should be to change, to get out of your damp clothes and, if possible, take a shower. This is where many racers err: they stand around and chat, and in so doing cool off and become chilled. A beeline for a change and a shower may spare you more than just discomfort.

THE WHEREWITHAL

You'll probably find that racing is really superb self-instruction in skiing, with many spinoffs that benefit your everyday ski touring. In racing a distance you would have to be strongly immune to the entire spirit of putting on a bib and com-

mph. But the racer covers more track, and attains a speed of 8.8 mph. Note that the two skiers are skiing with almost identical tempos—the racer is only slightly ahead of the skilled recreational skier

in starting the next kick. Speed comes from improved technique, not always from the rapidity with which it is done. *Fletcher Manley*

peting, not to work a good deal harder than you would just to tour that same distance over the same track. Skiing at speed contracts the time allowed for each maneuver, which sets a premium on smooth, efficient technique. Meeting these challenges, the extra requirements of racing above and beyond those of pleasure skiing, are among the joys and benefits of participation.

Just as good cross-country ski technique is a suitably slowed, less extreme version of racing technique, racing technique is nothing more than a speedier version of good cross-country technique. If you already ski well, little more need be said, save that skiing fast uses energy rapidly, and the penalties paid for inefficient movement are correspondingly high. Ski efficiently is the maxim of racing.

There is no one, correct racing technique, as speedy movement amplifies, rather than reduces, individual differences. No two racers ski exactly alike; never try to imitate another racer exactly, no matter how skilled he appears to be. Good racing technique can best be described as a skeleton of no-waste movement around which you can build the body of your own racing style.

The best way to learn something of good racing technique is to watch good racers race. See what they do, and, more important, what they don't do.

You'll probably note that the better racers all have a relaxed, forward-leaning body position, with virtually no bob and sway as they ski. Seen in motion the body appears to hang suspended in space, as arms and legs swing, pendulumlike,

RACER

SKILLED SKIER

DOUBLE POLING

The greater thrust of a more complete and more rapid pole maneuver is what gives the racer speed. Here the time scales don't match exactly as they did for the diagonal stride sequences: the skilled skier took 1.4 seconds to complete the double poling shown, while the racer took 1.2 seconds. But in

DOUBLE-POLE STRIDE

Here the skilled skier and the racer are again skiing with about the same stride tempo. The elapsed time for one stride, or the difference between the first and last frames of the above sequences, is 1.3 seconds. But the racer covers half again as much track as the skilled skier for each stride, mostly because of a

RACER

SKILLED SKIER

those times the racer covered 18 feet of track, compared to the skilled skier's 12 feet of track. The skilled skier is still moving at 5.8 mph, but the racer's speed has jumped to 10 mph. *Fletcher Manley*

more rapid and powerful poling, followed by a longer glide on one ski. The skilled skier's speed has gone up slightly, to 6.2 mph, which is evidence of the value of added pole thrust in the stride. But the racer is still at a high 10 mph. *Fletcher Manley*

In all strides the racer stays right over the skis and
the tracks. *Fletcher Manley*

forward and back to propel the body forward.

You'll also notice that racers "stretch out" more, that their arm and leg movements are more extreme. This is a consequence of faster skiing, of kicking "harder" with each stride. It's specifically *not* "giant steps." Recall what you do when you want to speed up on foot: you don't stretch the forward leg out front more, you push off harder, or kick more forcefully with each step.

In the diagonal stride both your stride length and your tempo, or rate of striding, contribute to your skiing speed. Mathematically your speed is simply the product of your stride length and tempo:

Skiing speed = stride length × stride tempo

For instance, average, skilled skiers, skiing on the flat with stride lengths of about eight feet and tempos of about eighty strides a minute, ski at a speed of:

8 feet per stride × 80 strides per minute
= 640 feet per minute = 38,400 feet per hour
= 7.3 miles per hour

Increasing each stride by six inches—about half a boot length for many adult skiers—increases overall skiing speed by half a mile an hour. Stepping up tempo by five strides per minute, no more than one extra stride every twelve seconds, produces the same result. But if both stride length and tempo are increased by these amounts, speed jumps to 8.2 miles per hour.

So to ski faster, kick both harder and faster. The "stretch" you see in good racers will come by itself. As is the case in running, your more forceful movements will include active forward movements of your arms and legs; you want to get them there where you need them, faster than if they just swung forward. Good racers have extremely active forward arm and leg movements on uphills, and, to a lesser extent, on flats.

Finally, you'll note that racers *really* direct all their movements down the track, in the direction they are going. If you ever doubt that a little side-to-side arm movement, say, eats up much energy, stand still and move your arm from side to side for the length of time you would do so in a race. You'll probably tire quickly. Wasted movement wastes energy; wasted energy tires you more rapidly; when you tire, you no longer can kick or pole forcefully enough to maintain your speed; you then tire more quickly. It's a vicious circle: poor technique tires you rapidly, and when you're tired, your technique gets poorer. So concentrate on nowaste movement, your best friend in racing technique.

One of the more subtle skills in racing is to match your technique to the track and the terrain, continually changing stride tempo and length, and type of stride, always "shifting gears" to suit what's underfoot. There's no way to describe how this is done in the pages of a book, as it depends completely on the terrain you ski and the tracks you face on the day of a race. The best way to learn is to ski behind someone who apparently masters the terrain and the track better than yourself, and imitate his or her movements, up and down hills, on the flats, and through bumps and dips, turns and bends. Be a kid and enjoy it. That's part of the joy of racing, too.

8
FITNESS AND TRAINING
How to Get More Out of Skiing

Plain walking is a route to fitness.
Michael Brady

Cross-country skiing is one of the more easily enjoyed winter recreations. But it also can be done in a way that makes it among the most strenuous. Full enjoyment of the sport comes only when you are physically prepared to ski well at the level you choose.

To understand why preparation is desirable even if you only ski for pleasure, consider an average cross-country ski trip at a major cross-country ski center: about 5 kilometers (3 miles) from the parking lot to a cabin or trail end, and back. Not much, those six miles; many who live in cities walk as much on weekend strolls. But cross-country ski trails are seldom level: they climb and dip, and often one end is higher or lower than the other, with a 750-foot difference in elevation being typical. A total of 750 feet gained and then lost is equivalent to walking halfway up and then down super skyscrapers like the World Trade Center in New York or the Sears Tower in Chicago. Combine that stair climb with the six-mile walk and you have a trip that few would attempt with no preparation whatsoever.

Although preparation for skiing is desirable, it need not be specialized, unless your skiing is specialized. To prepare for a few walking-pace ski tours per season, you don't need to run or even jog vigorously; you just need to walk a lot. In fact, you may already be active in several ways that themselves are good exercise and good preparation for skiing.

GAUGE YOURSELF

Exercise is most effective when you know how it affects your skiing. In other words, if you must embark on an exercise program to supplement your daily activities, then it's best to be specific. Therefore your first step in approaching exercise is to gauge your abilities, needs, and goals.

Start with the most obvious questions: *Should I start an exercise plan?* The answer depends on your present condition and medical history. In general, if you are under 30, have never smoked, are not overweight, and have no past history of heart, lung, or other major internal organ difficulties, then you probably can start exercise. But if you are older, particularly if you are over 40, overweight, a smoker, have had any heart or lung difficulties or any previous medical history that makes you reluctant to exercise, you should consult your physician before starting an exercise plan.

When you have decided to start exercise, determine your goals and your starting point. This is the critical phase, the place where most failures occur. Resolutions to "get in shape," followed by a day of hard exercise that results in soreness, stiffness, and lack of sleep, have driven people away from exercise in droves. Don't set your sights too high too soon. The secret is to tailor your exercise to your needs, and to build gradually on what you can do.

If you are a recreational skier, a person who skis for pleasure only, then your exercise goal is to equip yourself to enjoy skiing more. Your off-snow exercise can be done in, or may already be a part of, your natural daily routine, in and around your home, or between your home and where you work or go to school. It need not involve special running or jogging of prescribed distances, weight lifting, or any sports facilities or equipment. You can do it with the most obvious piece of equipment at your disposal: your own body.

If you are a racer, or will start serious racing next season, your aim is to improve your capability to ski at speed. Your exercise, or training, program will be more specific than that for a recreational skier, and you will spend more time at it, sometimes with special equipment, or in selected, suitable places.

RECREATIONAL SKIERS— KEEP IT SIMPLE

How much you should exercise to prepare for recreational skiing depends on your abilities and needs. You can start by classing your exercise level much as skiers class their skills: beginner, intermediate, or advanced.

BEGINNER: You will take up cross-country skiing for the first time this season, or you started last season, skiing only a few times. You are not active in any sports, and you exercise only infrequently.

INTERMEDIATE: You have been cross-country skiing for one or two seasons, or have been active in other outdoor sports for several years. This past summer you were frequently active outdoors.

ADVANCED: You have been cross-country skiing for several years, and are active in outdoor sports year-round. You probably spend your summer vacations hiking or cycling, and you have followed exercise programs in the past.

Finally, determine your goal, how frequently and how far you wish to ski this winter. The more you intend to ski, the more miles you will cover, and the more you should prepare before snow comes.

There are no set rules for how much exercise you need to prepare for your skiing, but a general rule of thumb is that you should be able to cover the same dis-

BENEFIT AND ENJOY

The values and joys of physical activity are now well known, and have been described by many. Here's a sampling of expert opinion on the subject:

"Play has no purpose, but it gives meaning to life."
Dr. George Sheehan,
on describing exercise

"Athleticism must be, and should be, adult 'play.' It is when we make it work—dull, routined, scheduled, treadmill work—that we depart from the natural, the joyous, the exhilarating."
Renowned Australian running coach
Percy Wells Cerutty,
in *Athletics, How to Become a Champion*

"Passive fitness, the mere absence of any illness, is a losing battle. Without activity, the body begins to deteriorate."
Dr. Kenneth H. Cooper, in *Aerobics*

"Mens sana in corpore sano. (A sound mind in a sound body)"
Anon., from the Latin
(and now the motto of the Olympics)

tance on foot as you intend to ski. This means, for instance, that if you intend to ski a six-mile trail at a cross-country ski center, you should have walked six miles at least three or four times before the snow falls.

THINK SKIING

When you cross-country ski, all the major muscle groups in your body are active—arms, legs, chest, back, abdomen. As your body's major muscle groups act to propel you forward, your internal organs act at a

Conditioning Table

EXERCISE	EQUIPMENT	PURPOSE	HOW DONE	
Walking or jogging	Comfortable shoes, clothing for weather	Build endurance, strengthen leg and trunk muscles	In walking, stand straight, stride actively, swing arms, stretch trailing leg with each step, as in skiing. In jogging, strive for longer stride, constant pace; swing arms, but keep them low, hands no higher than your lower ribs.	
Push-ups	None	Strengthen back, arm, chest muscles; aid muscular endurance	Prone position, back straight, raise body by straightening arms, then lower to start position. If you can't do any, start with alternate push-ups.	
Alternate push-ups— on incline	Sturdy chair, bench, or table, edge 24″ to 36″ above floor	Same as for push-ups; build ability to do push-ups	Same as for push-ups, except start with inclined body, hands on edge of table or chair.	
Sit-ups	None	Strengthen abdominal muscles, build muscular endurance	Knees bent, roll upper body up and forward to nearly vertical position, back down again slowly. Hands clasped behind neck.	
Dips	Sturdy chair, bench, or table, edge 16″ to 24″ above floor	Strengthen triceps, important in poling; build muscular endurance	Start in up position with arms straight. Bend at elbow, lowering body, then straighten arms to return to starting position.	
Leg extension stride	Slight hill or flight of stairs	Build endurance; enhance flexibility for ski stride	Stride up hill or up stairs; always straighten trailing leg as if on skis, swing arms as if using poles.	
Back lifts (Seek physician's advice before doing if you have or ever have had back troubles of any sort)	Table, padded with mattress or blanket, strap around table at ankles, or someone to hold your feet.	Strengthen back muscles, vital in all strides on skis.	Lower body, from hips down, supported, upper body free. Start horizontal, sink down as far as comfortable; return to starting position. Hands clasped behind neck. Don't go above horizontal; a swayback position is undesirable.	

corresponding rate. Therefore fitness for cross-country skiing involves all the physical capabilities that comprise fitness: *endurance,* or heart-lung capacity and efficiency, *muscular strength, muscular endurance,* and *flexibility.*

In skiing you need overall endurance to ski without tiring. Muscular strength enables you to perform the movements of skiing, and muscular endurance enables you to perform them many times. To understand the difference between overall endurance and muscular endurance, think of what part of your body usually is the first to tire on early season ski tours—your arms. Many summertime activities contribute to overall endurance, and many build arm strength. But few contribute to arm muscular endurance, which is one reason why you should think of skiing when exercising. In exercising your arms, which, along with your legs, provide your forward power in skiing, think of how they act when you ski. What connects them with your legs, with which they work? Your trunk, the muscles in your abdomen and back. That's why the best exercises for cross-country skiing aim to build muscular strength and muscular endurance for all your skiing muscles, and, as an additional plus, aid the flexibility that you need to assume the various positions of skiing maneuvers.

A word about strength. In cross-country skiing, bulging biceps or bodybuilder bulk are useless. In fact, they may work against you, as greater muscle bulk means that you have more weight to haul along the track. For the cross-country skier, strength means being able to perform the movements of skiing, and being able to perform them many times. That's why exercises that benefit skiing should be done many times: they aim to give you muscles that *do,* not muscles that *show.*

HOW MUCH, HOW OFTEN?

How much you should exercise depends on your abilities and needs. To determine your abilities, you may start by testing yourself to set your own personal dose, the amount of exercise that is best for you. Retest yourself once a month, and readjust your "dose" of exercise as you improve.

BEGINNERS TEST: See how far you can walk in half an hour and how many repetitions of each exercise shown in the table you can do. EXERCISE: Walk half of your half-hour maximum distance at least twice a day, and do half of your maximum* for each exercise, at least once a day, preferably after you have warmed up by walking.

INTERMEDIATES TEST: Walk or jog at the best speed you can comfortably maintain for 45 minutes, and see how many repetitions of the exercises shown in the table you can do. EXERCISE: Walk or jog at two thirds of your maximum speed, for at least half an hour, once a day, and do two sets of half your maximum quantities* of the exercises, preferably after you have warmed up by walking or jogging. Do each set completely, starting with push-ups and ending with back lifts; do not follow any one exercise with more of the same exercise.

ADVANCED TEST: Jog or run at the best speed you can comfortably maintain for an hour, and see how many repetitions of each exercise shown in the table you can do. EXERCISE: Jog or run at two thirds of your maximum speed, for at least 45

*If your maximum for an exercise is an odd number, round off to the next highest whole number in doing half the total: if you can do three push-ups, do two each time you exercise.

minutes, once a day, and do three sets of half your maximum quantities* of the exercises, preferably after you have warmed up by jogging or running. Do each set completely, starting with push-ups and ending with back lifts; do not follow any one exercise with more of the same exercise.

How often you should exercise depends on what you wish to achieve. For the initial stages of fitness plans, fitness experts recommend daily exercise sessions for four weeks, followed by two or three sessions a week. This is because you need daily exercise to build condition, and as deconditioning sets in after three days of inactivity, you should never go more than three days without exercise if you wish to maintain the condition you have built up.

So, to prepare for winter skiing, start daily exercises at least four to five weeks before your first ski tour. Then, during the ski season, exercise at least twice a week between skiing weekends, to maintain and build on the head start your exercise gave you for the season.

THE BODY MACHINE

Cross-country skiing at speed places a premium on overall physical fitness. Overall physical fitness cannot be measured exactly, but it is determined mostly by how well your body functions, by its cardiovascular capability, or how well your heart, lungs, and other internal organs act to fuel the muscles that keep you moving. The "fuel" for motion involves oxygen and a "burning" of carbohydrates and fat. It is termed "aerobic" from the Greek, meaning "with air." The more oxygen your body can supply to your

muscles, the greater your *aerobic capacity,* or overall physical fitness.

Physiological measurements have shown that cross-country ski racing requires the highest level of aerobic capacity, ahead of distance running, cycling, and swimming. This means that in cross-country skiing at speed, your body essentially functions as an aerobic machine. So vital is this measure of performance, that cross-country ski racers and other distance-event athletes often measure their aerobic capacities using specially equipped treadmills or cycle ergometers in human-performance testing laboratories.

In the aerobic process each gram of fat burned liberates about two to three times as much energy as each gram of carbohydrates burned. But fat burning is the more complex, and the body "prefers" to "burn" its carbohydrate reserves before "burning" any fat. In most normal adults the body's carbohydrate reserves, in the form of glycogen, will fuel approximately half an hour of fast skiing. Thereafter the body gradually begins to "burn" its fat reserves. This is why there are no chubby cross-country ski racers. In Scandinavia, where cross-country ski racing reigns supreme as a winter competitive sport, there's an old adage that a good weight (in kilograms) for a cross-country ski racer is body height (in centimeters) minus 100 to 110. This means that your racing weight should be 154 to 176 pounds if you are 5'11" tall, 132 to 154 pounds if you are 5'7" tall, and 110 to 132 pounds if you are 5'3" tall.

In activities such as sprinting up a hill or at the start of a mass-start citizens' race, the body must transform energy in excess of that which can be supplied by the somewhat slower aerobic process alone. It then starts with or shifts to another "combustion" process which in-

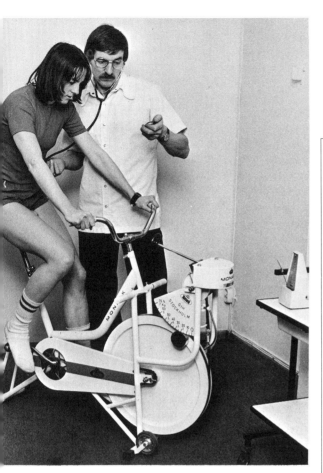

Cycle ergometers test aerobic capacity. *Frits Solvang*

NO BIBS

When you exercise or train for skiing, view it as part of the ongoing joy of the sport. Leave the stress of your daily life behind; do not compete. Whatever you think of when walking, jogging, or running, do *not* count the miles you cover each week or month. Leave that to the lunch-break marathon buffs. If someone passes you when you are out on your daily tour, suppress the urge to keep up or overtake again. Remember, you are preparing, not competing. If you wish to compete, do so later: put a number bib on and race in a classified or citizens' race. But leave your bibs off when you exercise or train.

LOW PULSE?

You may have heard that a low pulse rate is a badge of excellence for distance endeavors, much as the ability to press so many pounds is revered as a sign of strength for weight lifters. True, top-conditioned cross-country ski racers, including Olympic medalists, have been tested as having resting pulse rates ranging from 34 to 54, with a median in the mid 40's. But the resting pulse rate, which you may measure when lying in bed, before getting up in the morning, is no reliable indicator of endurance. The recovery rate, or how fast the pulse drops back to its resting level after sustained exertion, is a better physiological indication of performance potential in cross-country ski racing. However, if you have an abnormally high resting pulse rate, it's advisable to consult your doctor before taking up an endurance training program for cross-country ski competition.

volves little or no oxygen. Termed *anaerobic,* literally "without air," this process is sometimes said to be accompanied by an "oxygen debt," because the product of its "combustion" is lactate, which can build up in the muscles, and must subsequently be removed by the circulatory system. The two processes are similar to those in an automobile engine. A car battery "fuels" an electric starter, without combustion, to start the engine. An engine running, burning fuel and consuming oxygen, then recharges the battery.

If you wish to ski fast and far, you need both aerobic and anaerobic capacities. Your aerobic capacity is what keeps you moving most of the time, while your anaerobic capacity is the reserve that enables you to sprint at the start of a race, or put on extra power to climb hills rapidly.

You must also be capable of exploiting your overall fitness to your best advantage. This means that you should be suitably strong in all the motions of cross-country skiing to perform efficiently for as long as you ski. This is where many skiers err in preparing for racing, and where almost all skiers have, at one time or another, felt a weakness. If your arms have ever "gone dead" when you otherwise are skiing well, or your legs have felt sore and stiff after you have skied hilly terrain, you know the penalties of strengths deficient compared to your overall skiing ability.

RACING—SPECIFIC AND MORE

Being "in shape" for racing has many connotations. For young, athletic racers, it means being able to win. For most cross-country skiers who race in citizens' races for fun, it means enjoying racing without feeling hampered by their own limitations.

Physical conditioning for "getting in shape" involves *training*, which can best be described as regular, specific, goal-oriented exercise, performed according to some plan. Training is preparation, the off-season "tune-up" that determines your potential capability as a racer on skis.

Training does not necessarily involve strain, grunt-and-groan effort, or discomfort, nor does it require an athletic "gift." Training can be done by any skier. In fact you probably do some training without knowing it, just as the recreational skier may find that some summertime exercise actually directly benefits wintertime skiing. *Training is any physical activity that improves or maintains your physical performance ability.* So whenever you walk, jog, cycle,

swim, paddle, cut wood, garden, or otherwise are physically active, you are training. This means that the *exercise plans* for recreational skiers described earlier in this chapter are really *training programs.* But for most people the very word *training* connotes preparation for competition, so it is used in that sense here. This use, or misuse, as some purists might maintain, may be fortunate, as it provides a scale of activity: a recreational skier *exercises* to achieve the fitness to enjoy skiing, while a racer *trains* to race well. In any case, *training* in its purest sense, be it exercise for recreational enjoyment or preparation for competition, is and should be an enjoyable, varied spectrum of activity. Almost anything goes, so long as you, the skier, benefit. If you can't stand jogging, don't do it. Forsake the asphalt-bound plod of the jogging boom, and cycle, paddle, or wilderness-hike instead. In so doing you not only spice up your activities, but you may also discover other joys, new aspects of other sports.

One of the side benefits of regular, measurable training is that it offers personal challenge. To train well is to see your own progress, to feel satisfaction in a form of self-competition where the rewards are measured in well-being.

Whatever your goal, from personal improvement to honing your competitive edge, you should always aim to train fitness into, not out of, yourself. Although not as serious as abstaining from exercise completely, overtraining can actually dilute your abilities. This is where inexperienced racers often err: if training for racing fails to produce the improved results they seek, they train more, sometimes attaining ridiculous totals for hours spent or "miles covered" per week, only to achieve still lesser results in competition. Often, in such cases, the problem is skiing, as it's

Hikes are good summer conditioners. *Michael Brady*

STRAIN, MAYBE; PAIN, NO

Beware the frequently repeated clichés "The pain of the distance runner," "Overcoming the pain barrier," and so on. They are, at best, misleading.

To those skilled in the distance events, pain is associated with physical injury: if you feel pain in exercising or skiing, stop, just as you would stop to take a rock out of your shoe on a hike.

Quitting is sometimes automatic. High levels of anaerobic exercise can produce lactic-acid buildup to the point of extreme discomfort, often sensed as pain. But when that point is reached, the muscles stop working of their own accord. No conscious desire, no determined "mind over body," will reverse that physical process. It's one of nature's ways to prevent extreme damage.

Strain, on the other hand, is something else again; that's part of the challenge of doing anything more strenuous than cardplaying. For any high-level physical performance, be it focusing your consciousness entirely on a short maneuver of skill and strength, as in skiing a tricky downhill, or utilizing your physical resources at their ultimate for a prolonged period, as in cross-country ski racing, strain is involved, both physical and mental. Pain may be an accepted part of pugilism and contact sports, which may be why it has infiltrated athletic jargon. But pain simply has no place in cross-country skiing. If it is not a part of your present awareness, learn to recognize the difference between strain and pain. Strain can often exhilarate. Pain is your body's warning signal that something is wrong, and you should never ignore those signals. Knowing the difference is one of your best personal guides to safe exercise.

always true that among otherwise equal racers, the one with the best technique always wins. Remember: training is *not* alchemy: it cannot change you into something you are not. It is what you employ to realize your greater physical potential.

THE WHOLE IS THE SUM

Time was when top cross-country ski racers all came from hardy peasant stock, tough farmers and lumberjacks whose everyday lives suited them for the level of competition of their day. Those days are gone. Racers with differing backgrounds, interests, and life-styles now combine various types of physical training to suit their needs. There are no standard training recipes, but the following training program ingredients are used by all racers. If you seriously contemplate racing, you probably are physically active year round, and need only alter or supplement your training activities to benefit your cross-country ski racing capability.

Training is broken down into different activities or *types of training,* each aimed to *primarily* enhance or maintain a particular physical capability. The word *primary* is important, as no type of training is absolutely specific, that is, has only one effect. A long hike in hilly terrain has its uphills that load muscles (strength training) and push up pulses for short periods (anaerobic training), strictly speaking training benefits differing from the most obvious, *primary* benefit of endurance (aerobic training). Stacking bricks or books or moving furniture *primarily* requires strength, but doing it for any period of time requires some endurance (aerobic training). And so on, throughout the range of training activities, all of which overlap to some degree.

For cross-country skiing, training is best broken down into *distance training, interval training, tempo training,* and *strength training.* These categories are the most widespread for the sport, both in North America and internationally.

DISTANCE TRAINING, as its name implies, aims to enable you to "go your distance" on skis. Therefore, it is the major form of training for cross-country skiers. It may be done on foot or on skis, while many skiers prefer to cycle instead of run on foot in the summer. There are two main types, whose names unfortunately are not yet standardized. Serious racers and coaches speak of *overdistance training,* continuous movement throughout an exercise period, of half to one-and-a-half times the maximum intended race duration.

The primary benefit is maintaining or increasing the body's ability to exploit its aerobic capacity over distance. Differing somewhat in purpose, *distance training* is regarded as training primarily aimed to increase aerobic and anaerobic capacities, and involves continuous activity at near-racing tempo, for durations of half of to full racing times. The difference between the two is difficult for most skiers to observe in practice, so in this book only the latter type will be discussed. In distance training (of the latter type), pace yourself to a constant speed throughout your exercise period, which may be from half to one-and-a-half times your intended race duration. In running off snow, seek the same type of terrain as that on which you ski. If possible, at least once a week, try to run the same trails where you ski. You will find that running a cross-country ski trail not only is good distance training, but also builds your sense for skiing terrain, enabling you to ski it better when snow comes.

INTERVAL TRAINING consists of exercise periods, spaced at intervals, broken up by "rest" periods. Its purpose is to maintain or increase your aerobic capacity. There are two types of interval training, *timed interval* training and *natural interval* training. In timed interval training, sprints and rests follow a definite timed sequence on a track or up and down a single hill, and may last from fifteen seconds to two minutes or more. In training, racers will repeat from a few such intervals to forty or more.

NATURAL INTERVAL consists of running in undulating terrain, at a fairly constant speed, so the uphills require more work than the flats or the downhills. It is the most commonly used form of interval

Running on ski trails builds sense for skiing terrain.
Frits Solvang

The uphill ski stride builds repetitive arm strength and may also be done as a form of interval training. *Fletcher Manley*

Summer arm exercises build poling strength. *Fletcher Manley*

training for cross-country ski racing, as it closely simulates the irregular effort required in racing on snow. Biking is also a close cousin to cross-country skiing through the natural interval connection, which may explain why some great cyclists have also been great cross-country ski racers.

TEMPO TRAINING aims to accustom you to the speed, the tempo, of a race, and therefore is sometimes called "speed training." Physiologically its purpose is to build anaerobic capacity, sometimes termed the ability to tolerate "oxygen debt." Tempo training uses the same

sprint-rest-sprint sequence of interval training, but is run faster, at your racing speed or greater.

STRENGTH TRAINING builds the muscles you use in racing. There's no escaping the simple fact that to ski fast you must be relatively strong, as kicks, polings, and in fact most of your movements on skis involve acceleration of body parts, and that acceleration is produced by muscle force. Muscle produces movement.

Strength training is a complex subject that has yet to be completely understood; many conflicting theories and schools of thought exist on how it should best be done. From the standpoint of the cross-country ski racer, strength training can be divided into two types, maximum strength and repetitive strength. Maximum strength is the goal of weight lifters, and although practicing it will equip you to lift weights, it's seldom ideal for cross-country ski racing. If you find you have particularly weak muscle groups, do, by all means, weight-train to strengthen them if you wish. The bulk of a cross-country ski racer's strength focuses on the muscles used in skiing, the way they are used in skiing. Just as muscle produces movement, movement builds muscle. For most active persons this means training arm and trunk muscles. Activities which require you to use your arms, such as canoe and kayak paddling, train arm strength and endurance. But for greatest benefit you should always include a few exercises specifically aimed to replicate skiing movements.

One of the most effective and most easily performed arm and trunk exercises is the uphill ski stride, done on foot with ski poles. First, walk up a gentle slope, stretching your legs out in back, pushing off from your toes, bending your forward knee, and swinging your arms, as if you were on skis. By adding ski poles, you are doing the cross-country ski diagonal stride. The uphill serves only to provide the resistance that makes your movements simulate skiing. Make the slope steeper, or stride faster, and you have the same simple and superb conditioner used by the best of racers. Start first with two half-minute walks up a hill, and work up to five one-minute walks over a period of one to two months. This exercise also aids on-ski technique by forcing you to kick correctly, when your body weight is directly over your kicking foot.

Another good way to exercise arm and back muscles is to use an arm exerciser. It's a device that offers resistance as you pull on it, simulating single- or double-pole motions. The simplest arm exerciser is a pair of old ten-speed-bike tire tubes cut and knotted together. Fasten the knot to a hook at about shoulder height on a wall or tree, or lay the knot over the top of an open door and shut the door to secure the tubes in place. Grip the loose ends, one in each hand, then step back until the tubes are taut and offer resistance. Pull on the tubes with both arms, either simultaneously or alternately as you would in poling on skis. Increase the number of repetitions each day to build your poling muscles.

If you are a serious racer, you may wish to train on roller skis. These devices are wheeled platforms, of aluminum or wood, fitted with cross-country ski bindings. One or more of the wheels are fitted with ratchets to prevent backward roll. Roller skis are used on pavement to simulate skiing on snow; both the diagonal stride and double poling can be done, so they are also useful for leg training. Roller skiing seems to be gaining in popularity, but don't be swept along with the fad before you thoroughly evaluate the value of roller skiing to your on-snow skiing.

Roller skiing has several drawbacks, some of which may be serious. First and most obviously, roller skiing is done on paved surfaces, usually roads where there is traffic, and therefore can be dangerous. Some counties and states curtail or forbid roller skiing outright for this very reason. Always check local regulations before you roller-ski. Second, roller skiing is more difficult than skiing on snow, as there are no tracks to guide your skis, and irregularities in pavement surfaces can send your roller skis off on strange courses. If you're not an accomplished skier on skis on snow, you'll find roller skiing difficult, and may fall frequently. As the penalties for falling on concrete or asphalt are usually greater than those for falling on snow, it's always prudent to be sure you can handle roller skis before using them for training.

Finally, roller skis are expensive, usually costing more than quality racing skis. Investing in them is a commitment to racing that not all skiers wish to make.

WARM-UP AND -DOWN

As in all other sports, warm-up before and warm-down after exercise are among the more vital, yet most frequently neglected, parts of training for cross-country skiing.

Young skiers, without the experience to appreciate the value of a good warm-up, unknowingly depend on resiliency to take the place of warming up. Were they older, the truth of the matter would be forced upon them, by protesting, if not damaged, muscles. Although there is an ongoing debate as to just exactly how much warm-up is necessary before distance events, virtually all physiological evidence to date indicates that warm muscles are substantially more efficient and stronger than cooler muscles. On that basis alone, cross-country skiers should be advocates of warm-ups, as efficiency is the name of the game in cross-country skiing.

Warm-downs are also important, as the body usually needs time to "recover." After training, go inside, take a shower, or a shower and a sauna, and cool off gradually. Change to dry clothing, and rest if you feel the need. Drink to replace the liquids you may have lost.

Roller skiing simulates skiing on snow.
Fletcher Manley

OPPOSITE. Make training recreation and fun a part of all training. *Michael Brady*

HOW MUCH?

How much, how often, and how long you should train depends on a myriad of factors, including your previous experience in training, your goals as a racer, the availability of suitable training terrain, and your personal dedication.

Some racers will train twice a day, five to seven days a week, year round, adding up monthly totals of 100 to 130 hours of training in the autumn. That sort of schedule takes dedication and, in our day—long after that of the idealistic, independently wealthy gentleman sportsman—financial support, which is one reason why ski teams seem always to be short of money.

Most citizens' racers, who are not full-time skiers, pursue a more modest training schedule, as outlined in the table. Whatever time you have available for training, always seek to distribute it evenly over a week: train frequently and enjoyably, not seldom and strenuously. Seek training in your daily activities; it counts.

Typical hours devoted to training per week for serious, adult citizens' racers.

Season	Hours per week devoted to:				
	DISTANCE TRAINING	INTERVAL TRAINING	STRENGTH TRAINING	SPECIAL TRAINING: ROLLER SKIING, ETC.	TOTAL HOURS PER WEEK
Spring-summer	3–5	0–½	½–1	0–1	3½–7½
Fall	4–6	½–1	1	1	6½–9
Early winter	6–8	½–1	0–½	0	6½–9
Winter—on snow	3–4 plus one race	1–1½	0	0	4–5½

9

SKIING IS FOR KIDS
It's Only Natural

With the family, it's kid stuff.
Michael Brady

A child, almost any child, is a "born skier." As the Austrian skiing prophet Dr. Stefan Kruckenhauser once observed, "If you want to learn to ski naturally, go watch a child do it; you will learn a lot." Teaching kids to ski, or participating with them in the sport, is then really nothing more than learning how they do it best, seeing how it fits into their world.

Cross-country is even more natural for children than it is for adult newcomers to the sport. Kids develop skills on skis as rapidly as they do on foot; they have none of the adult hangups about looking proficient on skis, falling, or balancing well or poorly. For them cross-country skiing can and should be just another way to play, another route to exploring the world. In that, too, adults can learn from kids, as the childlike joys of skiing are often the simplest, most straightforward, and most deeply rewarding.

Cross-country skiing must be the king of family wintertime outdoor participation sports. It's natural, easily and rapidly learned to the point where it can be enjoyed, available wherever there is snow, affordable for all, and as packed with opportunities to share experiences and joys as the whole outdoors itself. Teaching it to or sharing it with children is a reward in its own. It is probably easier than you think.

START EASY, KEEP IT SIMPLE

Wherever you live, however you first introduce a child to snow and skiing, keep it gradual, easy, simple, and direct. An urban child, driven to the snow of a Friday evening, and plunked on skis for the first time on Saturday morning to tag along behind parents, has little chance of success. Do this, and you may have a whining child on your hands, and find yourself thinking, if not saying, "Next time you're staying home!"

Introduce children gradually to snow and skiing. Remember, theirs is an expanding world; they should have time to investigate all that is new. If you live in the snow belt, the white winter stuff is probably familiar to them, unless, of course, you are so unfortunate as to live in a snow area during a snowless winter. If you travel to snow, let your children find out what it is first, firsthand. Let them run, romp, jump, and roll in the stuff. Then it will be less scary when they first put skis on. If you have toddlers along on a cross-country excursion, consider towing them in a *pulk,* an over-snow baby carriage. The more they feel at home with snow around, the more rapidly they will pick up skiing.

The best place for children to first be put on skis is where it is easy, on a level, fairly well-packed area, with a few bumps and dips for fun, and where there is a close tie to the familiar—your own backyard if you have snow, close to a ski-center building, with you or playmates around, and so on. Being introduced to skiing doesn't necessarily mean being put on skis right away: toddlers can ride a pulk for a winter before getting their first pairs of skis the next.

Keep their first steps on skis simple, no more complex than when they first stood up from a crawl and started to walk. Start them out without poles, which both complicate the new, unfamiliar movements, and can be dangerous in a fall. And kids fall a lot; they have no fear of it. Your first, and perhaps major, contribution to their instruction should be to teach them how to get up from a fall. Do that, and then turn them loose to play on their skis. You'll soon have little skiers around.

WHO AND HOW SOON?

Parents, even longtime skiing parents, often ask if there are any guidelines that tell when a child is "ready" for skiing, and, if so, what's the "right" age to start.

Ex-Olympic team skier and U.S. Nordic cross-country coach John Caldwell once remarked that he thought kids ought to start skiing "just before they learn to walk; that way they won't develop any bad habits in form." Caldwell may have stretched the point a bit, but there's no denying that his philosophy of an early start produced results: John and Hep Caldwell's brood of three boys and one girl all became skilled cross-country skiers, all became university team racers, and two became members of the U.S. Ski Team. That's a good argument, if competition is any measure.

Even if it's not, the earlier kids start, the more time they'll have to learn, and the less instruction they'll ever need. Kids teach themselves, as they do in other activities.

There's an ongoing parental concern as to how rapidly children "should" learn skills such as cross-country skiing, and, women's lib aside, a considerable amount of scientific research devoted to investigating differences by sex.

Entire fields of knowledge and books have been devoted to the subject; there's only room for the general, overall trends to be stated here:

Preschool boys and girls, three to four years old, can easily learn to ski, and some start even earlier, at two and a half or so. The boys usually are stronger, faster skiers than the girls, while the girls often pick up "good technique" more rapidly than the boys. The uncoordinated, strong boy skier and dainty little lady skier are known throughout the skiing world. By age seven these differences have lessened, and otherwise equal boys and girls are about even in skiing. Thereafter differences gradually develop again. By adolescence, boys are again ahead. Girls who could outski boys in preadolescence stop doing so at about age fourteen.

A FAMILY THING, PART OF LIFE

The more you dovetail skiing into other family activities, the more everyone concerned is likely to enjoy it. Cross-country skiing is perhaps unique in winter sports in being both utilitarian and egalitarian, in addition to being a recreational activity. If kids can play on their feet, off snow, then they can play almost all the same games on skis, on snow. If they walk to visit playmates or walk to school in snowless months, then they can ski those same routes on cross-country skis. Yes, believe it or not, there still are kids who ski to school! If you hike or walk with your children in the summer, you can do it on cross-country skis in the winter. In making skiing part of another accustomed activity, you add interest and challenge, and at the same time teach the ability to cope with snow and winter weather.

If you regard skiing as something extremely special, an activity complete in itself, then beware the risk of transmitting this view to your children. "We're not here to play, we're here to ski," or "You can look at (or do, or try, or whatever) that at home, now ski!" and similar parent-to-child commands have perhaps done more to ruin skiing for more children than anything else outside of not being exposed to the sport at all.

The key is to integrate skiing into your other activities, and always integrate other activities into your skiing with your children. Let the joy of being on snow on your cross-country skis be that extra-special something that makes skiing an enjoyable experience in sharing.

Plan your ski outings with children around their needs and growing interests; don't add their participation as an after-thought. If you do, you may be faced with kids more cranky than you ever dreamed would be possible on, say, a long car trip, an experience most parents know to be the greatest producer of wails going. Keep ski tours with children to lengths that they can manage comfortably, and always be aware of the weather. Weari-ness or chill may be only inconvenient to you, as an adult, but to a small child they are frightening. Many families solve this problem by touring with their children at major cross-country ski centers, where the interlaced trail networks can provide shortcuts back to the car whenever need-ed. Plan ahead: know the trail and know where you're going. Pick a time of the day that doesn't collide with any other accustomed daily activities, such as an after-lunch nap or a midmorning trip to the toilet, and you'll save a few frustra-tions.

Once your kids have "discovered" ski-ing, fuel their interest when you're off the snow. Let them watch ski races on TV, tell them about ski jumping, biathlon, freestyle Alpine skiing, the whole spec-trum of the sport. They'll soon zero in on what interests them most. Many families have found that there's no substitute for the childhood glee produced by looking at snapshots of family or friends skiing, or watching slide shows or home movies of skiing. If a child thinks pictures of skiing are fun, encourage participation; let the

On snow, two pulks instead of two baby carriages
. . . *Michael Brady*

kids take pictures of each other and of you.

Make skiing part of your family life, even if you can only do it a few times a winter, and it will become a way of life for your kids.

LEARN BY DOING

In all ski instruction for children there's only one rule: keep it simple, make it fun. The best instructor for children isn't al-ways the most technically proficient skier

Start 'em young. *Michael Brady*

around, but rather the more skilled on-ski companion for the kids, the one who continually thinks of new games, new things to do and see, while the kids go about learning by doing. And learning is something that most of them do at a rate that outstrips that of most adults.

In fact, left to play by themselves on skis, most kids will turn into perfectly capable skiers without any adult intervention at all. Kids rapidly discover ski techniques on their own, or by mimicking adults. Exploit their abilities as imitators whenever you can: capture their attention, ski a bit, and you'll find that they're probably doing just fine, without your ever having explained things. Above all, don't make skiing technical for them: remember, especially for the smaller tots, it may not have been so long ago that they learned the difference between right and left, between walk and run, or between foot and knee. Don't verbally instruct; do, and have them copy you.

If you are a newcomer to skiing yourself, or if for any other reason you feel unqualified to teach your own children to ski, then by all means seek a good cross-country ski school that has special programs for kids. Were you to travel to the major cross-country ski centers throughout the continent, you would be amazed at how many good programs for children actually are in operation, and how many of them are staffed by people who, in other professions, might be termed overqualified. Many of these instructors elect to teach kids because they enjoy it more than teaching adults, a response to a call that benefits kids in learning.

Always work instructional games in for kids—or, for that matter, anyone you instruct on skis. Play is one of the most enjoyable and quickest routes to learning new sports skills. Don't harp on perfection and don't watch initial maneuvers as the kids do them. Remember, they're more concerned with having fun than with looking "pretty" on skis, but if you hover over them, you may impede their progress-through-play. Even if you've thought up some wonderful games, be willing to improvise continuously to suit the day's conditions. If it's a warm day and you've got a slight downhill to ski on, you'll probably find yourself with a mob of downhill bombers. Let them zoom if they want to; it's all part of the game of learning to ski.

Vary your approach, your instruction.

Children have far shorter attention spans than adults, and seldom can be coaxed into long drills of any one skill. Always think in "kid time," how long things seem to them. And give them frequent breaks and "free periods," as especially new activity will tire them quickly.

Almost any on-foot game you can think of will work on cross-country skis. Here are a few standbys, all-time favorites:

HIDE-AND-SEEK: Need more be said? To an adult, the game may seem pointless on snow, as ski tracks will always show where someone is hiding. But that's exactly the point; that's how kids learn about tracks. And besides, after kids have played on skis in an area for a while, there are so many tracks around that nobody can tell which set was made last.

FOLLOW-THE-LEADER: A marvelous ruse for teaching technique and feeling for terrain. Make a loop track outside a figure-eight track with a few bumps and dips, uphills and downhills in each track. Start off, having the first child do exactly what you do. Ski a round or so, and jump in the track ahead of the second child at some crossing point, and it's you who are following the leader. Work your way back down the line until every child has had a chance to ski behind, and imitate you.

TREASURE HUNT: "Hide" a few easily identified and easily carried objects, such as mittens and caps, in a designated area, so the "treasure hunters" have to ski a couple hundred yards for each "treasure." Tell the "hunters" what the objects are, and turn them loose. Who finds the most, or the "golden treasure"?

FOX AND GEESE: A schoolyard game for generations, and, on skis, a good game for

THE NORWEGIAN WAY

According to legend Norwegians are born with skis on their feet. There's a grain of truth in that saying, because for decades Norwegians have believed that skiing, like walking, is something instinctive, easily learned from one's parents.

But today in Norway, as elsewhere, schools and classes are taking over more of the older, more traditional teaching chores once done at home. And this includes skiing, as Norwegian parents are now aware of the value of good instruction.

The largest children's ski school in Norway was started in Oslo some forty years ago by Tomm Murstad. The school, near Oslo's venerable Holmenkollen ski arena, site of the 1982 FIS Nordic World Ski Championships, is ideally geared to its purpose. It has its own illuminated areas for after-dark skiing, a cabin where small noses and toes can be warmed, and 24 instructors who can care for about 240 children a day between January 1 and mid-March. Children's classes are divided according to age, beginning with three-year-olds. Murstad has found that seven-year-olds are the most receptive to learning ski technique. He says that younger pupils, though eager, are usually more interested in play than learning skiing for its own sake. For these pupils, instructors focus on creating class activities that imbue ski technique.

Children cannot take just one lesson here;

introducing kids to speedy skiing. Make a circular track, about 30 or 40 yards in diameter, with a "safety house" in the middle. One skier is the fox and all the others are the geese. The "fox" chases the geese until one is tagged, or "caught." The captured goose becomes the fox and the game resumes. The center "safety house" holds a limit of two or three they must sign up for a package of at least six, the number Murstad has found necessary to instill the fundamentals of ski technique.

Aside from being a down-to-earth, practical ski instructor, Murstad is a theoretician, and has written several books on teaching children to ski. In all his instruction and writings Murstad stresses teaching youngsters that skiing is fun. "You cannot force a child to ski or learn," he says. "If a child is not interested or is unwilling to learn, then it's the instructor's job to evoke interest. This must be done carefully, for as soon as a child is placed under stress—even in an enjoyable learning situation—potential interest may be killed."

Murstad also feels that the right ski equipment can speed learning. He has found, for instance, that children learn the basic cross-country ski strides far more rapidly if they are shod with cross-country ski boots fitted to pin bindings.

"If a child wants poles, let him have poles, but not all the time." Children bring poles to Murstad's group lessons, but they often practice without them in order to learn correct rhythm, weight shift, and balance. Skiing without poles should not be prolonged, Murstad feels, as it may interfere with arm-leg coordination.

Murstad believes that little people, like the characters in the *Peanuts* comic strip, deserve little-people attention. His instructors treat their small charges like equals. One trick instructors use to gain children's confidence is to bend down when speaking to them.

Murstad's is a relatively small, private ski school; it cannot handle all the children in Oslo who wish to take lessons, and not all parents in that spread-out city of half a million can send their kids across town to a single school. *Foreningen til Ski-Idrettens Fremme*, or "Skiforeningen" for short, the country's largest skier organization, also runs ski schools in Oslo, teaching more than 5,000 children every winter at scattered neighborhood locations throughout the city. The courses are designed for children of three different age levels, and are run accordingly: midday for preschoolers, after school for school-age kids.

Skiforeningen promotes its schools with course announcements in newspapers and by sending annual invitations to all kindergartens in the city. For kids living far from ski-school locations, Skiforeningen also arranges for free bus transportation.

For parents who cannot afford frequent purchases of gear for growing children, various ski clubs in Oslo sponsor annual equipment swaps. Some of these swaps can take on carnival proportions, lasting some two days, held in gymnasiums or indoor tennis halls, and turning over some 1,500 to 2,000 pairs of skis and boots.

geese, who are "safe" from the fox as long as they remain inside. The players' ski poles can form the boundary of the "safety house" as this game, like the following ones where the players may crash into each other, is best played without poles, for safety. Poleless skiing in games also is good balance training for skiing.

HARE AND HOUNDS: An on-show adaptation of the old-time "paper chase," with many hares. Divide the group; tie paper streamer "tails" on the hares, and "release" them with one or two minutes' head start. Then turn the "hounds" loose to pursue the hares, "catching" by taking a "tail" from a "hare." Sides switch after ten minutes or so, hares becoming hounds and vice versa. Who catches the most hares or eludes the most hounds? When you're done, you'll have a well-tracked area, suitable for other games or skiing instruction.

PICKUP: Make a good downhill track that all the children involved manage well. Then take two or three pairs of poles, and set them in the snow as "gates," one on each side of the track, spaced a few yards apart. Face the poles with the wrist straps pointing downhill. Then support a single pole horizontally on the top of each "gate," by putting its tip through one wrist strap on one side, and its grip through the wrist strap on the pole on the opposite side. The "racers" ski downhill, ducking under the horizontal pole of each "gate" to touch and "pick up" snow, rising to a more erect position between "gates." Another version of the game is with spare mittens on the snow at intervals on either side of the track. Skiers try to maintain downhill speed, bending down to pick up mittens. Who can pick up the most without stopping? Vary the game by staggering the gates or mitten pickups, zigzag down the hill, and you have the start of a slalom course to teach the kids how to turn around obstacles.

SKI SOCCER: A good game for a larger group, divided into teams. Poleless skiers play soccer with hands instead of feet, and can only "kick" by tossing ball as in volleyball, not "run" with ball.

EQUIPMENT AND CLOTHING

Small-sized skis, boots, bindings, poles, and ski clothing are available, mostly imported from Europe. Shops still don't carry a full selection to outfit small folks,

but then, again, most shops didn't carry cross-country ski equipment at all a decade or so ago. While they're learning to respond to your needs, you may have to look around a bit.

One good place to start is at ski swaps, or at cross-country ski centers featuring children's programs. If you want to purchase used items, these are good places to start looking. Or even if you don't, it will give you a better idea of what's available than you will see in most shops.

SKIS: Two general varieties of skis are available for youngsters, *junior skis* and *children's skis*. The categories are sometimes mixed, so rely on the way the skis look and are made, not on their designation. Junior skis are scaled-down versions of adult models, intended for eight- to fourteen-year-olds, while children's skis are designed for tots through first-graders, more for on-snow play than for "serious" skiing.

Junior skis are sometimes slightly thinner, but otherwise resemble adult skis in profile, construction, and overall shape. Children's skis usually are relatively broad in relation to their length, are built to withstand punishment more than to perform in skiing, and are designed for simple strap or toepiece bindings. They are made to be relatively inexpensive, and thus have simpler constructions than do junior skis or adult skis. Some ultrabudget children's skis are made of one-piece molded plastic.

Waxless skis are best for a first pair. Kids can play on them without ever involving you in preparation. Children six to sixteen years old can select skis to grow into, floor-to-palm-of-upraised-hand in length to start (as for adults, see p. 168), shorter as they grow. It's always best to be on the short side rather than

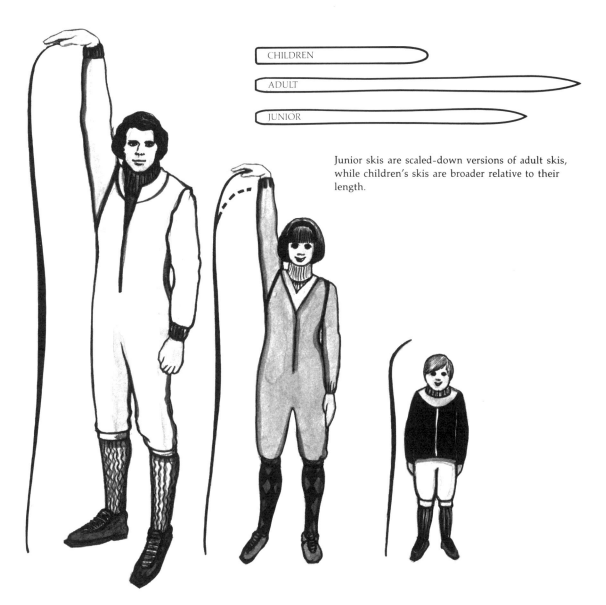

CHILDREN

ADULT

JUNIOR

Junior skis are scaled-down versions of adult skis, while children's skis are broader relative to their length.

Growing children can select skis to grow into, while tots should have short skis, for safety.

the long side in selecting children's skis. Skis for two- to five-year-olds should always be short, seldom much more than slightly over head height in length.

BOOTS: Unless you are among the wealthy, select children's ski boots to be as utilitarian as possible; shy away from the specialized varieties for the first pair. Tots can be fitted with standard galoshes, which fit into the simple strap bindings of children's skis. Older children are well fitted in 71-mm Nordic Norm boots with sturdy rubber soles that are flexible and comfortable enough for all-around winter use. Put these boots on the kids in the morning, and they're ready to ski anytime during the day. Also, you'll get your money's worth out of the boots before they're outgrown, if they are used year round, for hiking, playing outdoors, and on snow, as well as for skiing.

BINDINGS: Simple is the cardinal rule for children's bindings. The strap or strap-and-cup variety for tots is easy to manipulate, an important feature for youngsters just starting out on skis. The old standby 71-mm Nordic Norm pin binding has yet to have an equal for utility and the ability to withstand abuse: some models are virtually "childproof."

POLES: Start tots out without poles. If they notice that you ski with poles, discard yours, and set a good example. A preschooler's first pair of poles should have "safety tips," rounded plastic ends that cannot injure as easily as can the metal tips of standard, adult poles. For all kids, shorter is better than longer in poles; kids never have much of a problem bending over a bit more as they ski.

CLOTHING: Don't bundle kids up like little Eskimos, so they cannot move on skis. But remember that while an adult might tolerate the discomforts of being slightly too cold or too warm in anticipation of foreseen change, kids won't tolerate extremes very long. So for them, dressing in layers is even more important than it is for adults. The more layers, the more easily you can regulate their clothing by peeling.

Fancy clothing is no must for kids, although if they really take to skiing, knickers and knee socks are a sound investment. For almost all winter skiing, long johns, wool sweaters and pants, topped by waterproof ski pants and jacket, with a good knit cap and mittens are the basic garb for little folks, who are often in contact with the snow.

Always carry extra socks, mittens, caps, and sweaters when on cross-country ski tours with children. Change wet items and keep the kids dry and warm. In so doing you'll avoid the most common complaints kids have on tours, and with that bit of planning will have contributed

Even in China, cross-country is for kids. Here junior racer Wu Ming Su skis outside of Yangshou in northeast China. *Ned Gillette*

to the all-family fun that is part of the spirit of cross-country skiing.

A short race with lots of company makes the day for kids. Here, after finishing the 1.2 km course on Children's Day during the 1982 World Ski Championships, 5200 local Norwegian kids and those from 12 other countries were all awarded medals. *Michael Brady*

Outback, down south by far: Jan Reynolds on a
minor peak on an ice plateau in the Garden of Eden,
New Zealand. *Ned Gillette*

10
OUTSIDE AND AWAY
Safety and Survival Techniques

When you ski on a prepared track at a cross-country center, on a snow-covered local golf course, or go on a day tour in a familiar wooded area, wilderness seems far away. You are, after all, in well-known surroundings, or at least you have trail signs to guide and other skiers nearby to direct and aid you if need be. You feel secure, far from danger.

But what if you venture away from the familiar, further from the comforts of civilization, into the *back country,* the *wilderness*? Is it then that you need be prepared to survive? The answer is, of course, *yes,* but more so than most skiers believe. Because even if you don't deliberately forsake the familiar, the unfamiliar can come to you. Weather can change, turning your backyard into back country, and a familiar trail or track of woods into an unknown wilderness. This is why *survival* really seldom involves a long battle with extreme natural forces. Most of the time, in most skiing situations where survival skills are used, it simply means returning home, uninjured and unsung, by dark.

Survival, like seat belts in a car, might simply class as a preventive measure, the ounce of prevention in your skiing skills that's always there to be used if need be. Lack of any survival skills, on the other hand, can be potentially serious, wherever you ski. A few years ago, in New Jersey, a group of cross-country skiers failed to return by dark from a tour in familiar wooded terrain. A search mounted by the State Police, National Guard, Civil Air Patrol, and Naval Air Reserve found the group the next day, lost, exhausted, and frostbitten. They hadn't thought to take along maps or a compass, and afternoon winds had blown away their ski tracks. The search was estimated to have cost $200,000, and that was in early-1970s dollars. If it can happen in New Jersey,

it can happen anywhere skiers are on snow.

AVOID, BUT EXPECT

Just as the best way to handle skids in winter driving is to drive so you don't skid, the best way to deal with skiing emergencies is to prevent them. But just as knowing how to drive out of a skid is a necessary winter driving skill, every skier should know how to cope with the unexpected.

A sudden change of weather, cold fingers, hunger, or thirst half a mile from your car are usually just discomforts. Miles into the mountains their seriousness magnifies. The farther you are from the trailhead, the touring center buildings, your car, or whatever form of civilization you left behind, the greater the stakes.

Anticipate and avoid, but expect and be prepared to cope is the cardinal guideline for dealing with the unexpected outdoors. Perhaps the most common cross-country skiing mishap is getting lost. It can also be the most serious, as it can bring on other, greater hazards. The hazards of cold are always around you outdoors, winter or not. Darkness or extreme weather can stop you in your tracks; it's then best to bivouac out. Finally, snow, your friend in skiing, can become a lethal enemy if you get caught in an avalanche.

KNOW WHERE YOU ARE

Knowing where you are doesn't mean that you must always be able to pinpoint your location accurately. It does mean knowing where you are going, and how to get there from where you are, and knowing where you've been, and how you got to where you are. Simple? It is, if you simply extrapolate the basic rules for finding your way on a short day tour, as outlined in Chapter 6.

One of the more important things to do as you ski is to take note of your surroundings. Does another major trail intersect the one you're on as you ski out? Make a note of it, and you'll know which trail to take when you come to the intersection on the way back. Are there lots of uphills on the way out? They'll be downhills on the way back, and you'll probably ski them faster. But return uphills will be slower than outgoing downhills, calling for an earlier return. Note terrain features. How many small lakes did you cross? How many bridges? Did you pass any farms or other buildings? The legendary pathfinders had no superhuman senses; they just remembered where they had been before. Their trick will ease your route-finding.

Always do a bit of route finding before you ski. If you're skiing at a cross-country center or in a park, study the trail network map when you're still inside and warm. Talk to the locals; find out if the map is right for the days of your tour. Almost all maps can sometimes contain inaccuracies, as snows and weather conditions alter trail conditions. Topographic maps and park maps are almost always drawn for summer conditions, and not many show ski trails or routes. So know your route before you start, and know what to expect on the way. See if you can locate major landmarks, or "milestones," for your tour ahead of time. When will you reach the cabin? Will you stick to the wooded trail on a windy day, or seek the open meadowland on a sunny day? Will hilltops, peaks, creeks, bridges, or buildings tell you where you are? When you are out on skis, check each of

your "mileposts"; see what it looks like when you approach it, and as you ski away from it. Few terrain features, or even buildings, look the same from two opposite directions, and you can easily fail to recognize something you've seen earlier, when viewing it from another angle, in another lighting.

Use a good map to aid your mental picture of where you are and where you are going. "Reading" a map in terrain is more complex than reading a road map, where your only chore is to figure which of the marked lines represents the road you're on, and proceed accordingly. In terrain you can move in any direction, and as soon as you leave the convenience of a marked and maintained trail system, there are no signposts erected to guide you.

But there are other significant "signposts" you can use; you are literally surrounded by them as you ski. Ridges, hilltops, peaks, valleys, rivers, lakes, streams, stands of timber, and many man-made features such as roads, bridges, and buildings are shown on topographic maps. So whenever you stop to "read" your map, read the surrounding terrain first. Find the most prominent feature you can see, and locate it on your map. Visually orient your map using two or three such prominent features, and locate your position. Do this frequently enough, and you'll be able to keep tabs on your progress in terrain by following it on your map.

This is one of the most common ways that cross-country skiers use maps, and, fortunately, one of the simpler and more certain methods of wilderness orientation. The secret is simply always to start with and maintain "contact" with your map. You need not have been skiing long to know the difficulty of suddenly having to find where you are on even a simple sketch map at a strange cross-country ski center. You thought you knew where you were going, then something seemed wrong. Stop. Out with the map. "Now, let's see: Where are we now? Here? No! Here?" Keep that map contact; it's the only way your map can keep you from getting lost. Otherwise it's just a piece of paper.

Compasses are useful on all tours, and essential whenever you leave the beaten path. But having one along is no guarantee that you'll always find your way. And place little faith in stories you may have heard of skiers following compass bearings, through night, fog, or whiteouts, to successfully find their way home. They're good stories, no more. If you doubt that this is true, wait for the next whiteout at a familiar ski area, and try to ski a straight course across a large, open area following your compass. Then when the clouds lift, see how straight your tracks are. It'll be a convincer. In such situations, it's best to stay put and wait for better visibility. A compass is not a radar set.

Compasses are most useful when used along with maps, which is probably why *map and compass* is essentially used as a single word. The greatest use of your compass will be to aid you in orienting your map, providing a check on your visual orientation in terrain. In more remote regions or in mountainous areas, compasses are indispensable in large-scale orientation and in taking bearings on more distant terrain features, to aid planning the route ahead.

Maps and compasses are useful aids on all tours, and essential whenever you leave the beaten path. Their use is an art that cannot be learned overnight, and never can be learned on the spot, when you're standing outside, lost in unfamiliar surroundings. So if you intend to tour frequently, prepare by polishing your map and compass skills. Entire books, some as thick as this one, are available on the subject. But what you'll need to know for almost all cross-country ski tours is well documented in outdoor classics such as Kjellstrom's *Be Expert with Map and Compass,* and Chapter 5 of *Mountaineering, The Freedom of the Hills* (edited by P. Ferber, The Mountaineers, Seattle).

COLD: FRIEND AND POTENTIAL FOE

The cold that brings the snow that makes skiing possible can also debilitate and injure. Most people are familiar with the debilitating effects of cold: as it takes energy just to stay warm in cold weather, one tends to tire more quickly in cold weather than one does performing the same exertion in warmer weather. Cold accelerates fatigue.

However, the cold-induced injuries known as *frostbite*—a damage to tissue—and *hypothermia*—body temperature depression—are less familiar. This is perhaps because cold injuries are rare in everyday life, even though a hundred million or more persons routinely live part of the year in subfreezing temperatures in the northern USA, Canada, Alaska, Scandinavia, Siberia, northern Europe, and parts of Asia.

Much of the modern knowledge of the potential hazards of cold is based on military experience, as cold injuries have been far more frequent in warfare in subfreezing temperatures than in civilian life. Frostbite was common among the soldiers of both sides during Napoleon's Russian campaign and, more recently, during the Northern European campaigns of the Second World War and during the Korean War. Second World War air-force bomber crews, particularly waist gunners, were frequently injured by frostbite. At one time in 1943, their frostbite injuries were greater than all other casualties combined.

Early mountaineers and arctic-region pioneers suffered frostbite so frequently that it became part of the legends of these regions, almost an accepted part of outdoor activity in extreme cold. Fortunately, improved clothing, diet, and knowledge of the potential hazards involved have virtually eliminated the "routine" frostbite injuries, and injury is now rare, occurring usually only in accidents.

FROSTBITE is a freezing of body tissues, and most commonly affects the extremities—the toes and fingers and exposed areas of the head, such as the nose and ears. It can occur whenever a body part loses heat faster than it can be replaced by circulating blood.

Cold causes frostbite in two ways. First, and most obviously, a body part, such as a nose, exposed to cold and wind, loses so much heat that it starts to freeze. Second, when the body is chilled, it automatically acts to conserve heat by contracting blood vessels in the skin, particularly in the extremities, to lower skin temperature and cut heat losses. This is why the risk of freezing unexposed, insulated fingers and toes increases in persons exposed long enough or clothed so inadequately as to become chilled.

One of the first signs of frostbite is that the affected area becomes white. Pain is often, but not always, involved: toes and fingers will hurt, but you may be unaware of a frostbitten area in a sunburned face numbed by wind. Usually, a prickling sensation, similar to the numb "asleep" sensation in a foot or hand when temporarily impaired circulation is restored, is felt in and around the affected part.

Though uncomfortable, the pain and prickling are signs that there still is some normal function in the affected part. When they disappear, and other sensation is lost—you can't feel your toes or fingers, for instance—real danger sets in.

Small, superficially frostbitten areas, such as fingers, toes, cheeks, ears, and the nose, can be treated immediately by warming them against warmer skin: feet against another person's abdomen or armpits, fingers in your own armpits, parts of the face against a warm hand. Do *not* raise an affected part above body temperature, such as by warming it by a fire; too rapid warming can compound the injury or, worse, burn flesh too numb to be warned by the pain of heat. And despite any stories you may have heard, *never rub a frostbitten part with anything, particularly not with snow.* The abrasive action of rubbing will further damage frozen tissue, and snow applied to a frozen part will both freeze it further and rub sharp snow crystals into frozen skin, compounding the original injury.

Extensive or deeper frostbite—when the surface is white, hard, and has no feeling, and/or when skin doesn't seem to move over the underlying tissue—should be treated only indoors, preferably by qualified medical help. As cruel as it may seem, it's better to keep moving or transport a seriously frostbitten person than to risk refreezing following incomplete thawing. Frozen feet, for instance, can still function and be walked or skied on, while once thawed, they are usually too painful and too susceptible to further damage to be of any use in walking or skiing. The affected person then becomes a stretcher case, which may further burden the party, and raise the risk of increased cold injury.

The treatment of extensive frostbite is sometimes complex and almost always painful. The simplest treatment involves immersing the affected part in water warmed to just above body temperature, about 99° to 104°F., until thawed.

Sometimes blisters appear as frostbitten parts thaw. Leave them alone. Don't apply any salves or Vaseline to frostbitten or thawed areas. *Do* keep thawed parts warm by insulating with extra clothing, and do loosen any clothing that can constrict circulation to an affected part.

But the best treatment for frostbite is prevention: don't let it happen to you or others you ski with. In cold, windy conditions, keep an eye on your skiing mates, and warn them of any telltale white areas on their faces. Keep tabs on your own condition; avoid overall chill by dressing well, prevent the chilling of fingers and toes by putting on enough layers of clothing. Fortunately for cross-country skiers, who, in striding along, continually flex their feet and hands, activity in the extremities "pumps" blood into toes and fingers, lessening the chances of frostbite. But with the same clothing and no flex or motion, risk increases. If you stop skiing for long, put on an extra pair of mittens and stuff your feet (with boots on) into a pack to keep them warm.

HYPOTHERMIA (from the Greek, meaning insufficient heat) occurs when the body's core, or inner, temperature drops to dangerously low levels. It's the major hazard in what commonly has been called "exposure."

Hypothermia has been called a killer, and rightfully so, as in its acute stages it is the leading cause of death in outdoor recreational activities. Strange as it may seem, in many mountain areas, cases of hypothermia are more common in the summer than in the winter. Summer hikers or climbers, caught unprepared in a windblown rainstorm at temperatures a few degrees above freezing, quickly get thoroughly soaked in cold water and lose body heat rapidly. Also, summer hikers often are less well prepared for wet and wind chill than are wintertime skiers, which worsens their lot. In this tragic situation lies the secret of combating hypothermia. As it really strikes only the careless, the unprepared, the totally unaware, recognizing hypothermia and taking suitable precautions are the best means for avoiding it.

Hypothermia can occur whenever body heat loss exceeds body heat production. Body heat losses are due to convection, conduction, evaporation, and radiation. *Convection* heat loss occurs when warm air next to the skin moves, or is blown away. It is the major heat loss caused by wind, the *chill* of *wind chill* (see box, p. *tk*). *Conduction* heat loss occurs when the body loses heat directly to cold water, snow, or other colder objects. It can be a major loss when clothing gets wet. A skier starting a day clad in jeans may be well insulated, if enough layers are worn underneath. But a few hours and several falls later, the soaked jeans tap heat by conduction, and the skier is headed for hypothermia. *Evaporation* from the skin and exhaled air cools the body. External moisture, from snow, fog, or rain evaporating from garments also cools. The skier brushing snow off a parka isn't just being fastidious. *Radiation* is the direct transfer of heat by the emission of energy. In most skiing situations it is by far the least important of the heat losses. But, turned around, it is one of the more important heat gains: on a clear winter day the body can absorb up to as much as three times as much energy from direct sunshine as it can produce in its own metabolism. Aside from absorbed sunshine, the only source of body heat is

COMMON SENSE NINE

In Scandinavia, where wilderness ski touring has long been a national wintertime recreation, the guidelines for wilderness ski safety have been condensed into nine easily remembered, commonsense rules:

1. SKI WITHIN YOUR ABILITY.
   Choose terrain, route, and tour length within your ability. Prepare for longer tours. Avoid skiing to exhaustion.

2. SAY WHERE YOU ARE GOING.
   Leave note at home, hotel, or camp, of your approximate route and expected time of return. Always allow for unexpected delays: there's no sense causing undue worry, or being the object of a unnecessary search, when you're just skiing safely, but more slowly than anticipated.

3. ANTICIPATE WEATHER, HEED FORECASTS.
   Expect bad weather when it's forecast, and be prepared for it when it's not, as even the best of forecasts are sometimes wrong.

4. LISTEN TO LOCALS.
   They may not all be experts, but chances are that they can give you valuable information on routes, prevailing weather, snow conditions, and so on. You may be skilled, but in their area, you're foreign.

5. BE PREPARED FOR BAD WEATHER AND COLD.
   Always take spare clothing and emergency gear, even on shorter tours, and always take a snow spade on longer and/or mountain tours. Learn to bivouac. Remember: real danger comes long after acute discouragement, and spending a night out really isn't all that bad.

6. REMEMBER YOUR MAP AND COMPASS.
   The more practice you have with map and compass, the better. Attach both to your body, with lanyards, pins, or cords round the neck. Study your map route before starting a tour.

7. DON'T SKI ALONE.
   An obvious rule, with a hidden implication: a large, uneven group is no stronger than its weakest member.

8. TURN BACK IN TIME; IT'S NO SHAME TO STOP.
   Beware the "point of no return" philosophy when touring; nothing is lost in a safe return.

9. SAVE STRENGTH; BIVOUAC WHEN NECESSARY.
   Skiing in bad and/or cold weather, in difficult snow conditions, or just any skiing when you're lost, saps strength rapidly. Bivouac in safety, in time, rather than pushing on against odds.

from its available "fuels," the foods consumed. This is why eager touring skiers, skimping on breakfast and skipping lunch to press on to some goal, are frequently victims of hypothermia. Dehydration also plays a role in their plight, as body-fluid loss saps strength.

Fortunately hypothermia doesn't strike suddenly, like a lightning bolt from the blue. It occurs in progressive stages, often with overpoweringly obvious symptoms. It gives both you and those you ski with plenty of warning, well before it sinks to the irreversible, fatal level. Normal body core temperature in healthy persons is within half a degree of 37°C., or within one degree of 98.6°F. In initial, mild hypothermia, the body temperature falls a few degrees, to between 95° and 98°F. The victim feels undue fatigue, may shiver uncontrollably, and often fumbles or has poor coordination. This stage of hypothermia can be treated simply by reducing heat loss, as, for example, by putting on more clothing.

Left untreated, hypothermia can progress. When the body core temperature falls to between 91° and 95°F., the victim may feel a deep cold, be confused or apathetic, may stumble frequently, and may have slurred speech. Irrational or erratic behavior, disorientation, amnesia, muscle stiffening, exhaustion, and a decrease in shivering signal a further decrease in body temperature, to 86°–91°F. Then blue lips, dilation of pupils, slow or irregular pulse, drowsiness, signal the dangerously low level, 81°–86°F. Although the number of recognizable stages and their symptoms may vary, common for all is that the body is no longer able to cope with the ongoing heat loss, and heat must be added to reverse the pending hypothermic disaster. Unconsciousness and, subsequently, death usually follow if the core temperature sinks to 78°–81°F.

The obvious way to combat hypothermia is to react immediately to its first signs. Put on extra clothes, change wet socks, don wind garments, or seek shelter if you detect any signs of hypothermia. If you even suspect hypothermia, in yourself or someone else in your party, get that person warm, right away. Supply warmth: build a fire, brew some warm drinks. *Avoid alcohol:* it only accelerates heat loss by dilating blood vessels. Also avoid tobacco, which reduces circulation in the extremities. Imbibe or smoke if you wish, but only when you're indoors again, thawed, warm, and not at all hypothermic.

The best defense against hypothermia is to avoid it completely. Always dress properly for the temperature and wind conditions you expect to encounter on a tour. Never underestimate how rapidly wet feet, hands, or clothing can accelerate heat loss. Always ski within your endurance capability. If you feel tired, it's always better to stop early rather than being stopped too late.

DEHYDRATION, or liquid depletion, is a hazard often ignored by skiers. Sometimes this is because of the many myths and taboos that exist concerning liquid intake. Some may believe that as one shouldn't sweat as much in cold weather as in warm, liquid loss is less, and therefore liquid intake should be less in winter. Others may adhere to the "tough line," believing that as it's a pleasure to drink when thirsty, it's somehow sinful to do so. Still others may believe that by cutting liquid intake they reduce sweating, and hence cut body heat losses. None of these views is based on fact.

Exercise in cold weather requires more energy, and hence a higher metabolic activity than the equivalent amount of exercise in warm weather. Increased metabolic activity requires more water. Liquid loss in exhaled air can be enormous in cold weather, as cold, dry air is inhaled, warmed and moistened in the lungs, and exhaled as humid, warm air. Perspiration occurs whether or not you drink, at a rate proportional to activity, not liquid intake. Self-punishment through deliberate dehydration, whether induced by false belief or carelessness, may be good preparation for a mystical experience or a good step on the way to self-martyrdom, but it is a lousy way to ski anywhere.

Fluid loss can be dangerous for many reasons, aside from the simple discomfort of feeling thirsty. Fluid loss results in decreased blood volume and blood pressure, which, in turn, promote weakness and can accelerate collapse should hypothermia occur. Liquid loss automatically and unavoidably decreases physical performance. A liquid loss of only 2% of body weight, about five cups of water for a 125-pound person or seven cups of water for a 160-pound person, decreases work capability by 20%. No matter what you do, if you're 2% down on liquids, you're only 80% as powerful as you are with a normal liquid balance. Doubling the loss, to 4%, knocks physical performance down to half.

Avoid excess liquid loss and dehydration by drinking as frequently as you can. You'll find it's almost impossible to drink too much while skiing, while it's all too easy to drink too little. Even on shorter tours, you should always take along something to drink, and some provisions for melting snow to water should be in all emergency kits. One simple method is to fill transparent plastic bags with snow, and expose them to the sun, preferably on top of an exposed, warmed rock. The melted snow cocktail they produce is almost unpalatable, but it will do in a pinch.

Liquids cannot be discussed without mentioning salt, as there's a common belief that salt should always be taken to replace that lost in sweat when exercising.

Actually, when you sweat, you become "saltier." This is because the salt content of sweat is less than that of the blood inside the body, so sweating always causes greater fluid than salt loss. If you don't continuously drink to replace the liquid loss, your internal salt concentration goes up as you perspire. This means that additional salt should not be taken, especially in skiing situations where it's usually difficult to drink enough to avoid slight de-

hydration. If your regular diet contains adequate salt, there's no need for more, unless you engage in prolonged, strenuous activity and perspire profusely for a week or more.

ALTITUDE can pose problems for the cross-country skier. One of the more obvious difficulties cross-country skiers encounter in ascending to higher elevations is that their physical performance decreases: they either must breathe harder to keep going, or slow down to keep pace with their breathing. But other effects, and some hazards, are encountered by all who are physically active at altitude.

First, increased altitude increases liquid loss and thus accelerates dehydration. If you've skied at altitude you've probably noticed that you feel thirst more quickly than when skiing in similar conditions at lower elevations. There are a number of physiological reasons for the increased loss, the simplest of which is that respiratory rates increase with increasing altitude, and more liquid is lost as greater air volumes are exhaled.

Altitude may induce a number of illnesses, caused by the body's response to lack of oxygen. There are a number of classifications and descriptions of various altitude illnesses; altitude expert Dr. Charles Houston[*] points out that those of primary concern to persons exercising at altitude are acute mountain sickness (AMS), high-altitude pulmonary edema (HAPE), and cerebral (brain) edema (CE).

AMS is perhaps the most common altitude illness, often occurring after rapid ascents to over 5,000 or 6,000 feet. Its symptoms are headache, nausea,

[*]Houston, C. S., "Altitude Illness—Recent Advances in Knowledge," *The American Alpine Journal,* Vol. 22, No. 1, Issue 53, 1979, pp. 153–159.

Tents are necessary on longer tours—here in use on the Conway Saddle at an elevation of 20,670 feet at the head of the Duke of Abruzzi Glacier in the Karakorums; Gasherbrum Group in the background. *Ned Gillette*

weakness, shortness of breath, and, often, vomiting. Like a bad hangover, AMS doesn't last long and is only rarely fatal, though sometimes victims may wish it might be.

HAPE is probably the most dangerous of the common altitude illnesses. It results from filling of the alveoli (air sacs) of the lungs with fluid that has oozed through the pulmonary capillary walls. As the alveoli fill with fluid, they block oxygen transfer to the pulmonary capillaries, which, in turn, decreases oxygen concentration in the blood. Unchecked, HAPE can cause death by suffocation in 40 hours. HAPE usually comes on rapidly, after quick ascents to altitudes of 9,000 feet or more.

CE is less common, but more dangerous than HAPE. It is unusual below altitudes of 14,000 feet, but has been known to kill healthy persons at 10,000 feet. Its symptoms are a severe headache, staggering, uncoordinated movement, and ominous hallucinations. In its final stages it results in coma and death.

To date, little is known about susceptibility to altitude illness: there's no known reliable way to predict who will or who will not become ill at higher elevations. Physical fitness seems to have no deterrent effect, although fitter persons exercising at higher elevations perform more efficiently, and hence use less oxygen, than the less fit. Alpine skiers ride lifts up and ski down major western mountains, yo-yo fashion, at altitudes of 10,000 to 13,000 feet with little apparent incidence of altitude illness. One reason for this may be that Alpine skiers seldom exert themselves at high elevations, and they get down quickly, both of which lessen their oxygen demands. Cross-country skiers, on the other hand, work when they ski, and hence are probably more susceptible than are Alpine skiers at the same altitude.

Fortunately there's one known, simple cure for all altitude illnesses: *get down.*

Retreat to lower elevations as soon as altitude illness is noticed, and before it becomes serious.

FIRST AID AND EVACUATION

Considerable information is available on first aid and evacuation, in the form of books, lectures, and courses, some of which are for certification or even university credit. If you know no first aid, it would be wise to avail yourself of this wealth of information before you go on any longer ski tours, as the farther your skiing takes you from the beaten path, the more self-reliant you must be. Evening courses run by the Red Cross, various rescue groups, and outdoor clubs are to be recommended. It's always wise to supplement these courses, intended for all-around application, with some specialized first-aid skills for situations you may face. Excellent references on that subject are *Mountaineering First Aid* by Dick Mitchell, a small, ready reference useful for all touring skiers, and *Medicine for Mountaineering* edited by James Wilkerson, a handbook essential for extended tours or expeditions, both published by The Mountaineers.

Against this background only a few remarks particular to cross-country ski touring are necessary:

· Make up your own first-aid kit rather than rely on a ready-made kit of the drugstore variety. The contents of these kits are intended for household emergencies, and often are not exactly what you need in a skiing first-aid situation. For instance, you'll probably find that you have a great need for tape, but almost never any need for burn ointment while skiing.

· Always carry a plastic spare ski tip if you ski more than a few miles from the road or trailhead. Modern fiberglass skis break less frequently than did their wood predecessors, but when they break, it's usually at the tip. If you break a ski and don't have a spare tip, or if the ski breaks at some other place, your salvation may lie in reverting to the ski technique of a century ago. Wax the broken ski for good grip, or tie cord or tape around it for good traction on the snow. Wax your good ski for best glide. Use the broken ski as a kicker, pushing off on it as children do on a scooter or skateboard, and glide on the good ski.

· You can evacuate an injured skier on an improvised sled made from one or two pairs of skis. Lash a few cross-members, such as branches or ski poles cut in half for the purpose (this *is* an emergency!) across the skis at the bindings and the tips. Pad with packs, branches, and extra clothing. Lash ski poles to the tips to pull the sled.

· Always carry a knife, nylon cord, and tape with you, on all tours. A list of what these items have been used for by skiers would be greater than the content of this chapter: aside from being useful for fashioning an evacuation sled and repairing equipment, you'll certainly find uses that you never dreamed of for these three basic items.

· It's always a good idea to practice all emergency procedures, such as improvising a sled from skis, read instructions on all emergency supplies and medications, and know how to operate all your gear, from ski bindings to stoves, before you leave on a tour. A few minutes' head-scratching at home may save you subsequent discomfort outside when you try to figure something out in an emergency situation.

SNOW BIVOUACS

Skiers bivouac in the snow for two reasons. First, there are those who plan to do so in advance; they are snow campers, and are usually equipped with tents, stoves, sleeping bags and pads, and adequate amounts of food. You may never intentionally camp in the snow, and thus need none of the equipment for it. But knowledge of snow camping is useful on all longer ski tours, as accidents, sudden changes of the weather, or being caught unexpectedly by nightfall often dictate that it's more prudent to bivouac than to ski on.

No matter what anyone tells you, an improvised winter bivouac isn't much fun and is seldom very comfortable. It's just a way to survive until daylight or clearing weather allow you to ski on or return. So the most prudent approach to bivouacking is to avoid it; plan your day's tour conservatively, allowing adequate time for unexpected slow travel. Always set realistic goals for a day on skis, ones that the weakest skier can achieve easily, not ones that the strongest skier in the group wishes to achieve. But if you are caught by nightfall or bad weather, or must shelter an injured skier, it's almost always better to bivouac than to forge aimlessly ahead.

Fortunately, skiers are usually surrounded by excellent insulation for spending a night out: snow. The surface of a snow cover is always at the prevailing air temperature, whatever that may be, and is always exposed to the chilling effects of wind. But inside a snowpack the temperature is seldom lower than a couple of degrees below freezing, usually −1°C. (30°F.) or so, and there's no wind. The air trapped between snow particles is an excellent insulator, the secret of the warmth of an Eskimo's igloo.

But don't think that you must know how to build an igloo to survive a night outside. Igloos take skill, experience, and time to build and few besides Eskimos can do it well (and even among the Eskimos it's a waning art). What you need is not habitation, but an emergency bivouac.

Always allow at least an hour to fashion a bivouac, although you may be able to build one more rapidly if you have practice—which you should have if you go on longer ski tours where bivouacking may be necessary.

As soon as you decide to bivouac, start looking for a place to build one; it always takes more time than you think. Look for boulders for wind protection, fallen trees to crawl under, moatlike depressions around trees, or snowbanks to dig into. Take inventory of your gear to determine what can be used in your improvised shelter: skis and poles, covered with windsuits and snow, make a decent roof; packs become seats and foot warmers; skis, boots, and socks can insulate from the snow.

If you have a snow spade (again, one of your party should have one along if you are on a longer tour) use it to dig into the snow and fashion snow blocks; if not, use your skis to dig and cut snow. The most easily and rapidly fashioned in-snow shelter is a niche dug horizontally, straight into a compacted snowbank. If you cannot dig horizontally, dig down vertically, and then horizontally to make a niche. Dig a seat, as broad as you need for your party, and then a dome-shaped roof, for strength. Cover the opening with your skis and poles, piling snow blocks or

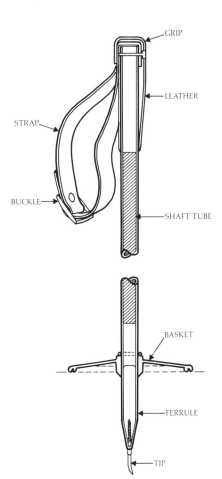

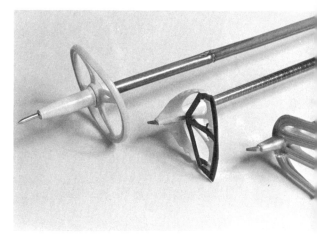

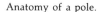

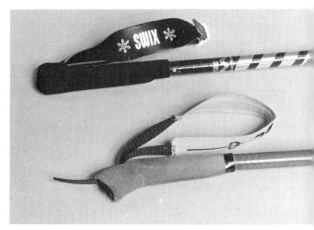

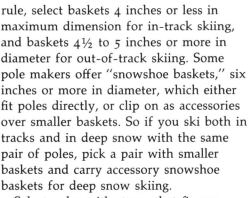

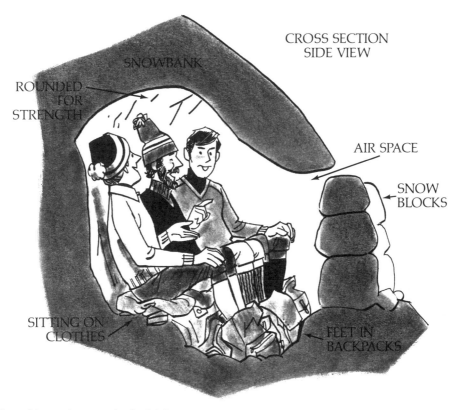

CROSS SECTION
SIDE VIEW

SNOWBANK

ROUNDED
FOR
STRENGTH

AIR SPACE

SNOW
BLOCKS

SITTING ON
CLOTHES

FEET IN
BACKPACKS

Never fear a bivouac in a snowbank. *Bob Bugg*

several inches of loose snow on the outside for insulation. Creep in from one end, and seal it up with smaller snow blocks. Sit on skis or packs on the seat, and stuff feet into the remaining packs for warmth. As soon as you've finished your bivouac and are prepared to settle down for the night, put on all your extra clothing. Put dry clothing next to the skin, and change any garments that got wet while you were building the bivouac. Stay warm from the start. If you have a candle and matches (again, which you should have along, just in case) light the candle. It may not provide much warmth, but it will help to keep you awake, as you should try not to sleep unless you have enough insulation to sleep comfortably. Tell jokes or sing songs to make the night pass. Eat in the evening if you have food and feel that you will get out the

following day, and be sure to drink plenty of water to avoid dehydration.

If you are in a wooded area, you may be able to build a fire to stay warm. Dry, dead branches, particularly the inner, lower branches of evergreen trees, make excellent firewood. To test for dryness, break twigs and branches: if they break with a snap, they are dry enough to burn. If they only bend, they are too wet. Build a small fire, just large enough to warm you slightly. A large bonfire may toast you on one side, and cause you to sweat, which is something you don't want to happen in a bivouac.

Finally, be cheerful; countless skiers before you have survived unprotected winter nights by bivouacking in the snow, and others may be doing it just as you sit in your bivouac.

AVALANCHES

Few cross-country skiers, even the most experienced, have ever been near an avalanche. But avalanches are not just the stuff of news reports, the catastrophes that sometimes eradicate Alpine towns. With each passing *normal* winter, more are reported, not because more now happen, but because more skiers now tour where avalanches can occur.

How much you need to know about avalanches and avalanche safety depends on where you intend to ski. Avalanches occur most frequently in steeper terrains, on slopes of 30° to 45° or more, although avalanches have been recorded on slopes of as little as 11°. So if you ski mostly in flat, gentle terrain, such as on the trails of many eastern cross-country ski centers, you need not worry about avalanches. You are probably more concerned about not falling into creeks or through the ice of frozen ponds or lakes.

But even in such terrain, and even in the East, you can be menaced by avalanches: if you tour in the floor of a valley that has steep slopes on each side, your danger of being involved in an avalanche is perhaps greater than it would be if you were up on the ridges above.

In the Rockies and other steeper cordillera of the West, avalanches are more frequent; if you tour there, you should know something about them.

The time you ski is also important. The highest avalanche hazard is always during and immediately after a snowfall. The hazard, or chance of an avalanche occurring, decreases as the snow settles. In the Pacific Northwest and the Sierras, snow usually settles relatively rapidly during warmer periods following snowstorms, and avalanche danger diminishes consid-

Avalanches can be giants, as is this one falling down about 1,500 feet onto the Ruth Glacier near Mt. McKinley. *Ned Gillette*

erably 24 hours after a snowfall. But in the Rockies and some of the Eastern ranges, cold weather often persists after a snowfall, so newly fallen snow settles slowly, sometimes remaining unstable, unsettled, for weeks, prolonging the period of maximum avalanche danger. This is why most Rocky Mountain ski tours are made in the spring, when the snow has settled, and avalanche danger has diminished.

Other factors influence the likelihood that a snow-covered slope will slide. *Wind* can pack snow into unstable slabs, form cornices which can collapse under their

Even seemingly innocent touring trails in wooded valleys can be threatened from above. *Michael Brady*

own weight, and erode the foundation that holds other snow in place. *Steeper* slopes are more likely to avalanche, but slope curvature is also important. A convex slope (bulging out) is more likely to slide than a concave (bowed in, like a bowl) slope, because the snow is under increasing tension in the downhill direction. *Ground conditions* can favor or impede slides. Rough surfaces, stands of timber, stable boulder fields, and the like favor stability. Smooth surfaces such as rock faces, mown meadows, or old slide slopes offer little purchase for snow and are potentially unstable. *Steep chutes and couloirs* are often ready-made avalanche paths, especially if they are exposed to the wind. *Snowfall rate* itself raises avalanche hazard whenever snow falls faster than it can compact and stabilize on the ground. Any snowfall of more than one inch per hour can create potentially hazardous avalanche conditions. The *history* of a snow cover determines its internal stability. Storms starting at lower temperatures, with snow falling as temperatures rise, can cause av-

alanches, as dry snow on the ground cannot support the heavier snow on top. Snow that has fallen on top of wind- or sun-crusted older snow is always unstable. Snow changes within a snow layer that create fragile deep hoarfrost can loosen the bonds between snow layers, triggering an avalanche.

The situation may sound complicated. It is. Most countries where populations are exposed to mountains and snow have permanent snow and avalanche research laboratories. Scientists have devoted their working lives to the subject, and volumes have been written on it. There are even professional journals devoted to snow and avalanche sciences. If you wish to know more, pursue some of the references listed in the back of this book.

Fortunately, a few basic precautions are all that most cross-country skiers need to avoid avalanche hazards. An Alpine skier, getting off a lift and whizzing down to put the first tracks in new snow, is in far greater danger of being caught in an avalanche than is a touring skier, who, more

35°– 50°

Slopes of 30° to 45° or more pose the greatest
avalanche hazard. *Bob Bugg*

slowly working with a touring party up a
valley, is more closely aware of snow
conditions because ski performance and
waxing depend upon them.

Avalanches are classed into two princi-
pal categories according to the snow at
the point of origin. *Loose snow* avalanches
start at a point, and fan out, growing in
size. *Slab avalanches* start when a large area
of snow starts sliding. They are of the
greatest concern, as almost all avalanche
accidents and injuries are caused by slab
avalanches, often triggered by the victims
themselves. Long avalanches may involve
more than one type of snow; the subclas-
sifications within the two main categories
are virtually endless.

In skiing, avoid potential avalanche

areas or routes that can trigger a slab avalanche. The combination of heavy snowfall and wind creates the greatest hazard,
so that's the time to stay home, or if you
are out on skis, stay far clear of any slope
that could possibly slide. Slopes in the lee
of the wind collect the most snow, and, if
they are also exposed to the sun, are the
most unstable. Don't trust them. Travel
on the windward side of ridgetops, well
away from cornices. Avoid traversing or
zigzagging on ascents or descents of
steeper slopes. Look for old avalanche
paths, vertical sweeps where the trees are
all gone. Avalanches can usually be
counted on to strike more than twice in
the same place. If the snow audibly re-
sounds under you as you ski, it's proba-

Skiers can start slab avalanches by crossing a
potential slide slope. Ski tracks can become slide
fracture lines. *Bob Bugg*

bly unstable and can slide. Seek cover in
sturdy stands of timber, on the down side
of ridges, or behind larger boulders if you
must cross what you believe may be a
potential avalanche path.

If you must cross a potential slide
slope, remove ski pole straps and any
safety straps you may have on your skis.
Unbuckle pack chest and waist straps;
loosen all your gear. Put on mittens and a
cap, and trail avalanche cord (a 100-foot-
long length of light, brightly-colored cord
that will "float" to the surface of a snow
slide, and lead others to you should you
be buried). Only one member of a party
at a time should cross a hazardous slope;
the others should watch and be prepared
to rescue if need be.

If you are caught by an avalanche,
don't try to outski it. Avalanches move
with incredible speed; only recently has
the world's record for downhill ski speed
equaled that of moderate avalanches.
When caught, try to discard your gear,
and stay on top by swimming on the
snow. Get your hands up in front of your
face, to beat out an air space so you can
breathe. Don't yell for help unless you
can hear the voices of searching skiers
nearby; snow deadens sound, and you'll
need your breath for breathing.

If you are a survivor, you are the victim's best hope of surviving. First, check
for further danger, then mark the point
where the victim was last seen. Quickly
search downslope from the last-seen

point. Even if there are only two survivors, a quick search must be made before going for help, and one should always stay and continue the search after the other has gone for assistance. If you are the sole survivor, you still should make a thorough search before going for help, unless help is only a few minutes away. A buried victim has only a 50% chance of survival after one hour. If you do go for help, be careful to mark or otherwise note your route. The rescue party will expect you to lead them to the scene of the accident and locate the last-seen points of the buried skiers, so ski back with the thought in mind that you must return.

SAFETY IS IN YOUR MIND

Potential hazards are part of the outdoor experience; they are the bad that goes along with the good, the enjoyment of skiing. Learning about hazards is not something skiers do for the same reason that they learn ski technique; wise skiers learn about hazards so they may appreciate and avoid them. It's just such knowledge that gives you the confidence to be calm, to use your "common sense" if something does go wrong.

11

EQUIPMENT
How to Select the Best

There's a lot in the spectrum
of cross-country gear.
Fletcher Manley

The cross-country skiing renaissance is in full bloom, which may be both good and bad news for the prospective purchaser of cross-country ski gear.

The benefits are obvious. The selection now is greater and the competition keener than ever, so the buyer benefits. But, on the other hand, so much is now on the market that even skilled skiers sometimes find evaluating the available options and combinations a mind-boggling task. Also, no book chapter, such as this one, could possibly contain all the details of the various makes and models of all items available in shops. If it did, it would be about as interesting reading, and about as thick, as a major city phone directory. And, because models now change annually or sometimes oftener, the content would be obsolete by the time you read it.

This is a chapter on the basics, what you need to know to find your way, informed, through the array of equipment now available.

START BIG, END SMALL

Here are a few general guidelines to consider before you get down to the nitty-gritty of finding out what you specifically want in the way of gear.

1. SKI AND SEE: Rent or borrow equipment until you are certain that you will stay with the sport, or until you decide what's best for your skiing. There's no substitute for on-snow experience with the items you contemplate using. Think: would you buy a car without test driving it?

2. THE GUIDING THREE: In selecting or buying, you will primarily be interested in three things: *performance, convenience,* and *du-* *rability.* What equipment and clothing do for you, on snow, matters far more than the specific technologies that went into their production.

3. LIGHT CAN BE RIGHT: Sturdy, heavy gear may be best for long wilderness tours with heavy packs. But few skiers ski this way all the time. If you jog, you know that light shoes are a joy, as with them you can jog faster and more easily, and therefore longer and with less fatigue than you can with heavier shoes. There's a parallel situation in cross-country ski gear: for in-track skiing at cross-country ski centers, the weight of the equipment on your feet greatly affects your technique. Shod with lighter gear, you may find that speedier skiing in tracks is an elation all its own.

4. SIMPLE'S BEST: Shy away from the ultimate in performance gear—that is, from racing equipment and clothing—unless, of course, you are a racer. It's more expensive, more difficult to use, often less durable, and more restricted as to where and when it may be used than its simpler siblings in the cross-country spectrum.

5. LOOK OFTEN: New gear appears every year, and the development of increasingly sophisticated equipment is an ongoing process. But the latest isn't always the best for all needs. As with other technologies, newly introduced ski equipment designs are often flawed, and need a few "generations" to work all the bugs out. So unless you want to experiment, stick with designs that have been around a few seasons. See what's used the season before you buy, or, if you're just starting out, ask skiing friends what types of gear they prefer.

SKI JARGON

As for all manufactured products, there's a vocabulary to describe the parts and features of skis. Here are the most-used terms.

BASE Bottom of ski that contacts snow surface.

BOX Synthetic ski structure, where structural fibers surround core.

CAMBER Upward curve of center of ski base above tip and tail.

CONTACT LENGTH Length of flattened ski base contacting underlying snow.

CORE Center section, inside ski; gives shape, but seldom strength.

GROOVE Longitudinal indentation in base, aids tracking.

HEIGHT Thickness, perpendicular to base, at midpoint of ski.

INJECTED SKI Ski made by injecting plastic in between top and bottom layers.

SANDWICH Wood or synthetic ski structure, built up, sandwichlike, of successive layers of material.

SHOULDER Broadest part of ski just back of tip.

SIDECUT Inward swing of ski side profile, as seen from above.

SIDEWALL Sides of a ski, between top and bottom.

TAIL Extreme rear end of a ski.

TIP Strictly, the extreme, pointed front end of a ski. In more common usage, the forward end of a ski.

TOPSHEET Uppermost layer on ski, usually decorated with ski maker's design, logo, or name.

WAIST Center of a ski; in a ski with sidecut, its narrowest point.

---

6. THINK SKIING: Your ski gear should function for you when you ski, so all your considerations and comparisons of materials, technologies, structures, and the like should focus on that goal. Your continual question when presented with anything new should be "Fine, but what does it do for me when I'm out on snow?" If you want to dig deeper into the subject of ski gear, there is a book on the subject: *Cross-Country Ski Gear,* published by The Mountaineers in Seattle.

BEST IS BEST FOR YOU

The best cross-country ski equipment and clothing is that which best suits your skiing needs. Determining your needs is the first and most important step in selecting ski gear. If you don't know your needs exactly, ask yourself the following questions. They're no Golden Rule for selection, but they'll help you on your way.

A. How proficient are you?
1. Just getting started
2. Experienced Alpine skier
3. Intermediate cross-country skier
4. Skilled cross-country skier

B. Do you cross-country ski for:
1. Recreation
2. Sport and/or fitness
3. Competition or adventure

C. What do you consider most important in your gear?
1. Convenience
2. Performance

D. Where do you intend to ski?
1. Prepared trails at cross-country ski centers, or local areas
2. Off-track, in wilderness
3. Special, selected places: race courses, ski mountaineering, etc.

E. How frequently do you ski?
1. Seldom, or, if you are an Alpine skier, only when the lift lines for the Alpine hill are unbearable
2. Every weekend you can during the winter
3. On long winter vacations, or several days a week each winter

In general, the more you tended to choose the first alternative each time, for a lower total score if you add the numbers, the more you'll be best served with simple, stable, care-free gear. The higher your score—you could add up to a 15—the more you should seek specialized, high-performance gear designed for specific skiing uses.

START WITH THE OBVIOUS

Skis are the first item of equipment that comes to mind when you think of skiing. So start selecting gear with the obvious, by finding the ski that best suits your needs.

TYPES FOUR

There's an ongoing discussion on the classification of cross-country ski equipment. Some manufacturers market their wares according to where they are used, such as *in-track* or *out-of-track*. Others speak of *performance* versus *recreational* skis (but that classification degrades: why can't a recreational skier expect performance?). So until superior terms replace them, the traditional four categories of *racing, light touring, touring,* and *mountaineering* will be used here, with the last being modified to *mountaineering/downhill* to reflect the trend of the major use of that end of the spectrum of cross-country gear.

RACING—IN TRACKS ONLY
Skis: Width: 44 mm (minimum regulation width) to 45 mm, little or no sidecut. Weight: 2 lb. 3 oz. to 2 lb. 14 oz. for a 210-cm pair.
Boots: Cut below ankle like jogging shoe, with leather or textile uppers. Soles of compact, hard plastic, 7 mm (about ¼ inch) thick.
Bindings: Minimum-weight metal or plastic toe clips, attach to snout on boot sole.
Poles: Ultralightweight carbon fiber, fiberglass, or aluminum shafts, various asymmetrical baskets, up to 3 inches maximum dimension.
Clothing: One-piece, knee- or ankle-length stretch suits.

LIGHT-TOURING—MOSTLY IN TRACKS, ON TRAILS
Skis: Width: 46 mm to 52 mm; 0–4 mm sidecut; Weight: 3 lb. 3 oz. to 3 lb. 12 oz. for a 210-cm pair.
Boots: Cut at ankle, some with groove around heel. Soles of hard plastic or foam plastic, 7 mm (¼ inch) thick, or plastic, rubber or leather, 12 mm (½ inch) thick.

If you were to go into a well-stocked ski shop cold, with no prior knowledge of the sport, you probably would find select-

Skis differ primarily in width. Left to right: racing, light touring, touring. *Fletcher Manley*

Bindings: Aluminum alloy or plastic toe bindings, attach to snout on boot or clamp around boot welt.
Poles: Tonkin, aluminum, or fiberglass shafts, baskets round or asymmetrical, approximately 4 inches diameter.
Clothing: One- or two-piece knit or poplin suits, or wool or corduroy knickers, with sweater and/or shell parka top.

TOURING—MOSTLY OUT OF TRACK
Skis: Width: 49 mm to 60 mm; 8–10 mm sidecut; Weight: 5 lb. 5 oz. to 7 lb. for a 210 cm pair. Some with metal edges.
Boots: Cut above ankle like hiking boots. Soles of foam plastic, rubber, or leather, 12 mm thick.
Bindings: 71-, 75- or 79-mm-wide aluminum alloy or plastic toepieces, some with heel-centering devices.
Poles: Same as light touring poles, but with larger, usually round baskets, diameters of 4½ to 6 inches.

MOUNTAINEERING/DOWNHILL—OUT OF TRACK, IN DEEP SNOW OR ON PACK
Skis: Width: 60 mm or more; 9–15 mm sidecut; Weight usually over 5½ lb. for a 210 cm pair. Usually have metal edges.
Boots: Single- or double-layer, many resemble touring ski boots or mountaineering boots. Foam plastic or rubber soles, often with lug pattern, 12 mm or more thick.
Bindings: 75- or 79-mm-wide, as beefed-up touring pin bindings, or resembling Alpine release bindings, for use with heavier mountaineering boots.
Poles: Shafts as for ski touring poles, baskets usually round, 4 to 6 inches diameter. For Nordic downhill use, poles may be shorter than normal all-around cross-country poles.
Clothing: Variable. For mountaineering, same as for mountaineering in similar terrain and weather, on foot. For Nordic downhill, anything goes.

All ski widths stated are waist widths, measured in the center of the ski, where the binding mounts.

ing cross-country skis incredibly confusing, because they are made with a greater variety of characteristics than any other item of sports gear, including jogging shoes, and you know how many of those there are. Here's a use-oriented way of

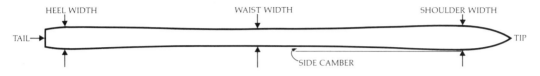

HEEL WIDTH   WAIST WIDTH   SHOULDER WIDTH

TAIL→   ←TIP

SIDE CAMBER

Anatomy of a ski.

classifying skis that will ease your way through the array of what's available.

Skis classify primarily according to 1) width and overall flex, 2) type of base, and 3) type of structure.

WIDTH AND OVERALL FLEX are determined by intended ski use. Generally, the wider a ski, the more area it puts on the snow, the less it sinks in, the more stable it feels in skiing, and the stronger it may be made. But it is also heavier, less respon- sive, and slower in turns. Generally, the narrower a ski, the lighter it can be made and the more its flex—the way it bends when you apply force—can be tailored for maximum response in faster in-track ski- ing. But narrower, lighter skis require more skiing skill. Because they are more responsive, they enhance your strides, but also amplify any error you make. With them you quickly know if you do some- thing right, or anything wrong.

Therefore there are several different categories of cross-country skis, differing from one another primarily by width, and secondarily by the flexes best suited to the uses for which the widths are de- signed. In order of increasing width, the categories are *racing, light touring, touring,* and *mountaineering/downhill* (see box, pp.158-59). The choice of ski guides the choice of other equipment items, as items should mate to best suit the use for which they were intended. For instance, ski-boot height generally follows ski width: below- the-ankle for racing, at the ankle for light

touring, above the ankle for touring, and above the ankle, often with a double boot, for mountaineering/downhill.

BASES: WAXLESS VERSUS WAXABLE

Your second, and perhaps most important, decision is whether to go with *waxable* or *waxless* skis. This is not a question of whether or not you intend to wax your skis for better performance, as do Alpine skiers and ski jumpers, but rather a deci- sion of the basic ski type you will use. Cross-country skiing requires that skis both grip and glide on snow, not grip only, as do shoe soles or automobile tires on asphalt, or glide only, as do Alpine skis or sled runners on snow. Cross- country skis are made with two different types of bases, or bottoms: *waxable* bases to which wax is applied for grip and glide, and *waxless*-base surfaces that grip and glide without wax.

The basic difference between the two types reduces to a question of perform- ance and versatility versus convenience and ease. The grip and glide of a ski on snow depend on how well its bottom sur- face suits the character of the underlying snow. Snow surfaces can vary in at least a thousand different ways. Therefore, wax- able bases are the most versatile and po- tentially the best performers, because dif- ferent ski waxes can be applied in varying amounts to suit the prevailing snow con-

Typical waxable (left) and pattern waxless (right) ski bases. *Fletcher Manley*

ditions. But the disadvantage of the type is obvious: you must wax every time, or almost every time, you ski. The basics of waxing are simple, but it is an art that must be learned to be practiced well.

A waxless ski needs no wax for general, all-round skiing. It's convenient, ready to ski when you are, with no preparation. But it has only one bottom surface, only one solution to matching all the different snows on which you may ski. It cannot accommodate to snow conditions, and is the same every time you ski. So its performance is both variable and limited, with few exceptions(see box, p. 163).This is why racers, who want the ultimate in cross-country ski performance, use waxable skis almost exclusively.

The *convenience* of the waxless base versus the *performance* of a waxable base is not simply a question of no-wax-at-all versus skiing-at-breakneck-speed. It's more a matter of your approach to your skiing:

· Waxless skis are best for those for whom convenience or transition-snow performance are paramount, such as:

—Persons who ski infrequently, and take only shorter trips
—Children learning to ski, especially in multi-child families or school programs where there aren't enough adults to wax all the skis
—Skilled cross-country skiers who need skis that work reliably in changing conditions, as common in the far West and central East Coast parts of the continent
—Alpine skiers who want to combine cross-country and Alpine skiing on their skiing weekends
—People who detest any form of equipment maintenance
—Skiers whose main problem in skiing is getting up hills

· The trade-off between convenience and performance is not as clear-cut as it once was. Competition among makers of the two categories of products has narrowed the gap. The performance of waxless skis has been improved since they were first introduced, so waxless skis are no longer only for beginners. Wax makers have developed more convenient waxing systems, so waxable skis are no longer for experts only.

· In terms of time, waxable skis may be the more convenient. Almost all waxless skis drag on the snow and glide less well than their waxable counterparts. So it takes more effort to push them forward, and your tours take correspondingly longer. The time you save by not waxing may be small by comparison.

· Waxless skis are not totally care-free. They can pick up dirt or ski wax from tracks and cease to function properly if they are not cleaned. Their bases, particularly the hair bases, can ice up if not kept meticulously clean.

·In general, waxless skis offer no advantage over waxable skis for snow conditions where waxing is easy, such as consistently cold snow. But when it's difficult to wax waxable skis, such as for rapidly varying snow conditions or snow just at freezing, waxless skis can sometimes outperform waxable skis.

·For best performance waxless skis should be waxed. Several companies offer sprays and/or brush-on liquids especially designed to improve waxless ski performance.

·There are so many waxless ski bases and waxless ski types on the market that you may find it more difficult to select the best one for your purposes than to select wax.

·Designing a *good* waxless ski is more complicated than designing a waxable ski of the same quality. In addition to all the design characteristics of the waxable ski, the waxless ski designer must put in the right length, location, and type of waxless surface in the base. A small error here, or a small error when the final user, the skier, selects skis, can loom large, as it cannot be corrected simply by altering the wax job a bit. In short: selecting a good waxless ski is difficult. It's best to try out as many types as possible, on snow, before you decide which is best for your skiing.

·Some waxless skis make a whining noise as they glide, which can be annoying. If you don't like to screech as you ski, listen first, buy later.

·Because wood absorbs water, and wax will not stick to a wet ski base, the waxing, and particularly the rewaxing, of wood skis can be difficult. Base preparation compounds, such as various synthetic

tars, are available to waterproof wood bases and partially cure the problem. Applying tars and fussing with occasionally wet ski bases can be messy. This is where waxless skis may offer an advantage. But modern fiberglass skis, with plastic bases that repel water, offer the same advantage: they need no messy tarring, and you can easily rewax out on the trail simply by scraping off the old wax and rubbing on the new.

·The ability to wax well for ultimate ski performance is an acquired skill. It takes time to learn. But if you start with one of the simple, convenient two-wax systems (see Chapter 13), you can wax satisfactorily from the start, for almost all snow conditions, simply by reading the manufacturer's directions. A season of skiing is all you will need to learn to use one of these wax systems well.

·Waxing does require some thought before you ski. Unless you are right at the snow, you should wait until you get there to wax: generally you cannot wax your skis at home, drive an hour or two to ski, and jump out of your car and ski right away. That sort of convenience is available only with waxless skis.

·Many skiers relish even difficult waxing, as an opportunity to meet nature on its own terms, and respond with skill, not just overpowering technology. Waxing well for tricky snows is like mimicking a bird song, and having a bird reply.

The final choice may depend on your dedication as a skier. If you're a newcomer to the sport and are in doubt as to which route to go, waxless is best. But later you may discover the joy of performance skiing and want to switch. Fair enough: most quality producers offer both

WAXING WAXLESS AND WAXLESS WAXABLES

When the waxing of waxable bases is difficult, such as whenever snow is in between wet and dry just at 0°C. (32°F.), waxless bases can be the best performers, which is why they have been successfully used in racing at these temperatures. However, these racing waxless skis would be more correctly termed *hybrids,* as they usually require some waxing, usually for glide. And, for many snow conditions, such as older, dirty snow, the center waxless sections of their bases usually are treated with a compound for maximum performance.

The opposite also occurs: traditional wood bases on wood skis do what they have done since skis were invented: grip and glide on cold, subfreezing snow, with little or no wax. In today's terms wood skis can be called the original waxless ski, which is just what they were before the first cross-country ski wax, a klister for wet conditions, was invented by Peter Østbye in 1913–14.

These are the two extreme cases: waxless skis that when waxed are top performers under certain conditions, and waxable skis that perform without wax under certain conditions.

types of skis, sometimes under differing brand or model names. If you're an avid skier who skis as much as possible each winter, then skiing performance and waxing are your best routes. If you're a sometimes skier, equally interested in other leisure activities in the winter, then waxless skis may be best. You probably will miss neither waxing nor the time it takes to be good at it. Again, cross-country is what you want to make it, in your own style.

STRUCTURE: WOOD VERSUS FIBERGLASS

Skis are classified according to the materials of which they are made in the same manner as buildings. Just as a wood frame house is still a frame house, even though it may have a brick facing, it's the material in the framework, or structure, of the ski that counts. Cross-country skis are now made with either wood or synthetic-fiber structures. Fiberglass is the most common synthetic fiber used, although other esoteric materials, such as carbon and aramid fibers, are used in high-performance competition skis. So wood versus fiberglass is the next major choice after you have selected your general category of ski and decided whether you will go waxable or waxless.

Wood skis, the traditional choice and dominant type up to 1975, are now the endangered species of skiing. There have been no wood Alpine skis produced for at least two decades, and no wood jumping skis for over a decade. Wood cross-country skis are fast disappearing. The demise of the wood ski is due chiefly to the advantages of modern fiberglass skis. A high-quality wood ski is still better than a low-quality fiberglass cheapie, but for skis of comparable quality, fiberglass skis now have the upper hand.

A SWITCH IN TIME?

Like it or not, the synthetics are here to stay. I love wood, cane, and leather as well as anyone, and miss them on the ski scene. But even with this nostalgia, it's difficult to agree with those who advocate a return to ski gear made completely from natural materials, solely on the grounds of exploiting renewable, rather than expendable, resources.

The "good old days" in ski gear really weren't all that good, for many reasons, including the few below:

- In producing wood skis, 65% to 75% of the wood a factory used was wasted; only a quarter or so actually found its way into finished skis. The rest ended up as sawdust, shavings, and discarded pieces. This waste was usually burned, as it came from too many different types of wood to make it usable in recycled products.

- Making wood skis required more glue than does the manufacture of modern synthetic skis, as glue joints bonded laminations into layers, and layers into skis. Good skis sometimes had 40 to 50 such glue joint bonds.

- Wood ski production involved more operations, and hence more power consumption per pair of skis produced, than does modern synthetic ski production.

- During their lifetimes, wood skis had to be frequently treated, top and bottom, with lacquers and tars, both, in the years after World War II, made exclusively of synthetic materials. So on a per-pair basis, wood skis may have used just as much expendable material as fiberglass skis, if not more.

- Wood ski production required more steps that required space, such as wood curing, than does fiberglass ski production. So wood ski factories were larger. For each pair of skis produced, more cubic feet of factory had to be heated than is the case for modern synthetic ski production.

- Tonkin poles required many factory operations and so, like wood skis, required more space, more factory heating, and more waste than is the case for synthetic pole production.

- The tonkin for pole shafts was cut in underdeveloped countries, usually by underpaid laborers, and shipped enormous distances, sometimes halfway around the world, before reaching the destination factory where it was used.

- As with shoes, hand-sewn crafting and leather soles were the answer when hides were plentiful, and both labor and energy were cheap. But were the old methods still in use, and were shoemakers to receive a decent industrial wage and work in comfortable conditions, few skiers would be able to afford their products.

- One factor in the high prices of natural-fiber garments, such as those of cotton and wool, is the transport cost and production cost of the raw material. Bulk wool and cotton must be transported to processing plants, and raising cotton and sheep requires energy. It would be interesting to see if someone could compute the total equivalent oil cost in a pound of wool versus the oil cost of the various synthetics that can, in combination, insulate and wick moisture away as well as the pound of wool.

In the little field of skiing, a speck in the worldwide energy-consumption picture, the use of synthetics may actually be what reduces the per-capita consumption of expendable resources. With the increasing popularity of the sport, perhaps we could not have afforded to continue with the old, wasteful construction methods for our ski gear. . . .

For comparable qualities fiberglass skis are stronger and more durable, and many models are guaranteed against breakage. Fiberglass skis usually perform better in both speed and turning ability, which is why they are now used exclusively in racing. Fiberglass skis are easier to maintain than their wood predecessors, which is a definite advantage for recreational skiers. If you have chosen the waxless route, your selection is virtually limited to fiberglass skis, as few, if any, wood skis with waxless bases are available.

Wood skis are objects of beauty, products of craftsmen. If you love skiing, you may enjoy handling and working on wood skis much as some sailors relish the care of wood boats. One argument in favor of wood skis is that broken ones can be repaired with ordinary carpentry tools and waterproof glues, but damaged fiberglass skis need more specialized, often expert, repair. Also, wood ski bases offer their traditional advantage of being able to grip and glide on subfreezing snow, with little or no wax, as compared to plastic bases in fiberglass skis, which won't grip at all without wax.

But these advantages are not adequate to stem the trend. Choose wood skis if you can find them, as they are still one of the few real bargains left in winter sports gear. In so doing you'll have the chance to participate in the sport as it once was. But otherwise stick to fiberglass skis.

WAXABLE BASES

In waxable skis there are two main choices of base: wood bases on wood skis, and plastic bases on some wood and all synthetic-fiber skis.

If you have chosen wood bases, then your selection is limited by what's still available as the breed of the wood ski dies out. Two woods, birch and hickory, are commonly used in wood bases. Hickory is the stronger and the more durable, but also the heavier and the more expensive. Edges on wood bases wear rapidly, so many wood bases have compressed hardwood edges, usually identified only by their trade names, such as *lignostone,* which is beech wood compressed to half its original volume.

Almost all ski base plastics are derived from three common plastics: *polyethylene (PE),* commonly used in household items such as bottles and shower curtains, *polypropylene (PP),* used in lightweight products such as ropes and other boating items that must float on water, and *ABS* (abbreviation for acrylonitrile butadiene styrene), used in impact-resistant products such as crash helmets.

Ski base performance depends not only on the base material itself, but also on how it is shaped and treated in production, how it is bonded to the ski, and how the ski's characteristics are designed to work with that base material. So there's no one answer for the best base, only general trends among ski makers:

The polyethylenes are the most frequently used in ski bases. The better polyethylenes offer the best performance, but are also the most expensive bases, and therefore are used primarily on high-end, high-performance in-track skis, such as racing skis.

ABS plastics withstand abuse, and therefore are used on skis intended mostly for out-of-track use.

Polypropylenes are somewhere in between these two extremes.

Ski makers may use these generic names or a variety of trade names to describe the plastic bases of their skis. The trade names are easy to remember and use, much as "aspirin," originally a trade name, is easier for most people to remember than "acetylsalicylic acid." But unless you're in the ski business, the trade names may be confusing. Take heart: there aren't very many of them, simply because only a few companies, perhaps no more than half a dozen worldwide, make the plastic parts from which ski makers make skis. And most often it's the plastic maker's, not the ski maker's, trade name that identifies the plastic. Here's how to decipher.

The trade name of a base plastic may have one or two parts, a name in letters and sometimes a suffix number. The name may be the generic one for the plastic used, or it may be a trade name for a particular brand or compounding of the generic plastic. Some common trade names are:

P-Tex, Fastex, Naltene, TKX, Kofix, for polyethylenes
ABS, Supernabutene for ABS-derived plastics.

If a suffix number is used and it is several hundred thousand or more, it indicates the *molecular weight* of the plastic. A higher molecular weight simply means that a plastic is built up of longer molecules, is denser, and, as a ski base, generally glides better. If the number is smaller, four digits or so, it's usually the manufacturer's catalog number of a particular molecular-weight plastic. Higher numbers usually, but not always, indicate higher molecular weights: P-Tex 2000, for instance, has a higher molecular weight, performs better, but is more expensive than P-Tex 1600.

WAXLESS BASES

There are three main types of waxless ski base, according to the type of surface ir-

regularity that grips, or gives the ski traction, on snow: *hair, pattern,* and *heterogeneous material.*

HAIR bases descend from the fur-based "kicker" skis of a century ago, and from the climbing skis that Alpine skiers used to ascend hills in the 1930s and 1940s, before all the big ski lifts were built. The principle is simple, and familiar to anyone who has ever stroked a cat backward. Hair is laid in the plastic ski base material in strips or small rectangles, with the nap angled backward. In the forward direction the hair slides, as does your hand when you stroke a cat from head to tail. But in the backward direction the hair stands up, as does cat hair when you stroke from the tail toward the head, and therefore can grip the snow. Natural or synthetic mohair and synthetic, trade-named hairs, such as Fibre-tran, are used. Hair bases work best in icy conditions and on hard pack and packed powder snow. But, like any fur garment, they can absorb water and freeze. When frozen they cease to work. Some synthetic hairs repel water fairly well, and silicone water-repellent sprays are available to treat all hair bases.

PATTERN bases have irregularities that, like sawteeth, glide in one direction, but bite in the opposite direction. The irregularities may be larger and spaced out along the base, or may be smaller and more closely grouped, like the teeth of a file, or *imbricated,* overlapping in sequence like roof shingles. The step, various trade-named patterns such as Fishscale, Crown-Cut, and T-Step, and other patterns molded, pressed, or otherwise machined into base plastics are either *positive,* where the pattern sticks up from the base, or *negative,* where the pattern is flush with or under the base surface. Pattern bases work best in slush, changing snows, and softer packed powder. They function by compressing the underlying surface for grip, much as a cat sinks its claws into a tree to climb. This means that they may perform less well on hard and/or icy surfaces, or in extremely light snow which won't compress to allow their irregularities to grip. Some patterns emit a squealing sound as they glide.

HETEROGENEOUS MATERIAL bases work like snow tires: small, denser parts, voids or particles grip, while the plastic of which they are formed or embedded in glides. The major advantage of heterogeneous bases is that the waxless grip action is a property of the material itself, and therefore is retained as the waxless section wears.

The performance of a waxless ski depends not only on the particular type of waxless base used, but also on the overall size, characteristics, and location of the waxless section, and on the way the ski's flex and camber are designed to work with the waxless base. In general, the more the waxless irregularities stick out, and the larger the area of the base they cover, the more they grip and the less they glide. All skis, both waxable and waxless, slip backward slightly before gripping when you kick. The slip can be so small as to be unnoticeable, such as on a well-waxed waxable base, or may be disconcertingly large for some waxless bases. For waxless bases of equivalent overall performance, smaller and more numerous irregularities tend to slip backward less and grip more quickly than do fewer, larger irregularities. Almost all waxless sections are located in the middle of the ski base for about a third of its length, just under your foot, where you most need traction on the snow. But the exact location of the waxless section and how far it extends forward of and back from your foot, influences how well it grips and how much it brakes to slow ski glide. Finally, the overall flex or stiffness of the ski influences how hard you must push down on your kick to get the waxless section to grip on the underlying snow. Skis too stiff for your weight and strength will have poor grip, while those too "soft" for you will grip all the time, and glide poorly.

So choosing a good waxless ski can be difficult. If you have the opportunity, select by trial. Rent different waxless skis and see how they work for you and your skiing, in the areas and under the conditions that you normally ski. Some major ski areas host on-snow ski shows when the snow first falls, usually around Thanksgiving. If you want to try the latest gear and are lucky enough to find a show with snow cover on the cross-country trails, give it a try. Even if you don't find exactly the waxless ski you're looking for, you'll be able to impress your friends with your firsthand knowledge of the latest gear.

SIDE SHAPE

Skis are made with various side profiles, which are most easily seen from above, when the ski is resting on a flat, horizontal surface. Traditional, and still most common, is *sidecut,* where the center, or *waist,* of the ski is cut in from its tip and tail, to an hourglass shape. The difference in widths at the waist and the tip and tail isn't much, seldom more than a tenth of the overall ski width, but the profile aids *tracking,* or how straight the ski runs when pointed in one direction, and turning, especially on downhills.

Racing skis have little or no sidecut, as they are intended for use in tracks, which guide the ski, and seldom need to be turned out of track. Their side shape is straight, or, in some extreme cases, spear shaped, for all-out, in-track speed. The opposite extreme are skis in the mountaineering-downhill-adventure skiing class, which have considerable sidecut, as they are intended for good tracking and ease of turning out of track. But sidecut or lack of it does not does not determine tracking and turning performance completely. Other ski characteristics, such as how well the ski resists twisting that can change its effective shape on snow, also influence its tracking and turning performance. In other words, there's no one answer as to how much or how little sidecut on a ski is good for a given skiing situation. If in doubt, rent or borrow skis with different sidecuts, and see how they ski for you.

Ski and pole length should suit you.

LENGTH

Select ski length to suit your height. Stand erect on a flat floor, wearing ski boots or low-heeled shoes. The best average ski length is from the floor to the palm of the hand of an upraised arm. For most adults, this is about 25 to 30 cm (10 to 12 inches) longer than body height. For instance, a person 5′ 11″ tall (182 cm) will usually select 210-cm skis. Even for U.S.-made skis, lengths are always stated in centimeters, and most skis for both children and adults are made in increments of 5 cm or 10 cm (2 to 4 inches).

Longer skis tend to be faster and more stable than shorter skis, while shorter skis are easier to maneuver in turns. So if you depart from the average ski length for

your height, it's best to go shorter if you are an average skier, and a bit longer if you are an expert skier.

Almost no skis are made in lengths longer than 220 cm, so supertall skiers, 190 cm (6′ 3″) or more tall, must ski on shorties.

FLEX AND STIFFNESS

Skis act like leaf springs, and bend according to how you apply your weight and other forces on them. This lively bending in reaction to your movements is one of the major factors that determine ski performance. Were this not so, you could strap a couple of two-by-one-inch planks on your feet and ski well.

Ski flex and stiffness should suit your weight, skiing ability, and the type of skiing you intend to do. More than in any other stage of the selection process, this is where you may need expert assistance. Flex and stiffness are not numbers, like

WEEDING OUT

The best assurance of purchasing quality skis is to deal with a shop that backs up the quality goods they sell. But lacking this assurance in purchasing, or if you want to check your present skis or a pair you consider buying yourself, you can look for the more common defects.

External blemishes are the most easily seen defects: damaged bases or topsheets, delamination, or marred sidewalls. Less obvious, and far more difficult to detect and far more important to ski performance, are structural or core defects. Some show up only in skiing, while many may be checked indoors. Those that you can find easily are twist and warp, splay, pair mate and closure, and flatness.

TWIST AND WARP. Twist or warp will cause a ski to *yaw*, or always turn or climb up out of a track instead of running straight. Check for twist by holding a pair of skis together and sighting from tail to tip when the tails are held together. Bases should touch over the entire width of the shovels. If there is a V-shaped gap, one or both skis is twisted. Even if the skis meet well, both may be twisted, in opposite directions. Check for this defect by reversing one ski, holding the pair with one tail against one tip, and resighting.

Check for warp by squeezing the midpoints of the skis together when they are held base to base. The ski sides should line up. If there is an offset, one or both skis are warped. Even if the sides do line up, both skis may be warped, in opposite directions. Again, check for this defect by reversing one ski, holding the pair together, tip-to-tail, and resqueezing the midpoints.

SPLAY. Hold the skis together, base to base, and watch what happens to the gap between the upturned sections of the tips as you squeeze the ski midpoints together. If the gap moves backward down the skis, the tips are splayed. Each time you weight a splayed ski, the tip will lift up from the snow, effectively shortening the ski, making it wander when gliding.

MATE AND CLOSURE. Sight between the bases as you squeeze the skis together at their midpoints. The bases should close at the same rate, evenly and smoothly, with no high points or low pockets, no gaps between points where the bases touch. Skis that don't mate may go in different directions as you ski. Bumpy bases wear wax or waxless sections unevenly, and glide poorly. With the skis held completely together, check pair mate: edges should line up along the entire length of the skis. Slight mismatch, 1/64 of an inch or so, has little effect. But greater mismatch may cause uneven tracking, or pull to one side.

BASE FLATNESS. Ski bases should be flat for best performance, although slight curvatures have little effect. Concave, or *railed*, bases wear unevenly and degrade ski grip; convex, or *bowed*, bases wear wax or waxless sections unevenly and, in extreme cases, degrade control and glide. Check base flatness by placing a steel base scraper or any tool with a good straightedge, on the base. Sight along the base with a light behind the straightedge. If there's an opening in the center, around the tracking groove, the base is railed. If there are openings at the edges, it is bowed.

clothing or shoe sizes, but characteristics that influence the way the ski behaves as you ski.

Expert skiers and skilled shop clerks usually have a feel for ski flex and camber, based on experience. They can flex a pair of skis, squeeze them together base-to-base, and match skis to skiers. Even if you don't consider yourself an expert, do try flexing skis before you purchase. Think: would you buy a guitar without first plucking a few notes? See how the skis "play" for you; knowing something about them is like knowing that a guitar will play well for you.

FLEX is short for the various *flexural stiffness* of a ski, the properties that determine how easily a ski bends or twists in use.

TIP FLEX is a measure of how easily the tip section of the ski bends directly upward in skiing. It can be felt by pulling the tip toward you with one hand, while supporting the ski away from you with the other hand, placed midway between the tip and the center of the ski. Softer tips "flow" easily over small irregularities in the snow, and therefore are faster in good tracks. But in loose snow, softer tips tend to dig in, causing skis to wander. Stiffer tips offer better ski control in out-of-track downhill turns. The length of the tip section that flexes is also important. A "longer" flex that bends more easily far back into the body of the ski follows the snow surface more easily, and therefore is easier to ski. A "shorter" flex is more responsive in tracks, and more suited to racing.

TAIL FLEX is equivalent to tip flex, just at the other end of the ski. It can be felt by angling the ski to a floor and pressing down on its midsection with one hand, while supporting the ski farther up with the other hand. Softer tails "flow" easily in tracks, but wipe out in out-of-track turns. Stiffer tails aid skis to hold their shape in out-of-track turns, but can chatter off bumps in tracks.

Select camber to suit your weight, strength, and skiing ability.

TORSIONAL FLEX describes how easily the front part of the ski, or the *forebody,* can twist relative to the center of the ski. It can be felt by holding the center of the ski with one hand, and twisting the tip with the other, as if you were trying to unscrew it from the ski. Torsionally softer tips give slightly when they hit the sidewalls of a track, and therefore help keep the ski in the track. But they also give when the ski is turned out of track, which degrades turning performance. Torsionally stiffer tips enable the ski to hold an edge in out-of-track turns, but also tend to ride up out of tracks more easily.

CAMBER AND STIFFNESS

Strictly speaking, *camber* is the upward arching curve of the middle of a ski and is what distributes your weight and the forces you apply at your foot over the ski, translating them into pressure on the underlying snow. *Camber stiffness* means the resistance to flexing along the camber curve. But the terms are used interchangeably, and are often combined with other adjectives, such as *hard camber* (relatively stiffer camber stiffness).

Overall camber stiffness is the property that determines how much force is necessary to flatten out the camber curve. When you ski, your weight and the forces of your motion push downward to flatten the ski out. Therefore you should select skis with camber stiffness that matches your weight and kicking force.

Because average body weights and overall strengths go up with heights, most ski factories produce skis with camber stiffnesses that increase with ski length. Each length of a particular make and model of ski is produced with a range of camber stiffnesses suitable for the average weights and strengths of skiers using that length of ski. For instance, adult male skiers 5′ 9″ to 5′11″ tall usually select 210-cm ski lengths, so most 210-cm skis are made in camber stiffnesses suitable for skiers weighing about 150 to 175 pounds, average for the heights involved. If you are light or heavy for your height, you may have to select shorter or longer skis to get a pair with the correct camber stiffness. Here is where you can depart the most from the average ski length for your height, as in most skiing it's far more important to ski with the correct camber than it is to ski with the average ski length for your height.

The more a ski is intended for faster in-track skiing, the greater its camber stiffness. This is because the faster you ski, the harder you kick to propel yourself forward. Racers often kick with a force of three times their body weight or more, but at average recreational skiing speeds, skiers usually kick with forces equal to

their body weights. Therefore racing skis usually have greater camber stiffnesses than do skis of the same length intended for use by recreational skiers of the same weight. Softer skis, those with less camber stiffness, are easier to flatten on the snow, so their wax or their waxless sections grip more easily, both in tracks and in off-track skiing in deep snow. Harder skis, those with greater camber stiffnesses, have the potential to perform better in tracks, but can be more work to use, especially if you're not strong enough, or are simply too tired to kick hard enough, to flatten out your skis' camber curves for grip.

With the correct ski your kick just flattens the midsection of the ski out so the irregularities of the waxless section, or the wax applied, grips on the underlying snow to give you traction. A ski that is too stiff for you will not flatten out when you kick, so it grips poorly and may slip backward. Like the spinning wheels of a stuck car, you waste power and get nowhere when you slip. A ski that is too soft will flatten out even when you don't kick, maybe even when you simply glide on both skis. Its midsection drags on the snow and grips all the time, slowing your glide. But if you err, it's best to be on the soft side: you may have slightly slow skis, but at least you'll make it up hills.

Snow conditions also influence ideal camber stiffnesses. The harder the snow, the more it can withstand the force of a ski being flattened out. The softer the snow, the more it tends to flow under the ski, to contact the midsection before it is flattened out. So stiffer skis are better on harder tracks, such as those set by machine at many cross-country ski centers. Softer skis are better for skiing in softer snow. This is why many racers have two pairs of skis: one "dry snow" pair for softer conditions, and one "klister" pair for use on hard, compacted snows, the usual conditions when klisters are used. This does not mean that you need two pairs of skis for recreational skiing. It means that you should compromise on a camber stiffness that suits you, your skiing, and the average snow conditions where you ski.

Whatever you choose in the way of skis, do not succumb to the temptation to purchase lightweight racing skis with racing ski cambers unless you intend to ski only in well-prepared racing tracks, at racing speeds, with a racer's vigor. The lighter weight of racing skis is achieved at a sacrifice of strength, particularly in the tip and midsections. Therefore, racing skis easily can be overloaded to the point of failure. Even a dip in a touring trail, such as where it crosses a creek bed, can be disastrous. In skiing through it on racing skis you risk your equipment just as certainly as you would the wheels (and maybe other parts) of an expensive, lightweight racing bike, were you to cycle straight through a deep city street pothole at full speed. Racing skis are no more made to withstand the punishment of touring trails than racing bikes are made to withstand the punishment of being ridden over curbs or through potholes. Because they are designed for use in well-prepared racing tracks, racing skis usually are far more difficult to turn out of tracks than are other types of skis. Finally, in addition to being relatively stiffer, racing skis often have a camber stiffness described as "double camber," which although actually a misnomer, describes the way the stiffness increases progressively as the camber curve flattens out. This property keeps the center of the ski base off the snow until it is literally punched down by a forceful kick. It's what allows

racers to wax ski tips and tails exclusively for glide, and midsections exclusively for grip, a combination for maximum in-track skiing performance. But to benefit from this property, you must either run like a racer or kick like a mule. So if you are not a racer or a mule, you may slip backward with every kick. For you, racing skis will be an expensive way to ski poorly.

SELECTING THE RIGHT CAMBER STIFFNESS: Computers may someday be programed to mate skis to skiers. But as yet there's no substitute for the human touch, for the experience of skiing and relating the way skis feel to the way they perform. There are also a few tests that you can make.

Squeeze test: For most persons, arm strength is proportional to leg strength and to overall weight. So squeezing skis, placed base-to-base together, gives you an indication of how well they may suit you and your skiing power. Hold a pair with your hands cupped around the skis at their midpoints. Squeeze the skis together. If you can flatten their bases against each other with both hands but not with one hand, the stiffness is about right for you, for recreational skiing. If you can flatten them together with one hand, they are too soft. If you cannot flatten them with both hands, they are too stiff.

Clamp test: Various calibrated clamps are available to read the force required to flatten one ski against a flat surface, or flatten two skis against each other. The clamps, or *ski testers* as they are called, are relatively expensive instruments, and are therefore used mostly in factories and shops. The instruments sometimes read in pounds, and sometimes in other units, which can be translated using charts to the equivalent skier weights for which the measured cambers are suited. Don't be-

Hand squeeze to test camber stiffness. *Fletcher Manley*

A ski camber tester is more precise. *Fletcher Manley*

lieve ski testers completely, just because they are instruments. Like any other instrument they require skill to use properly and interpret correctly, which, again, requires experience.

Paper test: Place a sheet of paper about four inches wide under the middle of one ski of a pair resting on a flat, horizontal, smooth, clean (*not* carpeted) floor. Stand with your weight equally divided on both skis, shoe tips at the ski balance points. With the average best camber stiffness for recreational skiing on most snows, the paper can be moved back and forth slightly out with moderate resistance. Stand still and have someone else try to move the paper, because if you bend over and try it yourself, you unbalance your weight on the skis and ruin the test. When your weight is all on one ski, the paper should be clamped fast between the ski and the floor. If the paper can be moved at all when you completely weight one ski, the skis are too stiff. If the paper cannot be moved when you equally weight both skis, then they are too soft.

The paper test is a good in-shop test.

None of these tests is one hundred percent certain. A pair of warped planks could, for instance, test well, but they would be miserable things to try to ski on. So it's always best to see how a camber stiffness test relates to your skiing. Find a pair of skis, by renting, borrowing, or whatever, that you think skis well. Subject it to one or more of the camber stiffness tests. Then you'll know what the tests can tell you. If you err, it's better to select too soft rather than too stiff. Excess stiffness can tire you rapidly as you ski.

BOOTS AND BINDINGS: TOGETHERNESS

In purchase or use, you should consider boots and bindings together, both because they are the only items of ski gear that must mate and work together, like a hinge between your foot and your ski, and because they are made according to different, incompatible systems. Some of the systems are industry standards—that is, they are not patented and therefore boots and bindings made by different makers interchange. Some of the systems are patented exclusives, with manufacturers and a few licensees offering boots that fit only the bindings that they make and vice versa.

The basic principle of all boot-binding systems is that the boot toe attaches to the binding, which is mounted on the ski at a point for correct boot location on the ski. The systems differ chiefly in the manner of attachment of the boot to the binding.

In the order of their appearance on the market, the systems are the Nordic Norm, Norm 38, Racing Norm and Touring Norm, System LIN, and Salomon. Their major features are compared in the table.

The NORDIC NORM descends from the basic pin binding that has been around since it was first invented in 1928. In pin bindings the boot toe is held by an overlapping bail that presses the sole down onto protruding pins that lock into sole recess-

Good cross-country boots in bindings are as flexible as running shoes. *Frits Solvang*

Five boot-binding systems, left to right: Nordic Norm, Norm 38, Racing Norm, LIN, and Salomon. *Fletcher Manley*

es. Nordic Norm pin bindings are available in a wide range of designs, in both metal and plastic, some light enough for racing, others sturdy enough for major ski expeditions or Nordic downhill skiing. Despite the multitude of available boots and bindings, all bindings fit all boots, which is the point of the Nordic Norm standard. There are three standard widths as measured at the pins of the binding or pin recesses of the boot, 71, 75, and 79 mm, with 75 mm being by far the most common.

The NORM 38 and RACING NORM systems were first developed for racing in 1975–

76, and have subsequently been made available in a variety of models of boots and bindings intended for recreational skiing. Both systems attach boots to bindings by a "snout" extension on the forward edge of the boot sole, and both have thinner, stiff plastic soles, 7 mm (about ¼ inch) thick, for lateral boot stability. The two systems differ basically in the shape of the snout and the binding, and in the method of attachment of snout to binding. The Norm 38 system is an Adidas exclusive, with a few models of boots and bindings being made under license by other makers. The Racing Norm system is not patented, so Racing Norm boots and bindings are available from several makers. The width of the Racing Norm system at the point of attachment is 50 mm and the thickness of the boot soles is 7 mm, so the system is sometimes called "50/7."

The TOURING NORM system is identical to the Racing Norm system, except that the boot sole thickness is 12 mm (about ½ inch), and the bindings are arranged accordingly. The greater sole thickness is intended to insulate better, an important feature for recreational skiers. The system is sometimes called "50/12."

The SYSTEM LIN works on the same general principle as the Norm 38 and Racing Norm systems, but relies on the snap fit of a rounded boot-sole toe-snout into the binding case. The system is patented and produced exclusively by Dynafit, a major Austrian producer of Alpine ski boots.

The SALOMON system differs from the other systems in that the boot toe is fitted with a rectangular metal clevis, which mates a metal tongue on the binding and is held in place by a plastic lever. The

Traditional Nordic Norm (left) is unsymmetrical, has a left and a right binding, while its offspring, the Touring Norm, like the other newer systems, is symmetrical and has no left or right. *Frits Solvang*

flex action is not in the boot sole as in the other systems, but in a flexible binding insert, which is offered in three stiffnesses to suit varying skiing proficiencies. The system is patented and produced by Salomon, a major French producer of Alpine ski bindings with a few models of boots being made under license by other makers.

If you are a newcomer to cross-country skiing, consider the Nordic Norm first. The system is proven, having evolved from boot and binding designs that have been around for generations. Also, you'll have a greater selection of models to choose among than in the other, newer systems, and probably will have a better chance of finding a good fit at a reasonable price. But as you gain skiing skill, or if you want in-track performance from the start, look into the other systems. They allow greater foot extension without lifting your ski off the snow, an advantage in uneven or shallow tracks. Also, they are lighter, always a factor to consider in a sport where you provide your own motive power.

BOOTS

If you are a skier or otherwise have walked around in snow for a while, you know that foot comfort and warmth are vital. Few things can mar your enjoyment of skiing more than sore, wet, cold feet. So if your budget is cramped, don't let it cramp your feet: splurge on good boots, and scrimp on your other gear purchases.

Boots should fit like good street or hiking shoes: snug at the heel and across the instep, with room at the toes for foot movement. For most skiers, this means that when wearing socks, toes should have about ⅜-inch clearance to the inner edge of the uppers. A good trick to check fit is to slip your foot into an unlaced boot, and push forward until your toes touch the front of the boot upper. You should then have enough room behind the heel for the first two fingers of your hand. Stand in the boot and flex forward, as if striding on skis. The toe of the upper should fold in several pleats, comfortably over your toes. A single large crease may skin your toes or blue your nails in skiing.

If the joints of your toes hurt when you ski, your boots probably are a bit too short and/or fitted too tightly into your bindings, so that the binding clamp mechanism impairs boot movement. Recheck your selection of boot length: you should have some space in front of the toes even when your foot is flexed, with weight on the ball. Binding clamp mechanisms, such as bails on Nordic Norm pin bindings, should fit boot sole welts no closer than about 1/16 inch from the boot upper.

Many boots are available in both unlined and fleece-lined models. The fleece is supposed to keep your foot warm, but as it cannot be removed, it lengthens the time wet boots need to dry. An extra pair of socks in slightly larger boots will insulate just as well, and can be changed when they are damp.

Leather is still one of the better all-around materials for boot uppers, as it is for the uppers of shoes and hiking boots, because it "breathes" to allow foot moisture to escape, yet is fairly water repellent. Textile uppers are lighter than leather, but usually less waterproof. On the other hand, they dry more rapidly. Some boot uppers are made of sandwiches of synthetic materials that contain a microporous laminate, such as GoreTex®, which will breathe yet hold moisture out.

Soles should flex longitudinally, the way your feet flex when you walk, yet resist sideways twist, to keep your heel lined up and bring it down on the ski as you stride. Bootmakers build these characteristics into quality boots in two ways. Shanks are used to reinforce thicker, softer soles. Thinner soles are made of materials stiff enough to resist twist, yet thin enough to permit the desired forward flex. You can roughly check boots by twisting them in your hands, but the real test is in how they behave when fixed into bindings on skis.

You can put a lot of torque on your feet in turning a pair of skis, so the heels of even the best boots can twist sideways off the ski as you turn, which, to say the least, often can ruin your turn. To cure the problem, boot and binding makers offer a variety of heel plates, which attach to the skis under the heel and have surfaces or protrusions that mate with the heel to hold it firmly in place when it is weighted and on the ski. The most common devices are serrated surfaces or pins that dig into the softer surface of the boot heel, wedges which mate into V-grooves in the boot heel, and a variety of restraint

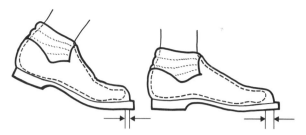

Toes need clearance as boot flexes in stride.

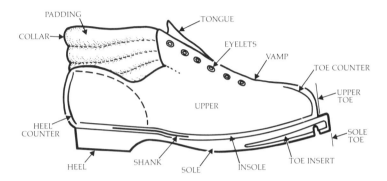

Anatomy of a boot.

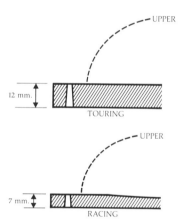

Two common, standard boot-sole thicknesses.

devices which mate to special extensions fastened to the rear of the heel. The more firmly the heel is held in place, the more control you have over your skis in downhill turns, which may sound like an argument for the most secure of the restraint devices. It isn't. Because, as almost all cross-country ski accident surveys conducted to date conclude, heel restraint devices are responsible for increasing the severity of twisting leg injuries sustained by skiers injured in falls when skiing downhill. So if you are a beginner or otherwise fear you may frequently fall on downhills, leave any use of heel restraint accessories until later. Stick with the devices routinely supplied by boot and binding makers with their wares, as most will free your heel when it's a quarter to three-eighths of an inch off the ski.

If you walk very much in your ski boots, you should consider their soles in view of this off-ski use. If you are purely a pleasure skier who puts on boots in the morning, walks or drives to skiing, skis all day with a few breaks, and then returns home, the thicker, softer rubber or foam plastic soles are for you. They grip well on hard surfaces, including the gas, brake, and clutch pedals of a car. They usually flex comfortably underfoot as you walk. Just as track spikes are made for running on tracks, the newer, thinner, hard plastic soles are made for a single purpose: skiing. Walking in them can be uncomfortable and, in some cases, dangerous. The hard plastics of which they are made are perilously slippery underfoot, and wearing them while walking up or down stairs or driving a car can provide excitement you hadn't counted on. Some bootmakers have remedied the problem by adding rubber inserts under the ball of the foot and under the heel.

BINDINGS

Just before the oldest of the newer boot-binding systems, the Norm 38 and the Racing Norm, hit the market in the mid 1970s, close to 40 Nordic Norm 75-mm bindings were on the market, most marketed with claims of exclusive, superior features. That's a lot of ways to press down the welt of a boot sole at the toe and hold it firmly in a holder 75 mm wide. Fortunately for the purchaser of Nordic Norm 75-mm boots and bindings, that situation has now eased somewhat, as designers have focused their attentions on new approaches to boot-binding design, not just on altering existing designs.

Once you have chosen a particular boot-binding system, you may or may not have a choice of bindings, as shown in the table. If you do have a choice, such as with the Nordic Norm, Touring and Racing Norms, and some Norm 38 models, check the action of the binding and its fit to your boots. You should find the binding easy to operate, and it should fit your boot snugly, allowing no sideplay. Sometimes boot soles or sole snouts are either a bit too small ("under tolerance") or worn, which leaves a gap between the sole edge and the binding. A gap means free play, and free play means a wobbly boot in the binding. If this is the case for your boots in bindings, check other models of bindings: some are adjustable, and can easily be snugged up to compensate for slightly smaller or worn boot soles.

Bindings must be mounted on skis.

This is a job that's best left for experienced workmen. But if you want to try it yourself, simply follow the directions packed with each pair of bindings. One word of caution: there's little agreement in the ski industry, and less among skiers, as to "binding location." "Where do you mount bindings?" is a question that always pops up at demonstrations and workshops. The question can be answered easily if you first think of the result of any binding mounting job: boot location. *Bindings should be mounted so the front edge of the boot upper locates just over the ski balance point.*

POLES

Poles seem relegated to the limbo of the ski equipment picture, for they are often overlooked, seldom discussed, and are almost never the subject of articles in ski magazines. The anonymity is unjust, as advances in poles have contributed to ski technique just as have advances in skis, boots, and bindings. A century ago skiers switched from one pole to two, which made the first true diagonal stride and double poling possible. More recently, lighter, stiffer, and stronger poles contributed to the precise poling that ups racing speed and cuts recreational skier effort. If you ever doubt how much a good pole can aid your skiing, try skiing with poorer poles that don't fit. Your tired arms will quickly get the message across.

In selecting poles, begin with the baskets, the disks that keep the poles from sinking into the snow when they are planted. Small, angled asymmetrical baskets are superb for well-prepared, packed tracks, as they ease pole plant and withdrawal in speedy skiing. But smaller baskets sink easily into soft, untracked snow. Here larger baskets are better. As a general

Boot-Binding Systems

SYSTEM	FEATURES	WIDTH OF SOLE AND BINDING AT ATTACHMENT POINT	BOOT SOLE THICKNESS, MATERIAL	INTENDED USE	COMMENTS
Nordic Norm	Binding clamps welt ahead of boot upper. Asymmetrical; has right and left.	71, 75, 79 mm depending on boot size, type, 75 mm by far most common	12 mm, rubber, softer plastic	light touring, touring, Nordic downhill	Widespread, older standard, products from many makers
Norm 38	Binding holds "snout" extension of boot sole. Symmetrical, no right or left.	38 mm	7 mm, hard plastic	racing, light touring	Adidas exclusive, some licensees also producing
Racing Norm	Binding holds tapered "snout" extension of boot sole. Symmetrical.	50 mm	7 mm, hard plastic	racing, light touring, touring	Widespread standard, products from many makers
Touring Norm	As for Racing Norm; has same profile, differs only in thicker boot sole. Symmetrical.	50 mm	12 mm, rubber, softer plastic	light touring, touring	Standard, products from several makers
System LIN	Springlike catch on rounded sole extension locks into mating binding. Symmetrical.	55 mm	7 mm, hard plastic	racing, light touring	Dynafit exclusive, no other makers
Salomon	Rectangular metal eye on sole toe mates tongue latch on binding. Symmetrical.	30 mm	7 mm, hard plastic	racing, light touring	Salomon exclusive, some boot licensees

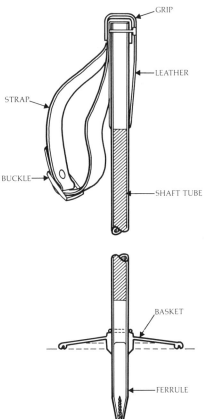

GRIP

LEATHER

STRAP

BUCKLE

SHAFT TUBE

BASKET

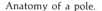

FERRULE

TIP

Anatomy of a pole.

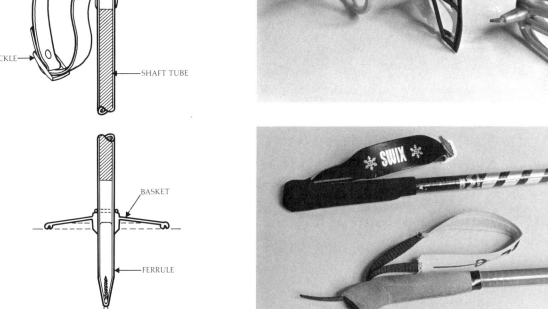

Typical pole types, left to right: conventional touring pole with round basket, and two types of racing pole with asymmetrical half-baskets (A), and two typical grips, angled Finnish type with nylon strap and straight Norwegian type with leather strap (B). *Fletcher Manley*

rule, select baskets 4 inches or less in maximum dimension for in-track skiing, and baskets 4½ to 5 inches or more in diameter for out-of-track skiing. Some pole makers offer "snowshoe baskets," six inches or more in diameter, which either fit poles directly, or clip on as accessories over smaller baskets. So if you ski both in tracks and in deep snow with the same pair of poles, pick a pair with smaller baskets and carry accessory snowshoe baskets for deep snow skiing.

Select poles with straps that fit comfortable, not only with your bare hands in the shop, but with your hands in all the combinations of gloves or mittens that

you intend to wear. Most quality pole straps are adjustable, so you may alter their loop lengths to fit your hands and what you have on them.

Pole shafts are made of tonkin cane, fiberglass, aluminum alloy tubing, steel tubing, or carbon fiber. Tonkin cane, the traditional pole shaft material, is now on the wane, like the wood ski, a disappearing breed. The synthetics are taking over, as they are in skis. Fiberglass shafts and metal alloy shafts are available in a wide range of strengths and qualities, ranging from poorer than the traditional tonkin cane, to stronger and more durable. Carbon fiber shafts are lighter than shafts of any other material. They are also stiffer, which aids precise poling. These features are why carbon fiber poles are most used in racing. However, they are also more expensive than other poles, sometimes as much as five to ten times as costly as poles with shafts of other materials. For most recreational skiing, fiberglass or metal tubing shafts are fine. Here, quality and shaft strength usually follow price.

Select proper pole length using the same sort of test as used for selecting ski length. Stand on a flat floor, with an arm outstretched horizontally from your shoulder. With the pole point, or *tip,* resting on the floor, the proper pole length is with the top of the grip just under your arm, or fitting snugly under your armpit. For most adults this works out to pole lengths 35 cm (about 14 inches) less than your height. For instance, a 5'11" (180 cm) tall adult will use 145 cm-long poles.

PACKS AND PULKS

Except for racers racing, few skiers travel without some baggage. *Packs* are handy for loads that exceed the capacity of pockets. *Pulks,* skier-drawn sleds, are used for loads too cumbersome or too heavy for packs.

If you've skied both with and without packs, you know that it's easier to ski without a pack, any pack. But if you've ever tried to stuff too many items into parka pockets, and then take off the parka and tie it around your waist when you get warm skiing, you know that skiing with a pack is far more comfortable than skiing with a jumbled parka twisted around your waist, its overfull pockets banging against your rump as you stride along.

Fanny packs, day packs, and tour packs are all suited for skiing. *Fletcher Manley*

The golden rule for pack selection is to pick one that suits you and the load you carry, and don't overload it. It's always more comfortable to ski with a lightly loaded, larger pack than it is with an overstuffed, smaller pack, balled up like a monkey on your back.

For shorter trips when you want to carry wax, a lunch, a camera, and other small odds and ends, choose either a small, frameless backpack or a fanny pack that attaches around the waist with a belt. The choice between the two types is mainly a matter of preference. The smaller backpacks, such as climbing rucksacks available from outdoor and mountain supply houses, carry well and leave your arms and body free. Fanny packs provide ready access, as you can swivel them around in front to delve into their innards and find what you want quickly. But when improperly adjusted or slightly overloaded, they can be uncomfortable.

For tours of a day or more, you'll need a larger pack. Here the selection is seemingly limitless and the varieties endless. So you may have a chore ahead of you in selecting a good skiing pack.

First, keep skiing in mind. Packs excellent for summertime backpacking on trails sometimes are uncomfortable and even dangerous in skiing. For instance, high pack frames carry loads far up, which is good for on-foot backpacking, but upsetting to a skier. In a fall, high frames can scoot forward, causing neck or head injury.

Kiddie pulks are over-snow baby carriages.
Michael Brady

A good skiing pack should fit the body well and not bounce or shift. A shifting pack will amplify any skiing error you make, and can fling you off balance in downhill turns. The pack should carry its load close into your body, and be narrow enough to allow full, free arm movement past the body in the cross-country poling maneuvers. Soft packs and interior-frame packs are best in this respect. The pack bag should be fitted with internal pockets, or dividers, so packed items stay in place and can be quickly located. The straps should include a waist and/or chest strap, so the pack will stay in place and not sway with body movement or ride up onto the neck in a fall. The pack straps, buckles, and closures should be simple, and easily operated with gloved hands. Here is where many pack designs fail: those clever mechanisms that work so wonderfully in the shop can sometimes be a horror when you try to manipulate them with cold hands or hands in gloves. Finally, good packs should be waterproof, to protect their contents, and light, to save you work.

When you pack a skiing pack, load the

Some pulks are large enough to carry provisions for extended expedition skiing, as is this one, loaded with close to 240 pounds, being drawn by Doug Wiens through the sea pack ice of the Robson Channel on the Ellesmere High Arctic Expedition. *Ned Gillette*

heavy items close in to the back. If any of them are sharp or hard, pad the back first with a sweater or towel. Place frequently used items, such as ski wax, sunglasses, suntan lotion, cameras, and so on, in outside pockets or on top for ready access.

Ski conservatively with a pack, any pack you carry. Remember, its weight adds to your weight, and therefore it can increase the severity of any fall.

You may find a *pulk,* the runnerless sled developed by the Lapps, handy if you want to transport heavy or bulky loads, or things you would rather not risk carry-

ing on your back, such as a small child. In Scandinavia pulks are used as over-snow baby carriages. Multi-small-child skiing families are also multipulk families, as nobody gets left behind on a true crosscountry ski outing.

Pulks range in size from kiddie pulks up to larger transport pulks, such as those used by expedition skiers. Still larger pulks, capable of carrying several hundred pounds, are used for rescue work and in transporting supplies. Drawn by dog teams, these giants of the pulk family are the Scandinavian equivalent of the Yukon dog sleds.

Even a century ago, clothing for cross-country was
varied and individual—reenactment of skiing of
1870s; skiers wearing styles of that period. *Jan Greve*

12

CLOTHING
Your Style,
Your Defense

Cross-country skiing can be and often is done in almost any clothing. The U.S. and Canada must be the world's leaders in the range of colors and garments worn at cross-country ski centers, spanning the outdoor clothing spectrum from the purely functional to the wildly bizarre. So, as with cross-country ski equipment, you'll probably easily find something that suits your skiing needs, taste, and pocketbook.

As is the case for many sports, from tennis to baseball, cross-country skiing is most functionally and comfortably done when you wear clothing specifically designed for the purpose. Many cross-country skiers, for example, ski in jeans, the great all-around leg covering. But jeans do have drawbacks for cross-country skiing. They are tight and constrain your leg movements, especially when wet. The cotton fabric of which they are made absorbs moisture easily, and wicks it up the leg, which makes them cold and clammy. Knickers, even in-expensive ones, are better. Knickers allow full freedom of movement in the cross-country strides, and most quality skiing knickers are made of fabrics that shed water and absorb little moisture. You'll be a lot more comfortable in knickers and knee socks than in jeans. And at the current prices for some designer jeans that one sees on ski trails, knickers are by far the less expensive alternative.

The main mission of cross-country ski clothing is to keep you warm while allowing you full freedom of body movement. There is no one ideal apparel: as with equipment, the best clothing is that which suits your personal skiing needs.

YOU AGAINST COLD

Stop sometime when you're skiing in cold weather, and gaze out over the snow-covered landscape. There you stand, probably comfortable and warm. But the only thing maintaining that warmth is your

WATCH THAT JOULE!

As more and more things, from weather forecasts to soft-drink bottles, switch to the metric system, the Calorie may soon be obsolete. The metric unit of energy is the *joule;* dietitians now speak in terms of *kilojoules,* and some food products in international commerce are now labeled using the unit.

There are 4.18 joules in a Calorie, or 4.18 kilojoules in a kilocalorie, the dietary unit, abbreviated to Calorie, with a capital C. The joule is particularly handy, as it can be easily related to other common units of energy in everyday use. One joule is equal to a power of one watt for a duration of one second. So a kilowatt-hour, what you buy when you pay your household electric bill, is 3,600 kilojoules.

A cross-country skier burning 540 Calories per hour has an energy consumption of 540 × 4.18 = 2,257 kilojoules, which is equal to 2,257 kilowatt-seconds. There are 3,600 seconds in an hour, so this energy corresponds to a power consumption of 625 watts continuously for the hour. One horsepower is equal to 746 watts, so the skier expends 0.84 horsepower, mostly as heat. That's one reason why cross-country skiers can stay toasty warm in cold weather. . . .

Skiers are warmer. *Bob Bugg*

own body, as all around you it's cold. Maybe a chilling thought, but it gives you an idea of what's involved in keeping warm in cold weather.

When you think of a warm garment, you think of how it feels when you wear it outside, on its effect in keeping you warm. Your body metabolism is your only stored energy, your only source of warmth, so "warm" clothing actually is a misnomer: clothing cannot warm you. It can only insulate, or conserve the heat your body produces. So, strictly speaking, there is no such thing as a warm garment, unless you mean one that you've just taken off an indoor radiator or out of a hot-air dryer. *Insulate* is the major thing clothing does for you.

The more you move, the more heat your body produces and the less clothing insulation you need to stay warm at a given outdoor temperature. An inactive adult burns an average of 65 to 83 Calories per hour (see box, p. 189). Average adult minimum daily requirements vary with weight, age, and sex, but are seldom more than 3,350 Calories, corresponding to 140 Calories per hour. Even moderate activity increases energy consumption considerably. For instance, a fast walk requires 315 to 430 Calories per hour, while a moderately active cross-country skier burns almost twice as much, 580 to 625 Calories per hour.

Only one quarter or less of the Calories you burn produce motion, while the rest are given off as pure heat. This means that moderately active cross-country skiers produce 425 to 510 Calories per hour of heat, equivalent to 500 to 600 watts. Think of this when you select clothing for cross-country skiing: *you're carrying a half-kilowatt electric heater along when you ski.*

This is why winter clothing suitable for

75% HEAT

0–25% MOTION

Only a quarter of the energy you use can go to motion; the rest is given off as heat. *Bob Bugg*

less active pursuits, such as walking, watching an outdoor game, or average Alpine downhill skiing, where you often stand in lift lines or sit or stand still on lifts, insulates too well for cross-country skiing. Even on a modest ski tour, you will probably find that you quickly overheat if you wear a down ski parka. Likewise, should you go for a leisurely ski tour in the same clothes that a racer would wear in a race in the same weather conditions, you'll be rapidly chilled, simply because you're not insulated well enough.

Clothing insulates because it traps still air in yarns, weaves, and between clothing layers. The more still air trapped, the better the insulation, and the more body heat is conserved. Clothing fibers themselves, without their trapped still air, are poor insulators. This is why garments where relatively few fibers trap relatively larger amounts of still air insulate best,

and because air is light, lighter garments are often the better insulators.

Removing the trapped, still air in a garment or around the body destroys insulation, and can accelerate body cooling. This is why you feel colder facing a wind, or skiing downhill at some speed: passing air removes the still, warmed insulating air around your body. This cooling effect is expressed in terms of *wind chill* (see box, p.194): for every combination of temperature and wind, there is an equivalent lower still-air temperature that produces the same body heat loss. For instance, a skier on a downhill moving at a brisk 25 mph at −7°C. (20°F.), a comfortable skiing temperature, suffers a cooling equivalent to standing still at −26°C. (−15°F.).

Also, wet clothing is a poor insulator, because water rapidly conducts heat away from the body, defeating the effect of clothing insulation. Therefore, clothing must be both dry and shielded from wind

WATTS IN CROSS-COUNTRY

The human body consumes more energy when exercising than when at rest. How much more depends on the activity, on how many muscles in the body are involved and how strenuously the activity is performed. Below are some numbers for various activities, as published by Health and Welfare Canada.

In comparison, the typical female of the table below consumes 65 Calories per hour (75 watts) at rest, and the typical male 83 Calories per hour (96 watts). So when you cross-country ski, you "burn" 7.5 to 9 times as much energy as when you stand still. This is why you should dress more lightly for cross-country skiing than you would for a sedentary activity at the same temperature.

Skiing faster takes more energy and ups energy consumption further. Racers can consume Calories at an enormous rate; typical are 1,200 Calories per hour (1,400 watts) racing averages, and up to 2,100 Calories per hour (2,500 watts) in sprints.

ACTIVITY	TYPICAL CONSUMPTION, 125 POUND FEMALE CALORIES/HOUR	WATTS	TYPICAL CONSUMPTION, 160 POUND MALE CALORIES/HOUR	WATTS
Fast walk	315	365	430	500
Run, 9 mph	670	780	1000	1160
Bicycle, 13 mph	460	535	670	780
Moderate tennis	375	435	460	535
Moderate cross-country skiing	580	675	625	725

Where the figures for Calories per hour have been converted to watts (1 Calorie per hour equals 1.16 watts).

to keep you warm. If you ski in wet, windy conditions, you need windproof and water-repellent outer garments.

Your own motion is your cold-weather friend, as it warms you. But it also can defeat this friendly service, as all activity will cause you to sweat. Sweat-wet clothing acts just as if it were wet from the outside: it conducts heat away from your body. You may not mind or be chilled by slightly sweat-wet clothes as you ski, but when you stop, the moisture may cool you uncomfortably fast.

In addition to your own activity, which determines how much heat your body produces and how much you perspire, weather conditions can change during a day of skiing. Temperatures rise and fall; wind force and direction change; sunshine varies in strength and direction. So on an average ski tour, you don't have one need for insulation, you have several. This is why the best attire for your varying insulation needs consists of many thin garment layers. Multiple layers insulate better than fewer, thicker layers, and allow greater clothing flexibility.

Another method of regulating insulation is to regulate ventilation by zipping or unzipping, buttoning or unbuttoning parkas, blouses, or shirts. Inadvertent ventilation, such as through gaps between garments, should be avoided, as it robs you of insulating air. Adjoining garments should overlap.

Clothe yourself in three layers. *Bob Bugg*

THE BASICS

There are no exact rules for what you should wear when you cross-country ski. But there are a few basic guidelines:

1. DON'T OVERDRESS

Match your apparel to your activity. Forget down or quilted parkas, heavy sweaters, or mackinaws. They're great to wear on your way to skiing and to put on afterward, but if they keep you warm when you're standing still, they'll burn you up when you ski.

2. SUIT THE WEATHER

Select clothing first for function, then style. What looks great on a shop rack may not be so great when you face a wind outside. Take the prevailing conditions where you ski into account. If it's windy, go windproof. If it's wet, look for water-repellent outer garments. If conditions change rapidly, take along suitable extra garments in a small pack. Always be prepared for the weather, not surprised by it.

3. MANY LIGHT, OVERLAPPING LAYERS ARE BEST

Multiple, light layers insulate better because they trap more air. Overlap them to prevent loss of insulation. Vary them to suit your activity, adjusting at the first sign of chill or excess sweating. This is the old eskimo trick: regulate continuously for comfort.

FROM THE SKIN OUT

With the three basic guidelines in mind, select cross-country ski clothing to suit your needs. Think of clothing yourself in three layers: inner, middle, and outer.

The INNER LAYERS next to your skin insulate and keep your skin dry. They may do this either by being permeable to moisture, transporting it outward, or by absorbing the moisture. Most active cross-country skiers prefer the transport-type garments, such as those trade-named Super-Underwear, Thermic, or PolySport, made of polypropylene tricot, a fabric which itself does not absorb moisture. However, many skiers prefer the feeling and extra insulating value of wool. Wool garments wick moisture away from your skin by absorbing it; a quality wool will absorb up to a third of its weight in moisture.

The choice between the two, *transportation* or *absorption,* is governed by how much you ski and by your own preference. If you ski fast and far and perspire heavily, select transport underwear, as the amount of moisture wool underwear could absorb under the same conditions may be inadequate. But if you are a recreational skier who seldom skis fast, wool is a good bet, as it retains some insulation value even when wet.

Avoid cotton next to the skin in winter, as cotton wets easily and when wet, insulates poorly.

The MIDDLE LAYERS provide most of your insulation and allow you great flexibility in suiting clothing to activity and weather. Middle- and inner-layer garments or middle- and outer-layer garments may sometimes be combined into single garments serving two functions. Typical middle-layer garments, which may also be the outer layer, are shirts and sweaters, knee socks, and knickers. All inner and middle layer garments should fit the body well, without binding or restricting.

The OUTER LAYERS protect you against weather and are the visible part of your attire, setting your style for the action of skiing. Outer action garments are made both of knitted and woven fabrics. The knits, now mostly of nylon or nylon blended with other fibers, are the more elastic and resilient, and therefore are preferred by faster skiers. However, the weaves, such as poplin, are more wind resistant, and hence the wiser choice for recreational skiers or wilderness skiers who may face severe weather.

IMPORTANT SPECIALS: Most women find a comfortable sports bra, of the type suited for jogging or active sports, ideal for cross-country skiing, although some favor the stretch-tube type. Men who prefer to wear an athletic supporter when skiing should shy away from the ordinary cotton variety, as perspiration wets cotton quickly, which can be a chilling experience just where you don't want it. Better to wear a pair of close-fitting, transport-type briefs for support. Most such briefs also have a windproof nylon front, a good extra protection, for both men and women, against wind-chill discomfort or frost damage of the groin, especially when this sensitive area is otherwise covered only with underwear and a thin stretch ski suit.

CLO GLOW

The insulation provided by body tissues and clothing is measured in *clo,* a unit in which one clo is the insulation provided by typical office clothing that keeps a sedentary person comfortable in an indoor environment of 21°C. (70°F.) at a relative humidity of under 50 percent with only slight air movement.

Furry animals are, as might be expected, the insulation champs. The weasel's fur provides 2 clo of insulation, while the caribou and grizzly bear get 7 clo of insulation from their pelts. But still better insulated are the wolf, with 7.5 clo, and the Dall sheep, with 9 clo of insulation in its fleece. Humans are poor by comparison: body tissues provide only 0.5 to 0.8 clo of insulation. No wonder, then, that humans have traditionally used animal fur to keep warm in cold environments.

Eskimos have long known how to do this well. The traditional double-layer, caribou-fur Eskimo garment is about three inches thick, and provides a total insulation of 12 clo. This is the secret to the Eskimo's ability to survive: 12 clo of insulation are adequate for sleeping outdoors at −40°C. (−40°F.).

At that same low temperature, even moderate activity reduces insulation needs. At forty below an average adult needs only 4 clo of insulation to stay warm while walking or moving around, as body-heat production is about three times that when sleeping. This is why the more standard of arctic dress, such as air force and army arctic uniforms, provide about 4 clo of insulation.

SELECTING

Of the virtually limitless selection of outer-layer garments, two main types are now dominant on the cross-country skiing scene: two-piece and one-piece suits.

For most recreational skiing, two-piece suits are preferable, as they allow the greatest flexibility in altering ventilation or changing clothing to suit activity and weather conditions. Also, if you're going to be in your ski suit all day long, sooner or later you will discover yet another advantage to this more conventional approach to your skiing attire: it makes answering calls of nature routine inside and only slightly uncomfortable outside.

A wide range of two-piece suits are now available in nylon knits, poplin weaves, and combinations of fabrics. Suits are available both with knickers that go to the waist and with higher bib knickers. Bib knickers are the best for all-around cross-country skiing in varying weather conditions, as they leave no gap when you bend over, and have no belt or elastic at the waist to constrain as you ski.

Expert skiers and racers favor one-piece suits for their minimum weight and maximum freedom of skiing movement. These suits are a far cry from paratroopers' jumpsuits or the women's wear fashioned after them: they are made of two-way stretch nylon tricot, and fit close, some like a second skin. Two types are now in use: knee-length knicker suits, worn by speedy recreational skiers and some racers, and ankle-length suits, now the standard of racing. The full-length suits offer the racer slightly more knee freedom and are slightly more comfortable on the leg, as they apply no pressure to hold knickers down or socks up at the knee. In cross-country skiing as in other sports, there's a steady trend of equipment and clothing first developed and tested in racing, showing up in the more recreational versions of the sport within a season or two. In a few years full-length suits may be the norm seen in cross-country centers.

If needed, you can add protective garments over your cross-country ski suit. Indeed, one more common combination used by cross-country ski instructors is a one-piece suit topped with a double-layer shell parka. They wear the parka when instructing, and peel it off when they want to do a bit of fast skiing on their own. Select parkas to fit well, but allow freedom of arm movement. A hood is essential if you plan on skiing more than a mile away from your car. Check all parka zippers and closures to be sure you can manage them with gloves on. What seems to work fine in the shop, when your fingers are nimble and warm, can be frustratingly difficult when you try to operate it out on the trail with colder, gloved hands. Select parka materials to suit weather, wind- and/or waterproof as needed. Many touring skiers always carry two-piece windsuits along on all tours. These utilitarian garments are usually lightweight, but can be surprisingly warm when worn over a cross-country tricot suit.

Racers and many recreational skiers find warm-up suits one of the most convenient items of outer cross-country ski apparel. A warm-up suit resembles a bulky two-piece jogging suit, and goes on over other clothing. Featuring full-length leg zippers, the pants can be put on or taken off without taking off your skis.

HEAD

The multilayer principle also applies to the head and the extremities: hands, fingers, feet, and toes.

Your headgear is vital in keeping you warm, because one fifth of the body's heat loss is through the scalp. "If your feet are cold, wear a cap," so the old saying goes. Knit wool caps are adequate for most skiing, but need to be covered by a parka hood if you ski in windy conditions. Don't fear overdressing your head; you can always peel off the extra layers and stick them in your pocket. One easy double-layer combination is a knit headband around the ears, topped by a knit cap. If you are literary, or even if you're not, you may appreciate one of the outcomes of the Crimean War battle celebrated in Tennyson's "Charge of the Light Brigade." The headgear worn by the Tartars there, at Balaklava, became the British balaclava helmet, essentially a knit cap that stretches down to the neck, with an opening for the eyes and nose. The balaclava is great for extreme cold: they're worn by expedition skiers and racers alike. During the supercold pre-Olympics in Lake Placid in 1979, balaclavas were so to speak the hottest thing going for cold racing heads.

HANDS

An average adult's hands comprise only about 5% of the total body area, yet in an otherwise clothed individual, they account for 20% of the total heat loss. This is why keeping your hands warm is important not only for hand comfort, but also for overall body warmth.

Gloves are handy for skiing, but mittens are warmer, as they keep fingers together, cutting heat loss. A good combination is a pair of wool mittens that fit into windproof poplin mitten shells. The best mittens and mitten shells for cross-country skiing have leather or extra-heavy poplin reinforcement between the thumb and forefinger to withstand the abrasion of ski-pole wrist-straps. Racers usually use special gloves that resemble bicycle or car-racing gloves with fingers.

The palms of these gloves are of leather to withstand pole-strap abrasion, and the backs are of fishnet mesh, or are perforated for ventilation.

Some skiers complain of uncomfortable hand perspiration when they ski, but fear skiing barehanded. You may ski barehanded at temperatures above freezing if it feels comfortable and your hands are tough enough to stand the abrasion from the pole straps. But thin gloves will save your hands. Some cross-country ski racers, notably Canadians from the far north, and Russians, grow up and are accustomed to cold to the extent that they often train and race gloveless at temperatures down to −15°C. (5°F.) or below. This practice is not recommended for persons who have not grown up in the Arctic.

LEGS AND FEET

Knee socks are available in wool, synthetics, and blends. Wool socks insulate well but tend to collect snow more easily than synthetic socks. Some socks have acrylic legs for water repellency and wool-synthetic stretch feet for warmth and fit. Select knee socks to come up above the bottom of your knickers so that they don't leave a gap at your knee. If you buy stretch-weave knee socks, always roll, never pull them on. This is because pulling stretches the sock too thin over the foot and heel, which decreases insulation and accelerates wear. A pair of socks, thin or thick depending on how much room you have, under your knee socks will add insulation for your feet. For added insulation put on overboots outside your ski boots. Several models are available: some of rubber for waterproofing; some of nylon knit; some of lined poplin; and

WIND CHILLS

When you feel cooled by the blast of an electric fan in the summer or chilled when riding a bicycle against the wind, you are experiencing *wind chill*, the cooling effect of passing air removing the still, insulating air around your body. Wind chill may be pleasant in warm weather, but at winter temperatures it can be uncomfortable or even dangerous.

For example, at −15°C. (5°F.), a fairly common midwinter skiing temperature, the effect of even a gentle breeze, a 10 mph wind, is equivalent to lowering the still-air temperature to −26°C. (−15°F.). Even if there is no wind, a skier whizzing downhill at 20 mph when the temperature is −15°C. (5°F.), is momentarily cooled at a rate corresponding to −36°C. (−33°F.) outdoor temperature. This is why lightly clad, speedy skiers sometimes suffer frost injury while others go unaffected at the same temperature.

In skiing, remember that wind is your enemy. . . .

Wind Chill Table

WIND				TEMPERATURE (°C)										
BEAUFORT SCALE		SPEED												
FORCE NUMBER	STATE OF AIR	METERS PER SECOND	KNOTS	ACTUAL AIR TEMPERATURE										
				0	−5	−10	−15	−20	−25	−30	−35	−40	−45	
2	Slight breeze	2	3.9	−2	−7	−12	−18	−23	−28	−33	−37	−44	−49	
3	Gentle breeze	4.5	8.7	−8	−14	−20	−26	−32	−38	−44	−51	−57	−59	
4	Moderate breeze	6.5	12.6	−11	−18	−25	−32	−38	−45	−52	−58	−65	−72	
5	Fresh breeze	9	17.5	−14	−21	−28	−36	−42	−49	−57	−64	−71	−78	Effective
6	Strong breeze	11	21.4	−16	−23	−31	−38	−46	−53	−61	−68	−76	−83	Temp-
7	Moderate gale	15.5	30.1	−18	−26	−34	−42	−49	−57	−65	−73	−81	−88	erature
8	Fresh gale	18	35	−19	−27	−35	−43	−51	−59	−66	−74	−82	−91	
9	Strong gale	22	42.8	−20	−28	−36	−44	−52	−60	−68	−76	−84	−92	

Winds above 43 knots have little additional effect

DANGER INVOLVED	Little danger	Increasing danger (flesh may freeze within one minute)	Great danger (flesh may freeze within thirty seconds)

some with down lining for use in extreme cold. Thrifty skiers sometimes fashion their own cold-weather overboots simply by pulling an oversize ankle-height sock over their boot, and cutting out the toe where the boot fits into the binding.

Wet feet are a common skier complaint. Even if outside snow and moisture keep their distance, your feet may sweat enough to get your socks uncomfortably wet on a tour. The best solution to feet wet from the inside is to carry a spare pair of dry socks, and change when you first feel your feet going clammy. If snow water works in, wetting your feet from the outside, you can retard its progress in several ways. First, try *gaiters,* snug coverings that fit around the ankle and down over the boot. They'll probably do the job well, as snow working down inside boots is one of the most common causes of wet feet. Second, keep your boots waterproof. If they're of leather, polish them often, or treat them regularly with waterproofing compounds. If they have textile uppers, spray them frequently with silicone spray.

PRACTICAL OUTFITS

Personal needs and preference, frequency of skiing, and pocketbook are all decisive in selecting clothing, so no one outfit can possibly meet all skier needs. Although no two skiers will dress exactly alike, there are typical combinations of garments which work well for most skiers. Here are two:

TYPICAL RECREATIONAL SKIER: an average adult on a day trip in typical winter conditions, freezing temperatures to a few degrees below, intermittent cloudy skies and sunshine, chance of wind and/or new snow during the day.

Inner layer: Full-length underwear, top and bottom, thin wool or transport-type synthetic knit. If you are sensitive to wool, select the transport-type synthetic and add wool on top if you need extra insulation. Thin, synthetic socks on the feet.

Middle, insulating layer: Turtleneck sweater or shirt, preferably light wool knit, close fitting. Knee socks, preferably a long-wearing, wool-synthetic blend, with wool feet for warmth.

Outer, visible layer: A two-piece knicker suit allows the greatest variation. Bib-type knickers are preferable, as they leave no gap between suit top and bottom as you ski. Poplin or poplin-knit combinations (poplin front, knit back) are best for windy conditions. Knits are fine as long as there's little or no wind where you ski. Wool mittens that fit well up over or under the cuffs of the jacket arms, an overlap that prevents gap. Spare mitten shells in a pocket or pack. Knit wool cap.

Outer and emergency layer: Always carry extra windproof, water-repellent garments and extra clothing in your pack. A two-piece, nylon-poplin waterproof suit, as used by runners, is lightweight and easily put on if you encounter bad weather. In purchasing such a suit, remember to try it on over the clothes you intend to wear skiing. Be sure that all zippers and closures can be worked with ease with gloved or mittened hands.

TYPICAL SPEEDY SKIER: a skilled skier or racer, out for a couple of hours to ski in tracks in a familiar area, at freezing temperatures to a few degrees below, little chance of the weather changing before return to base lodge.

Inner layer: Full-length underwear, top and bottom, of transport-type synthetic knit.

Middle, insulating layer: Short-sleeved, light wool or angora T-shirt over top, transport-type brief (men) or panty (women) with windproof nylon front for protection, worn under or over long underpants, thin, synthetic socks.

Outer layer: Ankle-length stretch nylon tricot one-piece suit, ankle-height wool socks, knit wool cap, perforated-back racing gloves.

Extra outer layer: Single-layer, poplin shell jacket, used when warming up, taken off and carried knotted around waist, to be put on for wind protection on long downhills.

13

WAXING AND CARE OF SKIS
It Can Be as Simple as You Wish

Even the Trolls of Nordic mythology wax their skis. *Sturla Kaasa*

WAXING THOUGHTS

Waxing is perhaps the most frequently misunderstood, yet most scientifically studied, aspect of cross-country skiing. Through the years many opinions have been voiced on the subject, especially after waxless skis became popular. Here are a few selected thoughts:

"The gliding of skis and sled runners on different snows is an extremely difficult subject."
> Fridtjof Nansen,
> Arctic explorer, 1930

"Waxing may be a little more complicated than making a peanut-butter-and-jelly sandwich, but the aim is to keep it simple."
> Ned Gillette, in *Cross-Country Skiing*, 1979.

"I thought cross-country skiing was a gas, until I found out you have to wax the skis every time you go out. Screw it."
> Young dropout from Yosemite School of Ski Touring, 1972, as quoted by author Hal Painter

"When everything else has failed, read the instructions. They are printed on the tin or tube in at least three languages."
> Erling Strom describing cross-country skiing in Canada in the 1930s, in *Pioneers on Skis*, 1977.

"Waxing is like foreplay: You can make do without, but it's so much better with."
> *Playboy* magazine article: "What's New in Cross-Country Skiing" January 1981

"The wax question is a deep secret into which it takes years to penetrate."
> In *Skiing*, in the Official Souvenir Book of the III Olympic Winter Games, Lake Placid, New York, February 4–13, 1932

"I feel that waxing is a part of the sport, that it adds to the challenges. Cross-country wouldn't be the same to me without it."
> John Caldwell, in *Cross-Country Skiing Today*, 1977.

Of all the skills required in cross-country skiing, waxing is the most overrated and most frequently misunderstood. Waxing can be as simple as you want to make it, and as straightforward as skiing itself. But just as enjoying good cross-country skiing requires learning some technique, achieving waxing ease calls for a few simple routines.

Correct waxing lets you stride easily on the flat, climb uphill without slipping backward, and ski downhill on easily sliding skis. The wax facilitates both grip, or traction, and glide, or slide under your skis. This is because wax, unlike oils and greases applied to metal parts of machines to aid sliding, is not a lubricant. Moisture under your skis, between your skis and the underlying snow, is the lubricant. Wax is what you apply to your ski bases to make that lubricating moisture behave the way you want it to, to give your skis good grip and glide.

To wax well, all you need to know is how wax works in general, what's available to put on your skis, how much of that you need for your skiing, and how to do it. No more. It's that easy.

THE WHY

Snow scientists have many theories to explain why skis glide on snow, and if you've been skiing for a while, you may have heard of some of them. Most are complex, and none are correct all of the time. The best explanation is still the simplest: when in motion, a properly waxed ski melts the underlying snow surface particles just enough to provide an ultrathin layer of moisture on which the ski glides.

When the same ski is motionless and weighted, as in the kick of the diagonal

WHAT GOES ON

Waxing involves everything you do to and put on the bases of your skis, save for repairing damage, which is a separate subject. Everything you intentionally apply is either wax, base preparation, base wax, or cleaner.

WAX: This is ski wax, the stuff that does the job on snow. Two general types are used:

Cross-country waxes: evolved from the traditional waxes of the sport, they both slide and grip, or give you traction on snow. The hotshots call them "grip waxes" because that's what they use them for.

Glide Waxes: used to increase ski glide speed, and therefore sometimes called "speed waxes."

You'll be most interested in the cross-country waxes, as they are used by all cross-country skiers. Glide waxes are used by expert skiers and racers to attain maximum ski glide. You can ski a lot without ever using or even knowing about them.

There are three types of cross-country wax:

Hard wax: for snow in its original condition. This includes new snow and snow that may have been on the ground for days or even weeks, but still has not melted and refrozen, or otherwise changed. Hard waxes come in small cans or boxes.

Klister: for snow that has changed from its original state to something else: slush, ice, crust, heavy "corn" snow, and so on. Comes as a tacky liquid in tubes, like toothpaste, or as a semisolid, in boxes.

Klister-Wax: for snows in between those suited for hard wax and those suited for klister. It looks like and is packaged like hard wax, but is tacky and behaves like a klister.

All wax cans, boxes, and tubes, and often the waxes themselves, are coded with colors for identification. The specific colors vary from brand to brand, but generally follow the visual color spectrum: "colder" greens and blues for cold snow, "warmer" yellows and red for warmer snow.

BASE PREPARATION. This includes the impregnating tars that protect and waterproof wood ski bases, and the paraffin waxes applied to plastic bases for speed. If you have wood skis, sooner or later you'll become acquainted with impregnating tars. If you have skis with plastic bases, you may or may not become involved with base paraffins. For most recreational skiing, you don't need them, as they go "under" the glide waxes that racers use for speed.

Base wax, also called *base binders,* go "under" cross-country waxes to bind them more securely to the ski base. They're most used for abrasive snow conditions to increase final wax durability.

Cleaners are special solvents used to remove wax. They're not just any *cleaner,* but special aerosols or liquid solvents, designed to dissolve wax, but not ski bases.

stride, the small irregularities in the snow surface don't melt, but rather dig into the wax, providing grip to give you traction. The whole art of waxing focuses on attaining grip and glide.

The only thing that makes waxing difficult is the unpredictability of snow. It can vary from heavy and wet to light and fluffy. It can blow like dust or harden into clumps. It can be moderately cold, like refrigerated food, or extremely cold, like things stored in a good freezer. Along with these differences go characteristics that affect the performance of skis.

Therefore, wax must be selected and applied to match the snow on which you ski.

Snow often appears soft and velvety, but is actually made up of tiny, hard, sharp crystals of frozen water. The hardness and sharpness of these crystals determine snow characteristics.

If the temperature is well below freezing, all the water in the snow is frozen. The snow is said to be *dry.* The lower the temperature, the dryer and harder the snow crystals.

If the temperature is above freezing, the snow crystals start to melt. The snow is *wet.* The higher the temperature, the wetter and softer the snow crystals.

There are two main types of wax to match these snows: harder waxes for dry snow and softer waxes for wet snow. If you want to keep your waxing simple, you can get along with one wax of each of these types: two waxes are all that you need to wax successfully for almost all snows. At the other extreme you can wax precisely for every snow condition you encounter by using a collection of different waxes of each of the main types. Some wax makers offer a collection of as many as 23 different waxes just for this purpose. So waxing can be as convenient or as complex as you care to make it.

THREE WAYS TO GO

The best route to successful waxing is first to select an approach responsive to your skiing needs. The cardinal rule is to keep waxing as simple as possible, no more complex than it need be for your skiing. Are you, for instance:

1. A beginner or a more experienced recreational skier who skis for pleasure only?

Typical two-wax systems. *Al Patrick*

2. An avid skier who skis frequently and far, piling up many miles per season?
3. An expert skier or racer, who wants maximum skiing performance every time you ski?

If you're new to waxing, or if you are a pleasure skier who doesn't want to fuss with a plethora of products, then one good wax of each of the major types is all you need for almost all cross-country skiing. You should opt for a *two-wax* system.

If you're an avid skier, a citizens' racer, or a snow devotee who skis from the first autumn snowflake until the tracks turn to grass and mud in the spring, then you're probably willing to sacrifice a bit of convenience for better performance. You should use those products that suit the snows where you ski best. You use *selected waxing,* using the five to seven waxes best for your needs.

If speed is your skiing game, wax performance is your goal. Each time you ski, you want the ultimate attainable, the best match of wax to snow. So you'll need a full line of waxes. You're into *performance waxing.*

Whatever approach you elect, start simple. If you are a newcomer to waxing, start with a two-wax system. A season's skiing is usually all you will need to build confidence with those two waxes, and then you can branch out, expanding your capabilities to using other types if you wish.

Outdoor thermometers are guides, but not always believable ones. *Bob Bugg*

Test snow by taking a handful and squeezing it (A). If it clumps to a snowball, it's wet (B); if it flows or blows away, it's dry (C). *Michael Brady*

LOOK FIRST

The first and most important step in waxing is to judge the snow. Temperature is a good guide. If the snow-level air temperature is well below freezing, 25°F. or below, the snow is almost certainly dry. If it's well above freezing, 34°F. or more, the snow usually is wet.

Temperature readings from outdoor thermometers can mislead, especially if the thermometers are mounted high above the snow or are exposed to the sun. In addition, new snow is often colder or warmer than the air temperature at a point only slightly above.

You can, of course, always ski at touring centers where you feel you can rely on the "wax of the day" notices posted there. But that doesn't add to your own waxing skill, nor does it help you if you rewax out on the trail or ski somewhere else. So it's always best to check for yourself.

The best way to check snow type is by squeezing a handful of it in your gloved hand. Get down into it: have no fear, it's nontoxic. If the snow is loose and powdery or blows away when you open your hand, it's dry. You then need one of your "dry snow" waxes. If it forms snowballs or large clumps, it's wet. You then need a "wet snow" wax.

ON WITH IT

Wax indoors if possible. It's more comfortable than standing outside, and wax goes onto and sticks to your skis better when both wax and skis are warm. Since different brands of wax require slightly different application methods for optimum results, check the directions on the wax you use before applying.

Always start with clean, dry skis. Wax doesn't stick to dirt or water. If your skis have wood bases, they should be prepared so that no bare wood shows. If your bases are waxed incorrectly for the day's snow, remove the old wax with a scraper.

Now you are ready to apply the wax.

HARD WAXES: Almost all dry-snow waxes and some wet-snow waxes of the two-wax systems come in cans or boxes, and classify as hard waxes. Start by exposing a bit of the wax from its container. Apply the wax in short, rapid strokes, covering at least a third of the ski base, from slightly behind the heel of the boot forward. You do not need to wax the tracking groove in the center of the base. Wax applied here may fill up the groove, causing the ski to yaw, or "swim" when gliding on snow. Rub the wax out with a waxing cork.

The lower the snow-surface temperature, the smoother the wax should be. So for very cold conditions, 25°F. or below, polish the wax smooth with a waxing cork. Do a good job here; even exactly the right wax can have exactly the wrong

Expose wax by peeling off a bit of the container.
Fletcher Manley

performance if you slap it on in clumps and leave it that way.

For warmer conditions, just below freezing, leave the wax surface slightly rougher, or add another layer. More layers give better grip, while fewer, thinner layers give better glide.

KLISTERS are not only tacky; if you don't know the ropes of the game, you may find them downright sneaky. They have their own way of getting on your hands, clothes, equipment—and any other place where you don't want them. So approach them with respect for the mess they can create if you're just a bit negligent, and they'll behave beautifully.

Klisters must be applied when warm. Cold, you cannot coax them out of the tube, not even with brute force. If klister is too cold to flow out of the tube when you squeeze it, warm the tube slightly, over a radiator or in your hand. Squeeze out a strip on each side of the tracking

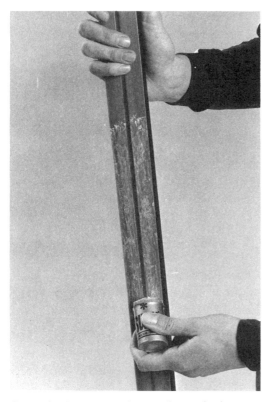

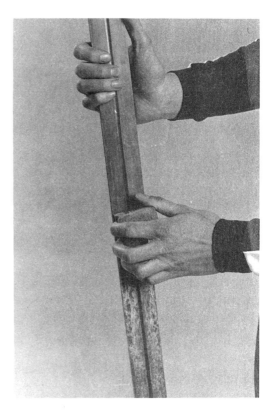

Crayon hard wax on in short strokes, and rub it smooth. *Fletcher Manley*

Apply klister evenly, and spread it out to a thin layer. *Fletcher Manley*

groove of the ski base, covering about a third of the base length, from just behind the heel of the boot forward. Then smooth it out with the edge of a ski scraper, or with the spreader paddle supplied with some klisters. Some skiers like to spread klister out and work it into the ski base using the heel of their hand, just below the thumb. If you don't mind the sticky result, this is an excellent way to get the job done.

The rule for applying klisters can be expressed in one word: THIN! Less may be too much; apply about as much as a coat of paint, no more. And when you've finished squeezing klister onto your ski bases, put the cap back on the tube, immediately. This one simple step will spare you most of the mess that the critics of klister maintain is its chief nuisance. After you have squeezed a tube, the klister can continue to flow, not to mention what it will do if you drop the tube on the floor and then step on it.

Avoid these problems with a little caution, and you'll probably become a klister fan. You may discover that klisters almost always grip better than hard waxes. If you have the right klister for the prevailing conditions, you're almost guaranteed good traction, while all hard-wax jobs, even those correctly matched to the prevailing snow, slip sometimes. Don't let anyone who has failed with klister discourage you from trying it. On the snows for which it is intended, nothing can match its performance.

KLISTER-WAXES: Most wet-snow waxes that come in cans or boxes like hard waxes for dry snow are klister-waxes, even though they may not bear that exact designation. When in doubt, check: dab your finger on top of the wax, and see if it sticks in tacky strings when you pull your finger

off. If it does, it's a klister-wax, or a close enough cousin to demand the same treatment.

Start applying klister wax as hard wax, by exposing a bit of the wax. But don't crayon the wax on as if it were hard wax; apply it in short strokes, or by dabbing the wax against the ski base, again for at least a third of the base length, from just under the heel forward. Don't rub it on, or the wax will come off in gobs, leaving your ski bases a lumpy mess. Finally, rub the wax smooth with a waxing cork, or if your hands are clean and dry and you don't mind the feeling, with the palm of your hand. As with klister, the rule here is THIN!

TAKING IT OFF

Cleaning skis, like waxing, is best done indoors. Always clean skis before applying new wax, preparing bases, or storing. Most waxes harden on skis when stored at room temperature for a few days, so if you're a weekend skier, it's best to clean your skis well after a weekend's skiing.

Start cleaning by scraping off as much old wax as you can with a ski scraper. Some skiers find broad-blade putty knives handy for this job, while others have become skilled in removing wax using the klister spreader paddles packed with klister tubes. The general rule here is not to use a metal scraper on a plastic base, as the scraper can dig into and damage the base.

After you have removed as much old wax as possible with a scraper, finish the job with ski cleaner, followed by wiping dry with a lint-free rag or wiping tissue. Always follow directions when using ski-cleaning fluids and use them in well-ventilated places. *Never* use lighter fluid,

WHAT'S IN A WAX

Ski waxes are blends of various raw materials, of type and quantity differing according to the desired properties. Many, such as Alpine ski waxes and cross-country glide waxes for cold snow, are blended, true to their name, almost entirely from various waxes. Some, such as fluid klisters, contain little or no wax.

To the scientist or the purist this presents a difficulty, essentially linguistic in nature. English, in contradistinction to the Scandinavian languages of the countries where skiing originated, fails to differentiate between *wax,* the general term for a large group of fatty solids, and *ski wax,* the substance you put on skis. But it's easy to live with this inconsistency, as no ski wax contains just wax.

The first ski waxes were concocted by hand from vegetable and animal compounds, such as tars, beeswax, and spermaceti (used by the 1848 California Gold Rush miners in downhill ski races). An aura of mystery, and sometimes correspondingly mysterious smells, surrounded these brews. Those days are gone, perhaps forever, as few modern waxes contain any of the traditional, natural ingredients. The larger wax makers use none at all.

HARD WAXES consist mostly of various petroleum waxes, which are obtained from oil in refining. As most petroleum waxes are hard and brittle, they are adulterated with oil and petroleum jelly for softness, and high-molecular synthetic rubber for adhesion.

KLISTERS consist mostly of synthetic resins and esters. As these raw materials are often hard when cold, they are softened with oils and petroleum jelly. The oil content is one of the major factors determining the final properties of the klister: red klister, for instance, is intended for wetter snow, and therefore contains more oil than does blue klister. Some klisters contain special adulterants for specific properties, such as metal particles in silver klister to increase surface hardness.

Remove old hard wax or old klister with a scraper.
Fletcher Manley

gasoline, or turpentine to clean ski bases. Aside from being dangerously flammable, these liquids can damage ski bases and degrade their wax holding ability.

TWO WAXES ARE THE FIRST RESORT

The *two-wax systems* offer the ultimate in waxing convenience. The waxes are specially compounded to respond to wide ranges of snow conditions, so you may use them to wax well for almost all snows. With only two waxes to keep track of, your selection is simple and straightforward: one for dry snow, one for wet. Though convenient and simple, these waxes are far from second rate: they are so reliable that they have been used on major ski expeditions. They are compounded to work well and ice little in the troublesome transition zone at freezing, 0°C. (32°F.), where snow changes so radically as to foul many a more esoteric wax job. So good is their adaptability that racers often use them for difficult conditions.

There are several two-wax systems. Almost all the major ones feature a hard wax for dry snow and a softer wax, or a klister-wax, for wet snow. Swix, for instance, offers a Gold for dry snow and a Silver for wet snow, while Jack Rabbit has a Blue for dry snow and a Red for wet snow. Skiers continually devise rhymes to remember which wax is which; a common one for Swix is "Gold for cold and Silver for slop," and one for Jack Rabbit is "Blue below, Red above." If such poetic eloquence escapes you, settle for reading the directions each time.

Start by following the manufacturer's directions, selecting and applying the correct wax for the conditions as you judge them. When in doubt, start by waxing for

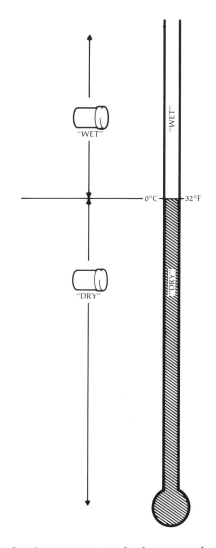

One for wet snow, one for dry snow makes it easy.

colder, dryer conditions. If you err, your skis will glide well, but not have enough grip. It's always easier to add wax for grip than to scrape skis for more glide.

Always test your wax by skiing. If your skis slip totally out of control in the first few yards, or if they ball up with snow before you even take your first stride, then you've missed completely. Go back and start over. But fortunately such drastic misses are seldom. So go out and ski about 500 yards, the distance your wax needs to "run in," before you judge your wax job.

If you need more grip, try extending the wax further along the ski until you have waxed the entire base. If you have already done this and it doesn't work, try adding another layer or two, especially in the middle section of the ski that is most important in grip. Let these coats of wax be a bit rough; it will give them more bite. If you still lack adequate grip, it's probably because you started with the "dry" wax on a day that called for the "wet." Just add a bit of wet on top, and you'll get the grip you need.

If you need more glide, try polishing your wax more with a cork. If that fails, remove a bit of the wax, especially that under the front and rear thirds of the ski base, with a scraper, and polish the middle third smooth with a cork. If you still don't have as much glide as you feel you should, then you've probably applied the "wet" wax on a day that called for the "dry." Scrape the *wet* wax off, switch to the *dry,* and you'll probably have plenty of glide.

Experiment with your two waxes; learn to know them well. If someone else has better results with another brand, you may or may not see an improvement if you switch brands. Most waxing problems arise from wax choice or application that doesn't suit the conditions, not from selection of any one particular brand. In other words, select one brand that is available where you live or where you ski. Getting to know its characteristics further simplifies and speeds your waxing.

A LEAP INTO THE ART

If you want improved performance for snows on the fringes of the capabilities of a two-wax system, you'll want to both supplement your collection of waxes and add to your techniques of wax application. You'll leap into the waxing art.

You may have first noticed that you

NO CHARTS HERE

In the early days of the cross-country renaissance in North America, wax tables or charts were necessary in books of this sort, to tell readers that there were several brands of wax products to suit the snows they might encounter, as they often could not find specific brands in shops. But there are no such tables or charts in this book, for a number of reasons.

First, the underlying need for them has passed. They are still useful in comprehensive waxing works, to show the spectrum of available products. But in books on skiing itself, readers are better guided by the selection in the shops where they deal.

Second, waxes have now been developed to such a degree of convenience, as in the two-wax systems, and sophistication—witness the great range of waxes available—that knowing the approximate equivalences between brands is seldom useful information. More often than not, changing application methods, rather than switching brands, will improve deficient waxing.

Third, wax makers now delete from, supplement, expand, or otherwise alter their range of products once a year, and sometimes more often. Therefore any information packed into a table in this book would be at least partially obsolete by the time it was read.

Fourth, wax makers seldom divide their ranges of waxes up equally: for temperature/condition ranges where maker A offers three products, maker B has only one or two, and vice versa.

Finally, waxing is now known as a part of the cross-country scene. It no longer needs the introduction it once did.

could use a bit more grip than the "wet" wax of a two-wax system gives, in skiing uphills in wet, spring snow. That's a signal for klister, usually the first addition when skiers expand their arsenals of wax.

If you ski predominantly cold-snow conditions, you may have felt that you could use more glide on extremely cold snows. That's the signal for acquiring a special cold-snow wax, such as one of the special greens. For almost all skiing you'll find that five to seven waxes will serve you admirably. If you doubt this, watch what the folks who carry those big wax kits use. The kits may hold the whole wax rainbow, but invaribly those skiers ski almost the entire season with five to seven waxes, just your prudent total.

If you ski long tours, or if you ski on icy, abrasive snows, or both, you may find that your wax jobs don't last as long as you would like: your wax wears off too quickly for your skiing. That's the signal to get involved with heat in applying waxes, and to add base wax, or binder, to your collection of wax products.

Heat is the simplest way to increase wax durability. Apply the first layer, and warm it onto the ski, to bond it better to the ski base. If it's a hard wax, warm with a moderately warm iron. The most frequently used tool for this job is also the most readily available: an inexpensive travel iron. Some wax makers offer handy iron heads that fit into standard 80-watt soldering irons that you can buy in a hardware store. All major wax makers offer rectangular aluminum irons with wooden handles, designed to be heated in a torch flame or over a stove burner.

Let the warmed-in wax cool at room temperature, and then smooth it out with a waxing cork. Apply subsequent layers without heat, so that they don't mix with the first layer.

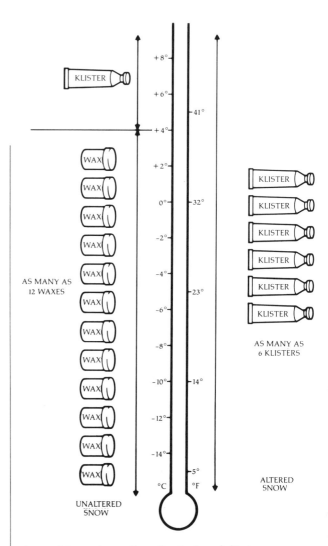

A complete spectrum allows fine tuning of skis to match snow.

If you're applying klister, don't use waxing irons. It's both messy and disastrous for the properties of the klister itself. This is when it's best to use the flame of a waxing torch fitted with a good flame spreader. Use the flame sparingly, just enough to cause the klister to flow on a horizontal, upturned ski base, and keep it moving, so as not to damage the bases. The polyethylene plastic used in many ski bases, starts to melt at 130°C. (265°F.), far cooler than the 175°C. (350°F.) temperatures commonly used in household ovens to bake bread. If you're reluctant to risk flame damage, you can try other sources of heat to warm in klister. Some skiers have used old, discarded hair dryers for this purpose. In any case, it's a good idea to get help the first few times you use heat of any sort on your ski bases. In so doing you'll probably avoid both mess and potential disaster.

For icy, abrasive snows, bond wax to ski bases with base wax, or binder. Start with an absolutely clean, dry ski base, as binder won't be much good if put on top of other wax. Binder is the tackiest of all products that come in cans, as its mission is just to bond, not to grip or glide on snow. Treat binder with even more caution than klister-wax, dabbing it on carefully in small amounts. If you can't seem to make the binder go onto your ski bases in anything less than unruly clumps, try cooling the can outside before application. Cold binder can often be crayoned on warm bases, just as if it were hard wax.

Spread, warm, and smooth the binder on the base with a warm waxing iron. The result should be a smooth, even, very thin layer. Let the skis cool to room temperature, and then set them outside to cool for a while. Some skiers prefer this to be overnight, applying binder in the evening for the next day's skiing. Give cooled binder a rapid polish with a well-used waxing cork. Don't use a new cork, whose surface may be rough and leave streaks, or worse, cork particles in the sticky binder. Then wax over the binder for the day's conditions. But do *not* use heat on the layers applied on top of the binder. Heat will cause the binder to work up into the wax covering it, which may drastically slow its glide, as raw binder has fair grip, but no glide at all.

You can apply binder over the entire length of a ski base, if you intend to final-wax the entire length. But the best general approach is to apply binder over the center third of the base, critical for grip. No sense working more than you absolutely must.

SOME TRICKS OF THE TRADE

CHANGE WAX only as needed. If yesterday's hard wax still works, leave it on and get a few more miles out of it. Klisters and klister-waxes pick up dirt, dust, pine needles, and other wax from the snow as you ski. After a day's skiing on klister, it's best to clean your skis.

WAX FOR THE COLDEST SNOW you expect to meet on a tour in variable snow conditions. If your skis slip on a sunny stretch, there are techniques of skiing, such as skating, herringbone striding, and double poling, that will bail you out. But if you've waxed too softly for the dry stretches, your skis may collect snow and ice up. No technique, except perhaps snowshoelike plodding, will save you then. You must stop, scrape, and rewax. So anticipate, and avoid this difficulty.

GLIDE DEPENDS primarily on how much the cross-country wax you apply drags, and only secondarily on how much any glide wax you apply glides. Glide waxes are, at best, a five-percent solution to good ski glide, so you can easily do without them, unless you are into racing.

WAX FOR MORE GRIP IN POWDER even if you are waxed correctly for the prevailing temperature and snow type, your skis may slip frequently if you ski outside of hard tracks, where the underlying snow isn't firm enough to withstand the pressure needed for ski grip. The situation is like that of sand: sand strewn on an icy road or sidewalk gives you great traction. But when you walk or drive in loose, dry

GLIDE AND GRIP— HOW MUCH?

Most skiers consciously or unconsciously rate the glide and grip of their skis usually as good or poor, and sometimes with adjectives unfit for print.

Both glide and grip depend on a ski's resistance to sliding on a snow surface. This resistance is caused by air resistance, displacement of snow (how much snow you plow up as you ski), and friction. Air resistance and snow displacement are familiar to most skiers, as they have many parallels in other activities. Friction is more subtle, more complex, and more important in overall ski glide and grip.

Friction (from the Latin *fricare,* to rub) occurs whenever two surfaces are in contact with each other. It's inescapable, both friend and foe. You couldn't walk without it. You use it when you write. You depend upon it when you strike a match. But it also wears car engines and can burn skin. Lack of it can cause cars to skid and wheels to spin.

In cross-country skiing, you need friction for grip. And although it opposes and therefore limits ski glide, you wouldn't want to do away with it completely, as you would have difficulty turning or controlling your skis unless there was some friction between them and the underlying snow.

Almost everything that can be said about friction can be expressed in terms of the *friction coefficient.* Strictly speaking, there are two main types of friction coefficient: *dry* and *wet.* The dry friction coefficient is the sort explained in high school science classes, the type you encounter in sliding furniture across floors, or in everyday walking. It's just the frictional force along the surfaces divided by the weight perpendicular to the surfaces. Wet friction is far more complex and far less well understood, depending also on the areas in contact and the viscosity of the wetting liquid (viscosity is a liquid's internal resistance to flow). Snow researchers know that neither dry friction nor wet friction completely describe ski grip or glide. Something in between, a mixed friction, is involved. As yet, nobody is certain about the "laws" of that mixed friction. Nevertheless, you can simplify matters if you just think of the old standby dry friction coefficient as a guideline.

Just how much or how little should the friction coefficient be for good ski grip and glide? Numbers alone mean little; it's their result that counts, that affects your skiing.

Think, for instance, of the admonitory warnings in state driver's manuals and safety campaigns: vehicle stopping distance goes up with increased speed and up still more on wet or icy roads.

The friction coefficient between good car tires and dry pavement is about o.8, which

sand, your traction is poor. So when skiing that fluffy stuff, wax as if it were a bit warmer, with a longer, thicker coat of the same wax, or perhaps a "warmer" wax.

WAX FOR MORE GLIDE IN GOOD TRACKS: Good tracks give your skis a hard, flat surface for maximum ski grip. In skiing in them you'll probably find that you can ski the diagonal stride up hills where you otherwise might have had to use the herringbone. So try for more glide in good tracks; wax as if it were a bit colder, with a shorter, thinner coat of the same wax, or perhaps a "colder" wax. Get the feel of maximum glide in tracks, and you'll become addicted to the joys it offers.

limits vehicle braking distance at the interstate limit of 55 mph to a minimum of 127 feet on a level road. Actual stopping distance is, of course, greater, as even the best brakes waste some stopping energy, and driver reaction distance adds to the total.

If the same road is wet, the friction coefficient drops to 0.5, which ups the minimum braking distance at 55 mph from 127 to 203 ft. An icy road, with a tire-to-road friction coefficient of 0.1, will further increase the minimum braking distance to 1020 feet.

In normal walking, you need a friction coefficient of 0.2 or more between your feet and the underlying surface. If that friction coefficient drops to 0.1, you instinctively slow down, feel uneasy, and take shorter strides.

For gliding skis, a friction coefficient of 0.1 is moderate to poor; one of 0.05 is good. To see the difference between the two, think of whizzing downhill at 25 mph and coasting out onto a flat in an even, level track. With a friction coefficient of 0.1, you'll stop in 210 feet. With a friction coefficient of 0.05, you'll coast 420 feet before coming to a halt. In terms of grip, you don't need much underski friction for good performance: a coefficient of 0.4 to 0.5 is usually adequate. What's slippery for a car on a wet road is good snow bite for a cross-country ski kick.

FROM THE BOTTOM UP is the rule in waxing for troublesome transition conditions just at freezing, 0°C. (32°F.). Start waxing assuming that the temperature is just below freezing, and test your skis. If they slip after you've skied 500 yards, go back and add a bit more "kicker," or wax for more grip. Keep going until you get sufficient ski grip. Going the other way, from the "top side" of freezing down, is more difficult, if not impossible, as you'll have to scrape off ice and snow each time you rewax.

ALTITUDE affects waxing, but altitude itself affects snow characteristics and waxing far less than do other climatic factors. More important is the source of the moisture from which the snow was formed. Snow falling on lower, coastal areas often comes from moisture evaporated from seawater, and may contain traces of salt and other impurities. Snow falling on high, inland mountain areas often comes from moisture evaporated from fresh water, and is purer. Dust, soot, and other contaminants in evaporated moisture also affect the characteristics of snow formed. You probably will note greater differences in skiing at the same altitude in different parts of the country than you will by changing altitude in one region.

MAN-MADE ARTIFICIAL SNOW differs from natural snow and sometimes may require different waxing. The major cause of the difference is that man-made snow usually is made from local ground water, which often contains minerals and other impurities, while atmospheric, natural snow is almost always more pure. So, just as salt lowers the freezing point of water, turning snow to water on subfreezing roads, minerals in man-made snows make them a bit "warmer" than natural snows of the same age at the same temperature.

MACHINE-MADE TRACKS often have snow surfaces that differ from the surrounding snow. This is because heavier packing and tracking machines often dig up older underlying snow, and mix it in with the newer, surface snow. The difference between in-track and out-of-track conditions is most acute when a thinner layer of new powder has fallen on top of older, frozen granular snow. Machines can dig up the older, more abrasive granular snow and mix it with the surface powder in tracks. You'll need base binder wax to ski even a short tour in these tracks, using the same wax that you otherwise could use for a day's skiing out of the tracks, up on the new powder.

FOG OR HIGH AIR HUMIDITY affects snow, making it "wetter" than it otherwise would be at the same temperature. All ski waxes are compounded for average wintertime humidities, so when the humidity is unusually high, or when you ski high in the clouds or in a fog, you'll have to wax "warmer" than the instructions on the wax container stipulate.

WIND COMPACTS SNOW, making it effectively dryer and harder than it otherwise would be at the same temperature. For wind-packed snows, wax "colder," "older," or "harder" than you would for the same snow that was not compacted by wind.

THE SUN HEATS SNOW, melting it and thus making it wetter than it otherwise would be at the same temperature. So you'll have to wax "warmer" or "wetter" for tours in sunshine than for tours in the shade. The difference made by solar heating depends on three factors: 1) How high the sun is in the sky, which is determined by latitude and time of year. You'll find solar heating of snow more pronounced in the spring than in midwinter, more pronounced in southern areas than in areas in the far north. 2) Cloud cover. It stands to reason that solar heating is most pronounced when the sun shines unobstructed on the snow. 3) The age of the snow. New snow reflects as much as 90% of the sunshine falling on it, while wetter, older snow may reflect only 50%, and therefore be warmed more quickly by sunshine.

ALWAYS DRY SKIS before waxing. Carry a piece of terrycloth toweling, about the size of a washcloth or half a small hand towel, in your wax kit to wipe moisture off bases. You'll be amazed at the time this rag will save.

BAG SKIS whenever you carry them on an auto roof rack. Road film, exhaust particles, and dust on ski bases degrade their wax-holding ability. The worst offender is saltwater, splashed up from salted roads: it etches bindings and ski bases so quickly that you may suspect that ski manufacturers are among those supporting its use on roads in skiing states. The solution is simple: always carry your skis in a ski bag when traveling. Many good, water-repellent bags are available on the market, most from ski manufacturers. Even the disposable plastic bags that airlines give away free to bag checked skis will do. If your car roof rack is one of the locking, hinged types intended to carry skis flat, side by side, best swap it for a simpler roof bar and a couple of rubber or shock-cord tie-downs. Toss the ski bag inside of your car if you fear theft when leaving your car unattended.

WAXING HIGH-PERFORMANCE SKIS

Getting the most out of high-performance skis, such as fiberglass, carbon-fiber, or Kevlar-fiber racing skis, requires waxing techniques that evolve from, but are slightly different from, those commonly used in recreational skiing.

This is primarily because high-performance skis have cambers and bases different from those of recreational skis. The cambers are relatively stiffer, and become more so as they close, in a fashion similar to a multileaf truck spring becoming stiffer as the truck is loaded down. The midsections of the bases of these skis contact the snow slightly or not at all when the skis are equally weighted, as in downhill skiing or in gliding after double poling. But when kicked vigorously down, such as in diagonal striding at higher speeds, the middle of the base is pressed against the underlying snow. The material of which the base is made, usually a high-molecular polyethylene, is most durable and glides best when waxed with paraffin wax. Therefore the middle of the base is most active in grip, and the tip and tail sections of the base are more important in glide. So on a high-performance ski base, there are three *zones:* a center *grip zone,* and two *glide zones,* one ahead of, the other behind the center zone.

FINDING THE MIDDLE

First, you should locate the center zone of your ski bases. It isn't in the center of the ski length, but rather in the center section of the camber curve, which falls in different places on different skis. So you have to test your skis to find out where it is located. Ski factories and shops can do this with ski testers. But lacking these refined methods, you can do just as well with a few checks.

Hold a pair of skis vertically, bases together, and sight through the gap made by the cambers as you squeeze the skis together with your hands placed just behind the bindings, or, for new skis, just behind the balance points. When the gap closes down to about 2½ feet, mark its front and rear points on the skis. The section of the base between these marks locates the center zone. In skiing you may find that you need to wax just these 2½ feet of the center zone, or maybe less, or sometimes more. The exact length of the center zone that you should wax for grip depends on your skis, your proficiency and skiing speed, and on the snow conditions. The only way to find how much you should wax in the center is to wax and ski and see. One quick skiing check is to wax your entire ski bases with cross-country wax, and ski about 5 kilometers in abrasive snow tracks. Where the wax has worn off locates the glide zones, and where wax is still on the skis locates the center zones.

PREPPING BASES

Always prepare new high-performance ski bases with paraffin wax. Repeat preparation whenever the glide zones feel dry or no longer feel "soapy," or whenever they appear a bit white. Base preparation and final glide waxing are essentially identical processes and use the same glide waxes— the only difference being that in preparation you work a bit more, so the paraffin wax bonds well to the base surface.

Heat is what makes it all possible. Molten paraffin wax and warmed ski-base polyethylene actually mix a bit, in a manner that chemists call a solution. The base polyethylene itself is *not* porous, as is often popularly assumed to be the explanation for its ability to hold wax. If it were, it would also act like a sponge and absorb water, which it doesn't: polyethylene is *hydrophobic*—it repels water. Heat is the catalyst that brews your paraffin-polyethylene solution, bonding the wax to the base.

Start preparing bases with your skis horizontal, bottoms up. If possible clamp them firmly in ski vises or on a waxing horse. Melt paraffin wax onto the skis with a heated waxing iron or electric iron, of the same type you use to melt-in cross-country wax. Hold the corner of the iron just above the base, press the wax against the iron so it melts and drip molten wax down to strips on either side of the tracking groove. Then smooth the wax out with the iron, warming it thoroughly in. Keep the iron temperature at 100°C. to 130°C. (212°F. to 266°F.), or *medium* to *high* on most ordinary electric irons.

Apply wax only to the front and rear glide zones, not to the center grip zone. Although some ski makers advise preparing the entire base, including the grip zone, you'll only make work for yourself if you do so. Cross-country waxes will not stick to paraffin wax. Applying glide wax in the grip zone makes as much sense as greasing a surface to be painted. If you paraffin-wax the center grip zone, you'll simply have to remove it all before you can wax for grip. In the center zone, cross-country wax warmed in prepares the base as well as can any paraffin you may apply, so the ski is both protected and treated as it should be.

Let hot waxed skis cool at room temperature until the wax has hardened, which usually takes 15 to 30 minutes. Then scrape the wax on the base to an ultrasmooth layer using a rectangular plastic ski scraper or, if you feel confident enough, a steel refinishing scraper. Beware of the potential danger of a steel scraper, though: if your hand slips, its edge can easily dig a trough in the soft plastic ski base. Scrape the bases until all the paraffin wax you applied seems to have been removed: only that which has penetrated, gone deep into the base material, should remain. Remove excess wax from the tracking groove with a round, soft object, such as the rounded corner of a klister spreader paddle.

BEWARE HEAT!

Always be about twice as careful as you think you should be in using heat on polyethylene ski bases. Heat can not only melt polyethylene, which is real destruction, but it can oxidize base surfaces, retarding glide.

Polyethylene bases glide well because, as mentioned before, polyethylene is hydrophobic. This property poses a problem in ski manufacture: it's difficult to get glues or inks to stick to polyethylene. Therefore, prior to gluing or printing, polyethylene sheets are usually treated with flames to oxidize their surfaces, which vastly eases glue or ink adhesion. This is why polyethylene bases with designs, logos, or lettering are actually clear sheets, printed on the reverse side that is also glued to the ski.

The same oxidation that promotes glue and ink adhesion will also absorb water, defeating the wonderful hydrophobic property of the polyethylene. Heat from a waxing iron or torch, or even excess sun, can oxidize polyethylene, so caution is the word. Telltale for oxidation is its color: chalk-white stripes or patches signal its advance. If you see oxidation, scrape it off with a steel scraper, and retreat the bases.

GRIP WAXING

Apply grip wax in the center zone, using the same techniques as for recreational skis, described on pages 202–4. As the wax applied functions mostly for grip, you can select slightly softer wax than you would use for recreational skiing under the same conditions, and apply less of it, over a shorter center section, or "kicker," in the center zone. For more grip, increase the length of the kicker, preferably a bit more forward than back, as most of your downhill glide is on the tail glide zone of your skis.

GLIDE WAXING

Glide waxing, or "speed waxing," as it's sometimes called, is what you do to the tip and tail glide zones to enhance glide. You may use either softer Alpine ski waxes or special cross-country glide waxes, but the special cross-country glide waxes are usually the better, for two reasons. First, they are compounded for maximum durability at lower skiing speeds than are Alpine ski waxes. An Alpine ski race seldom lasts more than a couple of minutes, and is run at high speed. A cross-country skier often is out for hours at a time, skiing at a lower speed than does the Alpine racer. Second, most manufacturers color-code their cross-country glide waxes to correspond to the color-coding of the cross-country waxes which are most frequently used under the same conditions as a grip wax. So to select, you just match colors.

Apply glide wax in the same manner as base-preparation wax. For best glide, always scrape glide-waxed zones carefully,

and finish the job by polishing with a smooth waxing cork.

A caution: Beware the overdo in glide waxing. This is where even skilled skiers sometimes fail: for more glide, they concentrate on improving their glide waxing. Remember: glide depends primarily on how much your grip wax drags, and secondarily on how much your glide wax glides, even when you zone wax. So to improve glide, work on your grip wax first, then on your glide wax.

BINDERS

For abrasive snows you should apply base binder wax "under" the cross-country wax in the *center of the ski only. Do not* put base binder wax on the glide zones: it will only slow glide. Here paraffin base preparation is the binder. Remember: *stick under grip, slide under glide.*

SOME MORE TRICKS, FOR THE CONNOISSEUR IN WAXING

There are easily a thousand different types of snow that are skiable, so even with an arsenal of 25 waxes and glide waxes, you may sometimes find that high ski performance is attainable only if you concoct your own brew for the day. Here are a few favorite brews.

SNOW'S DIFFERENT: Wax makers quite logically state the temperature ranges of their products as still air temperatures slightly above the snow. Few, if any, state snow temperatures. Think: if they did, then how would they state temperatures for use above freezing? The temperature of a snow surface can never go above 0°C.

OLE'S SPECIAL

Skilled skiers and racers are forever experimenting with ski wax and waxing methods, sometimes brewing their own concoctions for difficult snows. Here's one such blend, devised by Ole Mosesen, director of Ole's Cross-Country Center in Warren, Vermont, for the ultimate of tricky snows, falling new snow, +1° to +5°C. (34° to 41°F.), with glazed, slithering tracks.

    1 can Swix Red hard wax
    1½ cans Swix Yellow klister-wax
    6-inch strip of Swix Yellow klister, squeezed
        out of tube
    1 inch off bar of Toko Yellow glide wax

Heat ingredients gently, stirring continually, until completely molten and uniform pale red in color. Pour into wax cans, such as the ones originally containing the klister-wax, and allow to harden at room temperature. Apply and use like klister-wax. Recommended for new snow falling at temperatures above freezing, when tracks rapidly lose their shape, pack hard and smooth, and guide skis little, if at all.

(32°F.), or it would be water, not snow. But snow temperature does affect waxing, especially early in the morning, when the temperature close to the snow surface hasn't caught up with the sun-warmed air above, or whenever new, cold snow falls during a warmer day. For these conditions always check snow temperature, using a waxing thermometer. You'll often find, for instance, that green works best, while the prevailing air temperature may indicate a blue.

HARD TRACKS, NEW SNOW: One of the more difficult, but also more common, of the tricky waxing conditions in racing is hard tracks in older, wetter snow dusted with lighter, new snow. Tracks are often set in the afternoon or evening for an early-morning race, and powder snow often starts to fall in the early-morning hours, producing the condition. If you use klister that suits the wetter tracks, it will collect new snow and ice up, at best slowing your glide. If you wax for the new powder snow alone, you may get by if the race is short, 5 km or less. But over longer distances the abrasive, older snow in the tracks will remove your hard wax. So compromise: apply both klister for the hard tracks and hard wax for the powder. Start with the klister, selecting and applying it just as if the powder weren't there. Then cool your skis outside for half an hour or so. Select the hard wax that you would use on the powder, just as if the underlying older snow weren't there. Apply it sparingly, "covering" the klister, and smoothing it out with a fine, light touch of a cork. This is the reverse of the general rule that hard wax shouldn't be put on top of softer wax. Cooling is the trick that allows you to do it, and for the situation you face, it's about the only thing that will work.

COLD: CROSS-COUNTRY ALL THE WAY: Glide on extremely cold snow, −15°C. (5°F.) and below is poor, so the colder the snow, the less glide wax affects overall ski performance. The 1980 Lake Placid Winter Olympic 15-km run in cold, new snow, is a case in point. Much to the chagrin of many other racers, who had spent hours glide-waxing their skis, Thomas Wassberg waxed quickly, with no glide wax at all. He simply put hard cross-country wax for cold, dry snow on the entire length of his ski bases. And he won the race.

Typical corks and fluid wax-remover solvents. *Al Patrick*

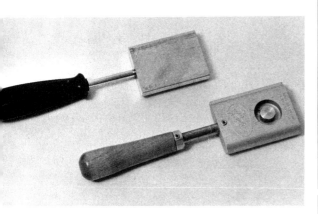
Typical waxing irons, intended for heating in torch flame or on stove. *Frits Solvang*

WAXING AIDS

SKI SCRAPERS are available in two types: smaller ski scrapers, often combined into a single unit with a waxing cork, for removing wax and scraping ice off of ski bases, and larger (about 3 by 5 inches, the size of a standard filing card) steel or plastic scrapers, used for scraping and repairing bases, and for scraping base-preparation wax and glide paraffin wax.

CORKS as the name implies, were once made only of natural cork. Synthetic waxing corks, made of expanded plastics (plastics blown full of bubbles), are now more common, and in many cases better for waxing than are natural corks.

SCRAPER SENSE

Steel refinishing scrapers used for working on ski bases dull with use, as do all tools with cutting edges. A good scraper will last a lifetime if regularly cleaned and sharpened. Here's how Stanley Tools recommends sharpening a quality refinishing scraper:

· First, clamp the scraper in a vise, one edge up at a time. File the edges square and straight by drawfiling with a smooth mill file. Round the corners slightly.

· Second, whet the edge, holding the blade square to the surface of the oil stone.

· Third, remove any burr left by edge whetting, by whetting the scraper flat on the oilstone. The final product should be smooth, sharp edges.

THERMOMETERS: Skiers use both larger, dial-face, wall-mount thermometers, with circular scales in degrees Celsius and degrees Fahrenheit, and sometimes with a scale to aid wax selection, and pocket-type waxing thermometers.

WAXING IRONS are usually small and light, and are available in a variety of types and models. Most common are solid rectangular aluminum blocks fixed to insulated handles, intended for heating with waxing torches. Electric waxing irons, and waxing-iron attachments to standard soldering irons, are also available, while some skiers simply use a small electric travel iron. *Caution:* if you travel outside of North America to ski, don't take an electric iron, unless it is a dual-voltage unit, capable of operation on the 220-volt supplies abroad.

WAXING TORCHES, used in warming-in wax and base preparations, and in cleaning skis, are available in a range of types, all fueled with liquefied petroleum gas. The most common types are those fueled by the propane cylinders, commonly available in hardware stores throughout the country, and those fueled by butane cartridges. The propane cylinders are heavier than the lightweight butane cartridges for the same amount of gas, but have the advantage that propane burns well down to −30°C. (−22°F.), while butane freezes at −1°C. (31°F.). The choice between the two depends on whether you are willing to carry a heavy torch that always lights, or opt for less weight, at the expense of having to heat it in your hands or inside clothing when it won't light in cold weather. *Caution:* If you go abroad to ski, forget the whole torch, and buy or borrow one there. For instance, European and North American torch heads are similar, and some are even made by the same companies. But the threads where the gas cylinders and the torch heads mate differ: you can't use a North American torch head on a European gas bottle, or fit North American gas bottles to European torch heads.

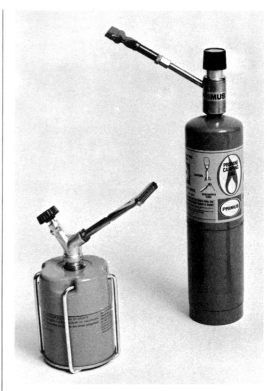

Typical wax torches. Taller unit runs on propane cartridges; smaller unit on butane cartridges.
Frits Solvang

WARNING: Federal and international regulations forbid the transport of all liquefied petroleum gases on passenger aircraft (see box, p. 219).

WIPING TISSUE, available from several major wax makers, is special lint-free, absorbent tissue, useful in cleaning skis and in polishing hard waxes on skis.

SPECIAL WAX-DISSOLVING HAND CLEANERS and most mechanic's waterless hand cleaners will remove wax from hands and clothing. Ordinary Vaseline is an acceptable solvent for klisters. Don't use these products to remove wax from skis, as they leave an oily residue that will repel wax subsequently applied.

WAX-REMOVING SOLVENTS are available from most major wax makers. These special solvents dissolve wax and evaporate rapidly, but do not damage skis or ski bases. Some are available in aerosol spray cans, but most are available as liquids, in bottles or cans containing about 6 to 12 fluid ounces of liquid.

WARNING: All such solvents are flammable, and most are harmful or fatal if swallowed. If swallowed, do not induce

It is illegal and extremely dangerous to take on board an airplane or check with your luggage any hazardous materials.

CAUTION

Specific instructions for shipping these materials safely by air can be obtained from your airline cargo office.

Aerosols—polishes, wax, degreaser, cleaners, etc.

Corrosives—acids, cleaners, wet cell batteries, etc.

Flammables—paints, thinners, lighter fluid, liquid reservoir lighters, cleaners, adhesives, etc.

Explosives—fireworks, flares, signal devices, loaded firearms, etc. *(Exception: small arms ammunition for personal use securely packed in fiberboard, wood, or metal boxes inside checked baggage, NOT permitted in carry-on baggage.)*

Radioactives—betascopes, radiopharmaceuticals, pacemakers not installed, etc.

Compressed Gases—tear gas or protective type sprays, oxygen cylinder, divers tanks, etc.

Loose Book Matches and/or Safety Matches *(Exception:* may be carried on person only)

Poisons

Each violation can result in a civil penalty of up to $10,000 or a criminal penalty of not more than $25,000 and/or five years in jail for the individual and the employer.

U.S. Department of Transportation
Federal Aviation Administration
Reprinting is authorized
For sale by Superintendent of Documents, U.S. Government Printing Office, Washington, D.C. 20402 SN 050-007-00460-5

GAS IS GROUNDED

Both federal and international aviation safety regulations forbid the transportation of liquefied petroleum gas aboard passenger-carrying aircraft. This means that you must leave the butane or propane fuel cartridges or cylinders for your waxing torch behind when you fly.

The reason for the restriction is simple and sound: seals on gas containers are designed to keep the gas inside when there's normal air pressure outside, provided they are undamaged. But if the outside pressure drops, as it does inside an aircraft at flying altitude, or if the container is damaged, as it might be if a piece of luggage bounces about or breaks open, then the gas may leak. And a fuselage full of gas is a flying bomb. Accordingly the federal regulations are strict, stating that a violation can result in penalties of up to $25,000 and five years imprisonment. Warnings, similar to the one reproduced here, are required to be posted by airlines.

What to do when you want to travel with your torch? Forsake flying and drive? You don't have to. Only the gas itself is grounded. Choose a torch that runs on common refills, such as the propane bottles sold in hardware stores throughout the country. Take your torch head along when you fly, and buy the gas bottle when you arrive, discarding it or giving it to a local skier before you return. At this writing, propane bottles cost only two and a half to three bucks in hardware stores, a negligible sum compared to the twenty-five grand it could cost you if you sneak one onto a plane, not to mention the far greater cost of the consequences of the type of accident the regulation is intended to prevent.

Posted FAA warning prohibiting transport of gas containers on passenger aircraft.

WHAT'S IN A WAX KIT
BESIDES WAX

After you've stocked your wax kit with the obvious items—wax, wax remover, scrapers, corks, a waxing torch and its fuel cylinder, and some wiping tissue—you'll probably toss in a few more items to ease waxing when on the road, away from home. Here's a few favorite extras carried by avid skiers, coaches, and racers:

SPARK LIGHTER: for torch; safer than matches, lessens danger of discarding burning match.

POCKET-TYPE WAXING THERMOMETER: one that you trust and have waxed with before.

REFINISHING SCRAPER: for trueing damaged bases.

POLYETHYLENE BASE-REPAIR "CANDLE": for repairing base damage.

SKI STRAPS: to strap skis together, especially useful when you must carry skis with klistered bases.

OIL STONE: for sharpening refinishing scraper and pole tips.

EPOXY GLUE: small tubes, for minor ski and pole repairs.

FEW EXTRA BINDING SCREWS.

POZI-DRIVE NO. 3 SCREWDRIVER: for tightening binding screws.

TRAVEL IRON: for ironing in hard and glide waxes. Several collapsible models available, some dual-voltage so you can take them abroad, with suitable adapter plugs.

FIBERGLASS TAPE: for repairing ski poles and, sometimes, skis.

PAINT BRUSH: for spreading warm klisters and for mixing klisters on skis.

AWL: for general repairs to pole straps and boots, an aid in mounting bindings.

SQUARE OF TERRYCLOTH TOWELING: for drying ski bases.

BAND-AIDS: for cut or burned fingers.

EXTRA POLE BASKETS AND HEAT GLUE TO PUT THEM ON.

MULTIBLADE KNIFE: for all-around use, from opening bottles to trimming around edges of repairs to skis.

PENCIL, SMALL POCKET NOTEBOOK: to make notes on waxing, etc.

SANDPAPER: for repairing ski damage, sometimes roughening bases.

NYLON SCOURING PAD: for final "scraping" of glide waxes used on extremely cold snows.

A FEW PAPER TOWELS: to clean up any mess left after waxing.

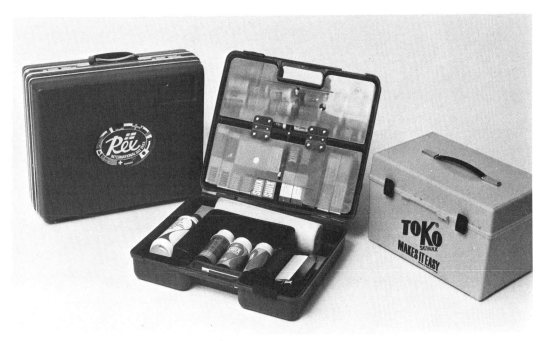

Wax kits can hold all waxing needs. *Frits Solvang*

vomiting. Call a physician immediately. Give air to an unconscious patient. *Keep out of reach of children!*

WAX KITS, as supplied by major wax makers, have hinged sections with compartments for storing wax and waxing accessories. Many skiers prefer to use a sturdy metal fishing-tackle box as a wax kit.

WAXING VISES clamp, in pairs, to tables or benches, and have padded jaws to hold skis firmly for waxing and repairs.

WAXING HORSES firmly clamp skis, bases up, at a convenient height for waxing and base preparation. Many models are collapsible for portability.

SKI CARE AND REPAIR

CLEAN both waxed waxable skis and waxless skis after use, but not necessarily after every day of skiing. Always clean skis that will stand for a few days or more, as wax and/or dirt on ski plastics hardens with time, and will be more difficult to remove later. Clean bases with a

Ski vises hold skis firmly for repairs and waxing. *Frits Solvang*

scraper and a solvent and wipe dry with rags or tissues. Clean tops and sides occasionally with solvent.

CHECK binding screws periodically, and tighten if necessary. Most bindings now mount with Pozi-Drive no. 3 screws. Screwdrivers for these screws are available from Alpine ski-binding suppliers, or from tool distributors. In a pinch use a Phillips driver, but don't do so often, as screw damage may result. If the screws are so loose that they don't tighten down, but just turn, take them out, and plug the holes with plastic plugs (available from ski shops) or homemade wood plugs, set in glue. If your skis have acrylic cores, use epoxy sparingly for this purpose, as epoxy can damage the core material. Redrill and redrive the screws when the glue has cured.

BASE GOUGES are best repaired immediately. First, thoroughly clean the area to be repaired, using wax removing solvent and tissue to remove all traces of foreign matter. Trim away any loose edges to the scar. Then, light the end of a polyethylene base-repair "candle" (available from ski shops), and drip molten polyethylene down into the gouge. Let the patch cool for at least half an hour, then scrape off the excess and flatten the base with a steel scraper. Finally, smooth the patch with fine sandpaper.

GOUGES AND SCRATCHES IN SIDEWALLS AND TOP: Clean the damaged area, and fill with two-component epoxy filler or glue. When the epoxy has hardened, scrape the patch flat with the surrounding surface. Sidewall repairs are often more urgent than base or top repairs, as sidewall damage may allow water to leak into the core of the ski, which can damage or even de-stroy the ski's internal bonds and thus degrade its strength.

DELAMINATION is the separation of sandwiched ski layers from each other. It occurs most often at the tail of a ski. First, spread the laminations from each other and block them apart with matchsticks. Clean all surfaces thoroughly, and allow the solvent to evaporate completely. Spread epoxy glue over the most accessible of the surfaces to be joined, remove the matchstick props, and close the laminations together. Apply pressure until the glue cures. C-clamps and blocks are the best method of applying pressure, but they're not part of the inventory of every skier's household. So simply wrap the ski with sturdy masking tape, starting ahead of the repair and working back, squeezing the laminations together and wrapping as you go. When the glue has cured, slit the tape along one ski edge with a knife, and remove it in one big unwrap. Then trim off any surplus glue that oozed out of the joint made.

WARNING: The epoxy fillers and glues that are best for ski repairs are also potentially hazardous and should be treated with caution. (See box, p. 223.)

STORING SKIS: Always clean skis before storing them for any extended period. Never store wood skis with base wood showing through: tar bases to a chocolate brown before storage, as exposed wood can absorb moisture, which destroys ski camber. Plastic bases can be stored with no further treatment, provided they are clean. High-performance polyethylene bases should be base-prepared with paraffin wax before storage. Some expert skiers simply apply the paraffin hot wax in the spring, and scrape in the fall when they take the skis out of storage.

EPOXY WISE

"Epoxy" actually isn't a substance. It's a chemist's shorthand name for a certain way that molecules can link together. Many different molecules of different materials can classify as "epoxy resins," the basic materials of the type used to bond synthetic fibers in laminates, and laminates together in skis and poles. Epoxy resins alone are useless. The properties that promote their use in ski and pole manufacture are brought about only when the resin is "cured" or "hardened" by other kinds of chemicals called, naturally, curing agents or hardeners.

The Public Health Service has identified epoxy resins and their hardening agents as occupational health hazards, causing allergies by sensitization, eye injuries, rashes, burns, unconsciousness, and other illnesses. Even though you may never use epoxies in an occupational situation, you should observe the safety rules for their use, even if only repairing your gear with commonly available, two-component "epoxy glue" or "epoxy filler."

Among the recommended safety procedures for using epoxies are:

- Don't be careless. Treat all products with caution.

- Don't let any of the products get or stay on your clothes. Stay clean.

- Don't take a chance on any material or spray getting into your eyes. Wear safety glasses.

- Don't inhale vapors of any solvents, resins, hardeners, or dilutants. Beware of dusts and powders from grinding or sanding. Ventilate well.

- Don't gamble with fire. Work away from all possible sources of ignition—cigarettes, lighters, open electrical heaters or motors, open flames, etc.

- Don't assume anything is clean enough. Keep contaminated hands, gloves, clothes away from eyes and mouth.

- Dispose of stirrers, mixing boards, and the like. Don't let your tools turn on you.

- Always read and follow the safety-warning-hazard statements on product package labels.

- Keep all tubes, containers, etc., covered. Don't chance a fire.

Recommended first aid:

EYE CONTACT. Wash/flush the eyes immediately with low-pressure flowing water for at least 15 minutes. Be sure the entire eye surface is flushed. Get medical attention at once.

SKIN CONTACT. Remove contaminated clothing at once. Use disposable wiping tissue or towels to take syrupy or thick liquids off the skin before cleaning. Clean skin immediately with soap and water or waterless hand cleaner. Do not use solvents to clean the skin. If there is any sign of redness, itching, or a burn, get medical attention promptly. Discard, do not reuse, contaminated leather articles (belts, shoes, watch straps).

DIZZINESS, NAUSEA, BLACKOUT from breathing of vapors: Get yourself or the affected person into fresh air immediately. Know how to administer and be ready to use artificial respiration if breathing should stop. Get medical attention immediately.

ILLNESS, NAUSEA from swallowing: Get medical attention immediately.

Want to know more? Obtain HEW Publication No. (NIOSH) 76-152, "Epoxy Wise is Health Wise," U.S. Department of Health, Education and Welfare, National Institute for Occupational Safety and Health.

All quality skis will retain their camber and stiffness in storage, regardless of whether they stand, lie, or are in any other position. Always store skis in a dry, cool place where temperatures do not go above 35°C. (95°F.).

14

HISTORY IN A NUTSHELL, MAJOR RACE RESULTS

Chronological Overview of Cross-Country Skiing in North America

Woodcut title page of Johan Scheffer's *The History of Lapland,* first published in 1674. *Reproduction courtesy of University Library, Oslo, Norway.*

The following is a chronological overview of cross-country skiing in North America, starting in 1840 when Norwegian miners first used skis in California. Ski history, which dates back some 4,500 years, is a subject in itself. For more on history, see the references listed.

CHRONOLOGY OF NORTH AMERICAN CROSS-COUNTRY SKIING

YEAR	EVENT
1840	Norwegian miners ski in California
1850	Miners organize downhill ski races in California
1856	"Snowshoe" Thompson carries mail over mountains in California
1861	Trysil Ski and Gun Club, world's first, founded in Norway
1872	Nansen Ski Club, first in United States, founded in Berlin, N.Y.
1883	Foreningen til Ski-Idrettens Fremme (Society for the Furtherance of Ski Sports), world's first ski-competition organization, formed in Oslo
1886	Aurora Ski Club founded in Red Wing, Minnesota, by 28 Norwegians
1887	Single pole replaced by two
1888	Fridtjof Nansen leads ski expedition across Greenland
1888	First 50-km cross-country ski race, Huseby meet (forerunner of Holmenkollen meet)
1890	First ski developed especially for cross-country ski racing
1890	First ski races in Colorado
1891	First laminated ski developed by H. M. Christiansen
1892	First Holmenkollen meet
1892	First toe binding developed by Svein Övergaard

1870s skier in Kiandra, Australia. *Courtesy J. Vaage archive.*

The first Holmenkollen was a combined meet (reenactment, 1979 centennial). *Jan Greve*

1894	First toepiece developed by Fritz Huifeldt
1902	Skis first listed in U.S. catalog, Alex Taylor of New York: ladies' skis $5, gentlemen's skis $8
1903	First ski wax sold, "Record" tar wax made by Thomas Hansen
1904	First U.S. national ski meet, jumping in Ishpeming, Michigan
1908	Norwegian Ski Federation, world's first, founded
1910	Dartmouth College Ski Club, first U.S. collegiate skiing, founded
1910	First women's cross-country, Auran Club in Finland
1910	First international ski congress in Oslo, The International Ski Commission, founded
1914	Klister patented by Peter Östbye
1920	First 3-layer laminated ski
1922	First Vasaloppet from Sälen to Mora in Sweden, 85.6 km (54 miles) long
1924	The International Ski Commission disbanded, FIS founded
1924	Toe irons patented by Marius Eriksen
1924	First Winter Olympics in Chamonix, France; Norwegian Thorleif Haug becomes world's first triple-gold-medal winner by winning 18-km and 50-km cross-country and Nordic combined, as well as taking bronze in jumping
1926	Rottefella binding patented by Bror With
1932	Winter Olympics in Lake Placid, N.Y., first time in United States
1933	Multilaminated skis patented by Splitkein
1933	First cross-country FIS relay, 4 × 10 km for men, Innsbruck, Austria
1939–40	First modern wartime victory for ski infantry, in Finnish-Russian "Winter War": Under Field Marshal Mannerheim, outnumbered Finnish ski troops successfully repulse invading Russians at Lake Ladoga, Suomussalmi, Salla, and Ivalo

Historic Finnish cross-country photo. Handwritten text on back of original: "Old-fashioned skirt and modern knickers clothing for cross-country girls. No. 102 is Elsa Kumpulainen, twice Finnish champ., no. 132 is Miina Huttunan, four times Finnish champ. Picture taken in 1923." *Courtesy Aamulehti of Tampere archive.*

1942–45	U.S. Army Tenth Mountain Division established and trains in Colorado and Alaska, first U.S. ski troops
1948	First international cross-country for women, Sweden vs. Finland
1948	Military patrol dropped as Winter Olympic event
1952	First women's cross-country in Winter Olympics, Oslo, 10 km
1954	First women's 10 km and 3 × 5 km relay in FIS, Falun, Sweden
1954	Men's 18-km race shortened to 15 km
1958	First world biathlon (cross-country ski racing and shooting) championships held in Austria
1960	Winter Olympics in Squaw Valley, California, second time in USA. Biathlon becomes Olympic event, with 20-km race
1962	Women cross-country skiers get three international events: 10 km, 5 km, and 3 × 5 km relay, in FIS, Zakopane, Poland;

BELOW. Alevtina Koltjina of Russia, the first woman skier ever to win three World Ski Championship events: 1962 FIS Nordic World Ski Championship 5 km, 10 km and 3 × 5 km relay races. *NTB*

ABOVE. Auran Club, Lemi, Finland, cross-country ski team, circa 1910. This is the first known photo of women on a cross-country ski team. *Courtesy Aamulehti of Tampere archive.*

Alevtina Koltchina, USSR, wins three gold medals in cross-country

1966	First World Biathlon Championships relay
1968	John Bower wins Holmenkollen Nordic Combined King's Cup, first American to win major international Nordic meet
1970	First major pattern-type waxless ski introduced
1970	First U.S. women in FIS Nordic World Ski Championships, Vysoké Tatry, Czechoslovakia
1971–72	Cross-country ski renaissance in United States: 350,000 pairs of cross-country skis sold in 1972 vs. 170,000 pairs in 1971, twenty times as many as in 1966
1972	Colorado voters reject 1976 Denver Winter Olympics on state referendum; International Olympic Committee picks Innsbruck, Austria, as site for XIIth Olympic Winter Games
1972	Winter Olympics in Sapporo, Japan, first time in Asia

Gjermund Eggen of Norway, the first cross-country
man to win three World Ski Championship events,
1966 FIS 15 km, 50 km, and 4 × 10 km relay races.
A-Foto

King Olav V of Norway, himself once a noted
Holmenkollen competitor, congratulating John
Bower, U.S.A., for winning the 1968 Holmenkollen
Nordic Combined King's Cup. *A-Foto*

Tim Caldwell, USA, just after placing second in the 1973 Holmenkollen 15-km race for juniors, then the best U.S. cross-country result to date. *Michael Brady*

Allison Owen and Martha Rockwell in the 1974 FIS World Ski Championships 4 × 5 km relay, Falun, Sweden, the first four-lap event for U.S. women skiers. *Michael Brady*

1973	First "American Birkebeiner" citizens' race, Cable, Wisconsin; forerunner of "World Loppet League"
1973	U.S. Army drops biathlon program
1974	Women's 3 × 5 km relay replaced by 4 × 5 km relay. Russian Galina Kulakova becomes world's first skier to twice win all events, repeating her 1972 Winter Olympic performance in the FIS Nordic World Ski Championships, Falun, Sweden; first major race wins on fiberglass skis
1974	First 10-km individual World Biathlon Championship race
1974	First World Cup in Cross-Country Ski Racing, won by Ivor Formo of Norway; second Juha Mieto of Finland; third Edi Hauser of Switzerland
1976	Winter Olympics held in Innsbruck, Austria, assigned by IOC after Denver default. Bill Koch places second in 30-km race, first American to win Olympic medal in cross-country. "Snout" boots and toeclip bindings first used in international racing
1978	First women's 20-km race in FIS Nordic World Ski Championships, Lahti, Finland
1978	New biathlon range standards: .22-caliber rifles on 50 meter range replace 5.6–8 mm (6.5 mm most common) rifles on 150 meter range
1979	First major international meet medal by racer using modern waxless skis: Norwegian Per Knut Aaland finishes second in Holmenkollen 50 km.
1980	Winter Olympics in Lake Placid, New York, for second time; third time in USA. Swede Thomas Wassberg wins 15-km race by one hundreth of a second, closest ever in cross-country ski racing
1980	First World Ski Championship 20-km race for women, Falun, Sweden
1980	U.S. ski explorer Ned Gillette twice in China, to teach cross-country skiing in Harbin in East, and to ski mountaineer on Muztagata peak in West; first western expedition so admitted to China

Bill Koch on his way to a silver medal in the 1976
Winter Olympic 30-km race, Seefeld, Austria; first
winter Olympic cross-country medal for U.S. skier.
Michael Brady

1978 centennial of the Holmenkollen meet, oldest in
skiing. Racer is Allison Owen, USA. *Michael Brady*

1981   Nordic downhill, called "Norpine" or
"Telemarking," well established in USA,
national championships held

1981   FIS officially recognizes and establishes
Cross Country World Cup on permanent
basis

1981   Bill Koch wins Engadin Ski Marathon in

Switzerland, first American to win
international "World Loppet" race

1982   FIS Nordic World Ski Championships in
Oslo, Norway, fourth time

1982   FIS Nordic World Ski Championship in
Oslo, Norway, fourth time for city. Bill
Koch wins Bronze medal in 30-km race;
his second WSC medal and second ever

Berit Aunli won three Gold and one Silver medal in the 1982 World Ski Championships, the most ever, anywhere, anytime, in any skiing discipline, for a competitor in World Championship skiing. Here she's racing the 20 km, in which she placed second and took the Silver medal, just 3.4 seconds behind the winner in a race lasting 1 hour and 6 minutes. *Michael Brady*

Skiers Tom Carter and Alan Bard on the Southern Cross Expedition, New Zealand, in 1979, the first major Alpine-type traverse. *Ned Gillette*

for a US racer in WSC cross-country. Norwegian Berit Aunli wins three Gold and one Silver medals in women's cross-country; most ever for any racer, anytime in a single Championships. Nordic Combined Team event added to program. Closest cross-country races ever: three dead heats in the relays in men's 4×10 km relay, Russia and Norway both awarded Gold; Finland and East Germany both awarded Bronze. In combined team event, Norway and Finland both awarded Silver. Americans become first racers ever from same country to win both official FIS cross-country and Alpine ski racing World Cups: Bill Koch from Vermont in cross-country, and Phil Mahre from Washington in Alpine.

THE BEST IN FIS WORLD SKI CHAMPIONSHIPS AND WINTER OLYMPICS

The International Ski Federation (FIS) is responsible for the skiing events of the Olympic Winter Games, held in leap years, and the FIS World Championships, held in even-numbered years between Olympic years. The FIS also arranged "Rendez-vous" races from 1925 to 1927, and "FIS-races" from 1928 to 1936.

The Olympic Winter Games are numbered consecutively with Roman numerals, starting with the first held in Chamonix in 1924. Following a 1965 FIS decision, all international races arranged by the FIS are regarded as world ski championships and are numbered consecutively starting with number one for the 1924 Olympic Winter Games.

The six best placings in the Olympic Winter Games (OWG), "Rendez-vous Race" (R-v-R), FIS race (FIS) and modern FIS World Ski Championships (no notation) are listed below. The international abbreviations for countries are:

AUT Austria	FIN Finland	SOV Russia
BRD W. Germany	FRA France	SUI Switzerland
BUL Bulgaria	ITA Italy	SWE Sweden
CAN Canada	GER Germany	USA United States
TCH Czechoslovakia	NOR Norway	
DDR E. Germany	POL Poland	

Men's Cross-Country

No.	Year	Country	Site	18 km		30 km		50 km	
1	1924	FRA	Chamonix	1 Th. Haug	NOR			1 Th. Haug	NOR
			OWG	2 J. Gröttumsbraaten	NOR			2 Th. Strömstad	NOR
			I	3 T. Niku	FIN			3 J. Gröttumsbraaten	NOR
				4 J. Maardalen	NOR			4 J. Maardalen	NOR
				5 E. Landvik	NOR			5 T. Persson	SWE
				6 P.-E. Hedlund	SWE			6 E. Alm	SWE
2	1925	TCH	Johannisbad	1 O. Nemecky	TCH			1 Fr. Donth	TCH
			R-v-R	2 Fr. Donth	TCH			2 Fr. Häckel	TCH
				3 J. Erleback	TCH			3 A. Ettrich	TCH
				4 J. Adolf	TCH			4 J. Adolf	TCH
				5 J. Bräth	TCH			5 J. Erleback	TCH
				6 G. Ghedina	ITA			6 J. Nemecky	TCH
3	1926	FIN	Lahti			1 M. Raivio	FIN	1 M. Raivio	FIN
			R-v-R			2 T. Lappalainen	FIN	2 T. Lappalainen	FIN
						3 V. Saarinen	FIN	3 O. Kjellbotn	NOR
						4 G. Jonsson	SWE	4 O. Hegge	NOR
						5 S. Åström	SWE	5 G. Jonsson	SWE
						6 M. Lappalainen	FIN	6 T. Niku	FIN
4	1927	ITA	Cortina	1 J. Lindgren	SWE			1 J. Lindgren	SWE
			d'Ampezzo	2 Fr. Donth	TCH			2 J. Wikström	SWE
			R-v-R	3 V. Schneider	GER			3 Fr. Donth	TCH
				4 J. Wikström	SWE			4 V. Demetz	ITA
				5 G. Müller	GER			5 H. Theato	GER
				6 E. Huber	GER			6 J. Nemecky	TCH
5	1928	SUI	St. Moritz	1 J. Gröttumsbraaten	NOR			1 P.-E. Hedlund	SWE
			OWG	2 O. Hegge	NOR			2 G. Jonsson	SWE
			II	3 R. Ödegaard	NOR			3 V. Andersson	SWE
				4 V. Saarinen	FIN			4 O. Kjellbotn	NOR
				5 H. Haakonsen	NOR			5 O. Hegge	NOR
				6 P.-E. Hedlund	SWE			6 T. Lappalainen	FIN

NO.	YEAR	COUNTRY	SITE	18 KM		50 KM		RELAY, 4 × 10 KM
6	1929	POL	Zakopane	1 V. Saarinen	FIN	1 A. Knuttila	FIN	
			FIS	2 A. Knuttila	FIN	2 V. Saarinen	FIN	
				3 Hj. Bergström	SWE	3 O. Hansson	SWE	
				4 O. Hansson	SWE	4 V. Liikanen	FIN	
				5 G. Jonsson	SWE	5 G. Jonsson	SWE	
				6 H. Haakonsen	NOR	6 Hj. Bergström	SWE	
7	1930	NOR	Oslo	1 A. Rustadstuen	NOR	1 S. Utterström	SWE	
			FIS	2 T. Brodahl	NOR	2 A. Rustadstuen	NOR	
				3 T. Lappalainen	FIN	3 A. Paananen	FIN	
				4 K. Hovde	NOR	4 M. Lappalainen	FIN	
				5 V. Saarinen	FIN	5 M.P. Vangli	NOR	
				6 M. Lappalainen	FIN	6 V. Saarinen	FIN	
8	1931	GER	Oberhof	1 J. Gröttumsbraaten	NOR	1 O. Stenen	NOR	
			FIS	2 Chr. Hovde	NOR	2 P. Vangli	NOR	
				3 N. Svärd	SWE	3 K. Lindberg	SWE	
				4 K. Lindberg	SWE	4 N. Svärd	SWE	
				5 H. Vikzell	SWE	5 Chr. Hovde	NOR	
				6 P. Vangli	NOR	6 H. Vikzell	SWE	
9	1932	USA	Lake Placid	1 S. Utterström	SWE	1 V. Saarinen	FIN	
			OWG	2 A. Wikström	SWE	2 V. Liikanen	FIN	
			III	3 V. Saarinen	FIN	3 A. Rustadstuen	NOR	
				4 M. Lappalainen	FIN	4 O. Hegge	NOR	
				5 A. Rustadstuen	NOR	5 S. Vestad	NOR	
				6 J. Gröttumsbraaten	NOR	6 S. Utterström	SWE	
10	1933	AUT	Innsbruck	1 N. Englund	SWE	1 V. Saarinen	FIN	1 SWE (P.-E. Hedlund,
			FIS	2 Hj. Bergström	SWE	2 S. Utterström	SWE	S. Utterström,
				3 V. Liikanen	FIN	3 Hj. Bergström	SWE	N. Englund,
				4 V. Saarinen	FIN	4 V. Liikanen	FIN	Hj. Bergström)
				5 S. Utterström	SWE	5 J.A. Persson	SWE	2 TCH (Svaz)
				6 F. Däuber	GER	6 P.-E. Hedlund	SWE	(F. Simunck, V. Novak,
								A. Barton,
								C. Musil)
								3 AUT (H. Gstrein,
								H. Gadner,
								B. Niederkofler,
								H. Paumgarten)
								4 GER (W. Motz,
								W. Bogner, J. Ponn,
								H. Leupold)
								5 ITA (F. de Zulian,
								E. Vuerich, S. Seilligo,
								S. Menardi)
								6 TCH (HDW) (F. Lauer,
								F. Kraus, A. Horn,
								F. Semptner)
11	1934	SWE	Sollefteá	1 S. Nurmela	FIN	1 E. Wiklund	SWE	1 FIN (S. Nurmela,
			FIS	2 V. Saarinen	FIN	2 N. Englund	SWE	K. Karppinen,
				3 M. Lappalainen	FIN	3 O. Remes	FIN	M. Lappalainen,
				4 A. Häggblad	SWE	4 A. Häggblad	SWE	V. Saarinen)
				5 K. Karppinen	FIN	5 J. Wikström	SWE	2 GER (W. Motz,

NO.	YEAR	COUNTRY	SITE	18 KM		50 KM		RELAY, 4 × 10 KM
				6 O. Hagen	NOR	6 H. Wikström	SWE	J. Schweiner,
								W. Bogner, H. Leupold)
								3 SWE (A. Karlsson,
								L. Th. Jonsson,
								N. Englund,
								A. Häggblad)
								4 NOR (L. Bergendahl,
								O. Hoffsbakken,
								H. Vinjarengen,
								O. Hagen)
								5 POL (B. Czech,
								S. Karpiel, S. Marusarz,
								A. Marusarz)
								5 teams started
12	1935	TCH	Hohe Tatra	1 K. Karppinen	FIN	1 N. Englund	SWE	1 FIN (M. Husu,
			FIS	2 O. Hagen	NOR	2 K. Karppinen	FIN	K Karppinen,
				3 O. Hoffsbakken	NOR	3 S. Brodahl	NOR	V. Liikunen,
				4 S. Vestad	NOR	4 M. Husu	FIN	S. Nurmela)
				5 M. Matsbo	SWE	5 K. Ogi	SUI	2 NOR (S. Brodahl,
				6 B. Iversen	NOR	6 M. Matsbo	SWE	B. Iversen,
								O. Hoffsbakken,
								O. Hagen)
								3 SWE (H. Moritz,
								E. Larsson,
								M. Matsbo,
								N. Englund)
								4 GER (M. Wörndle,
								H. Leupold, W. Motz,
								W. Bogner)
								5 TCH (Svaz) (C. Musil,
								B. Kudery, F. Simunek,
								A. Barton)
								6 TCH (HDW)
								(G. Berauer, F. Kraus,
								J. Ackermann,
								O. Berauer)
13	1936	GER	Garmisch-	1 E. Larsson	SWE	1 E. Wiklund	SWE	1 FIN (S. Nurmela,
			Parten-	2 O. Hagen	NOR	2 A. Wikström	SWE	K. Karppinen,
			kirchen	3 P. Niemi	FIN	3 N. Englund	SWE	M. Lähde,
			OWG	4 M. Matsbo	SWE	4 H. Bergström	SWE	K. Jalkanen)
			IV	5 O. Hoffsbakken	NOR	5 K. Karppinen	FIN	2 NOR (O. Hagen,
				6 A. Rustadstuen	NOR	6 A. Tuft	NOR	O. Hoffsbakken,
								S. Brodahl, B. Iversen)
								3 SWE (J. Berger,
								E. Larsson, A. Häggblad,
								M. Matsbo)
								4 ITA (G. Gerardi,
								S. Menardi, V. Demetz,
								G. Kasebacher)
								5 TCH (C. Musil,
								G. Berauer, L. Mihalak,
								F. Simonek)

NO.	YEAR	COUNTRY	SITE	18 KM		30 KM		50 KM		RELAY, 4 × 10 KM
										6 GER (F. Däuber, W. Bogner, H. Leupold, T. Zellev)
14	1937	FRA	Chamonix	1 L. Bergendahl	NOR	1 P. Niemi	FIN			1 NOR (A. Ryen, O. Fredriksen, S. Röen, L. Bergendahl)
				2 K. Jalkanen	FIN	2 K. Karppinen	FIN			2 FIN (P. Niemi, K. Karppinen, J. Kurikkala, K. Jalkanen)
				3 P. Niemi	FIN	3 V. Demetz	ITA			3 ITA (G. Gerardi, A. Compagnoni, S. Confortola, V. Demetz)
				4 S. Hansson	SWE	4 K. Jalkanen	FIN			4 SWE (S. Hansson, B. Stridsman, A. Hägglund, A. Dahlqvist)
				5 J. Kurikkala	FIN	5 L. Bergendahl	NOR			5 TCH (C. Musil, G. Berauer, R. Vrana, F. Simonek)
				6 A. Dahlqvist	SWE	6 F. Smoleij	JUG			6 SUI (A. Freiburghaus, J. Sonderegger, E. Berger, A. Limascher)
15	1938	FIN	Lahti	1 P. Pitkänen	FIN	1 K. Jalkanen	FIN			1 FIN (J. Kurikkala, M. Lauronen, P. Pitkänen, K. Karppinen)
				2 A. Dahlqvist	SWE	2 A. Rantalahti	FIN			2 NOR (R. Ringstad, O. Ökern, A. Larsen, L. Bergendahl)
				3 K. Jalkanen	FIN	3 L. Bergendahl	NOR			3 SWE (S. Hansson, D. Johansson, S. Nilsson, M. Matsbo)
				4 M. Matsbo	SWE	4 P. Niemi	FIN			4 SUI (A. Freiburghaus, A. Gamma, E. Anderegg, E. Soguel)
				5 M. Lauronen	FIN	5 K. Karppinen	FIN			5 GER (E. Haberle, G. Merlz, W. Bogner, H. Leupold)
				6 J. Kurikkala	FIN	6 T. Tiainen	FIN			6 ITA (G. Gerardi, G. Bauer, A. Jammeron, V. Demetz)
16	1939	POL	Zakopane	1 J. Kurikkala	FIN			1 L. Bergendahl	NOR	1 FIN (P. Pitkänen, O. Alakulppi, E. Olkinuora, K. Karppinen)
				2 K. Karppinen	FIN			2 K. Karppinen	FIN	2 SWE (A. Hägglund, S. Stenvall,
				3 C. Pahlin	SWE			3 O. Gjöslien	NOR	
				4 K. Jalkanen	FIN			4 P. Vanninen	FIN	
				5 L. Bergendahl	NOR			5 P. Niemi	FIN	
				6 P. Niemi	FIN			6 A. Hägglund	SWE	

							J. Westbergh, C. Pahlin)
							3 ITA (A. Compagnoni, S. Compagnoni, G. Bauer, A. Jammeron)
							4 NOR (O. Odden, M. Fosseide, E. Evensen, O. Hoffsbakken)
							5 SUI (A. Freiburghaus, E. Soguel, V. Borghi, A. Gamma)
							6 GER (G. Lochbihler, R. Wöss, L. Bach, A. Burk)
17	1948	SUI	St. Moritz OWG V	1 M. Lundström SWE 2 N. Östensson SWE 3 G. Eriksson SWE 4 H. Hasu FIN 5 N. Karlsson SWE 6 S. Rytky FIN		1 N. Karlsson SWE 2 H. Eriksson SWE 3 B. Vanninen FIN 4 P. Vanninen FIN 5 A. Törnkvist SWE 6 E. Schild SUI	1 SWE (N. Östensson, N. Täpp, G. Eriksson, M. Lundström) 2 FIN (L. Silvennoinen, T. Laukkanen, S. Rytky, A. Kiuru) 3 NOR (E. Evensen, O. Ökern, R. Nyborg, O. Hagen) 4 AUT (J. Gstrein, J. Deutschmann, E. Hundertpfund, C. Rafreiden) 5 SUI (N. Stump, R. Zurbriggen, M. Müller, E. Schild) 6 ITA (V. Perruchon, S. Confortola, R. Rodighiero, S. Compagnoni)
18	1950	USA	Lake Placid Rumford	1 K.-E. Åström SWE 2 E. Josefsson SWE 3 A. Nyaas NOR 4 A. Kiuru FIN 5 P. Lonkila FIN		1 G. Eriksson SWE 2 E. Josefsson SWE 3 N. Karlsson SWE 4 A. Törnkvist SWE 5 H. Maartmann NOR	1 SWE (N. Täpp, K.-E. Åström, M. Lundström, E. Josefsson) 2 FIN (H. Hasu,

| --- | --- | --- | --- | --- | --- | --- | --- | --- | --- | --- |
				6 V. Vellonen	FIN			6 P. Vanninen	FIN	V. Vellonen,
										P. Lonkila,
										A. Kiuru)
										3 NOR (M. Stokken,
										E. Dahl, K. Björn,
										H. Hermansen)
										4 FRA (M. Mora,
										G. Forestier,
										R. Mandrillon,
										B. Carrara)
										5 USA (S. Dunklee,
										R. Townsend,
										L. Hawkenson,
										D. Johnson)
										6 CAN (C. Richer,
										I. Wahlberg,
										A. Alain,
										T. Dennie)
19	1952	NOR	Oslo	1 H. Brenden	NOR			1 V. Hakulinen	FIN	1 FIN (H. Hasu,
			OWG	2 T. Mäkelä	FIN			2 E. Kolehmainen	FIN	P. Lonkila,
			VI	3 P. Lonkila	FIN			3 M. Estenstad	NOR	Korhonen,
				4 H. Hasu	FIN			4 O. Ökern	NOR	T. Mäkelä)
				5 N. Karlsson	SWE			5 K. Mononen	FIN	2 NOR
				6 M. Stokken	NOR			6 N. Karlsson	SWE	(M. Estenstad,
										M. Kirkholt,
										M. Stokken,
										P. Brenden)
										3 SWE (N. Täpp,
										S. Andersson,
										E. Josefsson,
										M. Lundström)
										4 FRA (G. Perrier,
										B. Carrara,
										J. Mermet,
										R. Mandrillon)
										5 AUT (H. Eder,
										F. Krischan,
										C. Rafreider,
										J. Schneeberger)
										6 ITA (A. Delladio,
										N. Anderlini,
										F. deFlorian,
										V. Perruchon)
				15 km						1 FIN (A. Kiuru,
20	1954	SWE	Falun	1 V. Hakulinen	FIN	1 V. Kusin	SOV	1 V. Kusin	SOV	T. Mäkelä,
				2 A. Viitanen	FIN	2 V. Hakulinen	FIN	2 V. Hakulinen	FIN	A. Viitanen,
				3 A. Kiuru	FIN	3 M. Lautala	FIN	3 A. Viitanen	FIN	V. Hakulinen)
				4 F. Terentjev	SOV	4 S. Jernberg	SWE	4 M. Stokken	NOR	2 SOV (N. Koslov,
				5 T. Mäkelä	FIN	5 T. Sipilä	FIN	5 E. Landsem	NOR	F. Terentjev,
				6 V. Räsänen	FIN	6 E. Tilli	FIN	6 F. Terentjev	SOV	A. Kusnetsov,
										V. Kusin)
										3 SWE (S. Larsson,

No.	Year	Country	Site	15 km		30 km		50 km		Relay, 4 × 10 km
										S. Jernberg,
										A. Olsson,
										P.-E. Larsson)
										4 NOR
										(H. Brusveen,
										O. Lykkja,
										M. Stokken,
										H. Brenden)
										5 ITA
										(V. Cchiocchetti,
										A. Delladio,
										F. deFlorian,
										O. Compagnoni)
										6 FRA
										(R. Mandrillon,
										S. Mercier,
										J. Mermet,
										B. Carrara)
21	1956	ITA	Cortina	1 H. Brenden	NOR	1 V. Hakulinen	FIN	1 S. Jernberg	SWE	1 SOV (F. Terentjev,
			d'Ampezzo	2 S. Jernberg	SWE	2 S. Jernberg	SWE	2 V. Hakulinen	FIN	P. Kolchin,
			OWG	3 P. Kolchin	SOV	3 P. Kolchin	SOV	3 F. Terentjev	SOV	N. Anikin,
			VII	4 V. Hakulinen	FIN	4 A. Sheljukhin	SOV	4 E. Kolehmainen	FIN	V. Kusin)
				5 H. Brusveen	NOR	5 V. Kusin	SOV	5 A. Sheljukhin	SOV	2 FIN (A. Kiuru,
				6 M. Stokken	NOR	6 F. Terentjev	SOV	6 P. Kolchin	SOV	J. Kortelainen,
										A. Viitanen,
										V. Hakulinen)
										3 SWE (L. Larsson,
										G. Samuelsson,
										P.-E. Larsson,
										S. Jernberg)
										4 NOR
										(H. Brusveen,
										P. Olsen,
										M. Stokken,
										H. Brenden)
										5 ITA (P. Fattor,
										O. Compagnoni,
										I. Chatrian,
										F. deFlorian)
										6 FRA (V. Arbez,
										R. Mandrillon,
										B. Carrara,
										J. Mermet)
22	1958	FIN	Lahti	1 V. Hakulinen	FIN	1 K. Hämäläinen	FIN	1 S. Jernberg	SWE	1 SWE (S. Jernberg,
				2 P. Koltjin	SOV	2 P. Koltjin	SOV	2 V. Hakulinen	FIN	L. Larsson,
				3 A. Sheljukhin	SOV	3 S. Jernberg	SWE	3 A. Viitanen	FIN	S. Grahn,
				4 S. Jernberg	SWE	4 A. Viitanen	FIN	4 A. Tiainen	FIN	P.-E. Larsson)
				5 H. Brusveen	NOR	5 A. Tiainen	FIN	5 E. Kolehmainen	FIN	2 SOV (F. Terentjev,
				6 F. Terentjev	SOV	6 V. Hakulinen	FIN	6 P. Koltjin	SOV	N. Anikin,
										A. Sheljukhin,
										P. Koltjin)

No.	Year	Country	Site	15 km	30 km	50 km	Relay, 4 × 10 km
							3 FIN (K. Hämäläinen, A. Tiainen, A. Viitanen, V. Hakulinen)
							4 NOR (H. Brenden, O. Jensen, M. Stokken, H. Brusveen)
							5 ITA (F. deFlorian, O. Compagnoni, M. deFlorian, G. Steiner)
							6 FRA (V. Arbez, R. Mandrillon, B. Carrara, J. Mermet)
23	1960	USA	Squaw Valley OWG VIII	1 H. Brusveen NOR 2 S. Jernberg SWE 3 V. Hakulinen FIN 4 G. Vaganov SOV 5 E. Östby NOR 6 E. Mäntyranta FIN	1 S. Jernberg SWE 2 R. Rämgård SWE 3 N. Anikin SOV 4 G. Vaganov SOV 5 L. Larsson SWE 6 V. Hakulinen FIN	1 K. Hämäläinen FIN 2 V. Hakulinen FIN 3 R. Rämgård SWE 4 L. Larsson SWE 5 S. Jernberg SWE 6 P. Pelkonen FIN	1 FIN (T. Alatalo, E. Mäntyranta, V. Huhtala, V. Hakulinen) 2 NOR (H. Grönningen, H. Brenden, E. Östby, H. Brusveen) 3 SOV (A. Sheljukhin, G. Vaganov, A. Kuznetsov, N. Anikin) 4 SWE (L. Olsson, J. Stefansson, L. Larsson, S. Jernberg) 5 ITA (G. deFlorian, G. Steiner, P. Fattor, M. deDorigo) 6 POL (A. Meteja, J. Rysula, J. Gut-Misiaga, K. Zelek)

No.	Year	Country	Site	15 km	30 km	50 km	Relay, 4 × 10 km
24	1962	POL	Zakopane	1 A. Rönnlund SWE 2 H. Grönningen NOR 3 E. Östby NOR 4 M. Lundemo NOR 5 E. Mäntyranta FIN 6 J. Stefansson SWE	1 E. Mäntyranta FIN 2 J. Stefansson SWE 3 G. deFlorian ITA 4 H. Grönningen NOR 5 E. Östby NOR 6 A. Rönnlund SWE	1 S. Jernberg SWE 2 A. Rönnlund SWE 3 K. Hämäläinen FIN 4 A. Tiainen FIN 5 H. Grönningen NOR 6 J. Stefansson SWE	1 SWE (L. Olsson, S. Grahn, S. Jernberg, A. Rönnlund) 2 FIN (V. Huhtala, K. Laurila, P. Pesonen, E. Mäntyranta)

No.	Year	Country	Site	15 km	30 km	50 km	Relay, 4 × 10 km
							3 SOV (J. Utrobin, P. Koltjin, A. Kuznetsov, G. Vaganov)
							4 NOR (M. Lundemo, H. Brenden, E. Östby, H. Grönningen)
							5 ITA (G. Steiner, G. Stella, M. deDorigo, G. deFlorian)
							6 FRA (F. Mathieu, R. Secretant, V. Arbez, J. Mermet)
25	1964	AUT	Innsbruck OWG IX	1 E. Mäntyranta FIN 2 H. Grönningen NOR 3 S. Jernberg SWE 4 V. Huhtala FIN 5 J. Stefansson SWE 6 P. Koltjin SOV	1 E. Mäntyranta FIN 2 H. Grönningen NOR 3 I. Voronchikhin SOV 4 J. Stefansson SWE 5 S. Jernberg SWE 6 K. Laurila FIN	1 S. Jernberg SWE 2 A. Rönnlund SWE 3 A. Tiainen FIN 4 J. Stefansson SWE 5 S. Stensheim NOR 6 H. Grönningen NOR	1 SWE (K.-A. Asph, S. Jernberg, J. Stefansson, A. Rönnlund) 2 FIN (V. Huhtala, A. Tiainen, K. Laurila, E. Mäntyranta) 3 SOV (I. Utrobin, G. Vaganov, I. Voronchikhin, P. Koltjin) 4 NOR (M. Lundemo, E. Steineide, E. Östby, H. Grönningen) 5 ITA (G. Steiner, M. de Dorigo, G. deFlorian, F. Nones) 6 FRA (V. Arbez, F. Mathieu, R. Pires, P. Romand)
26	1966	NOR	Oslo	1 Gj. Eggen NOR 2 O. Ellefsaeter NOR 3 O. Martinsen NOR 4 Bj. Andersson SWE 5 K. Laurila FIN 6 E. Mäntyranta FIN	1 E. Mäntyranta FIN 2 K. Laurila FIN 3 W. Demel BRD 4 I. Sandström SWE 5 A. Akentjev SOV 6 F. Nones ITA	1 Gj. Eggen NOR 2 A. Tiainen FIN 3 E. Mäntyranta FIN 4 O. Ellefsaeter NOR 5 H. Taipale FIN 6 V. Vedenin SOV	1 NOR (O. Martinsen, H. Grönningen, O. Ellefsaeter, Gj. Eggen) 2 FIN (K. Oikarainen, H. Taipale, K. Laurila, E. Mäntyranta)

No.	Year	Country	Site	15 km		30 km		50 km		Relay, 4 × 10 km
										3 ITA (G. deFlorian, F. Nones, G. Stella, F. Manfroi)
										4 SWE (Kj. Lidh, Bj. Andersson, K.-Å. Asph, I. Sandström)
										5 SOV (I. Utrobin, V. Vedenin, A. Nasedkin, A. Akentjev)
										6 SUI (K. Hischief, J. Haas, D. Mast, A. Kaelin)
27	1968	FRA	Grenoble OWG X	1 H. Grönningen	NOR	1 F. Nones	ITA	1 O. Ellefsaeter	NOR	1 NOR (O. Martinsen, P. Tyldum, H. Grönningen, O. Ellefsaeter)
				2 E. Mäntyranta	FIN	2 O. Martinsen	NOR	2 V. Vedenin	SOV	
				3 G. Larsson	SWE	3 E. Mäntyranta	FIN	3 J. Haas	SUI	
				4 K. Laurila	FIN	4 V. Voronkov	SOV	4 P. Tyldum	NOR	
				5 J. Halvarsson	SWE	5 G. deFlorian	ITA	5 M. Risberg	SWE	
				6 Bj. Andersson	SWE	6 K. Laurila	FIN	6 G. Larsson	SWE	2 SWE (J. Halvarsson, Bj. Andersson, G. Larsson, A. Rönnlund)
										3 FIN (K. Oikarainen, H. Taipale, K. Laurila, E. Mäntyranta)
										4 SOV (V. Voronkov, A. Akentjev, V. Tarakanov, V. Vedenin)
										5 SUI (K. Hischier, J. Haas, F. Koch, A. Kaelin)
										6 ITA (G. deFlorian, F. Nones, P. Serafini, G. Stella)
28	1970	TCH	Vysoké Tatry	1 L. G. Åslund	SWE	1 V. Vedenin	SOV	1 K. Oikarainen	FIN	1 SOV (V. Voronkov, V. Tarakanov, F. Simasov, V. Vedenin)
				2 O. Martinsen	NOR	2 G. Grimmer	DDR	2 V. Vedenin	SOV	
				3 F. Simasov	SOV	3 O. Martinsen	NOR	3 G. Grimmer	DDR	
				4 G. D. Klause	DDR	4 P. Tyldum	NOR	4 F. Simasov	SOV	
				5 P. Tyldum	NOR	5 G. D. Klause	DDR	5 L. G. Åslund	SWE	
				6 V. Tarakanov	SOV	6 L. G. Åslund	SWE	6 W. Demel	BRD	2 DDR (G. Hessler, A. Lesser, G. Grimmer, G. D. Klause)
										3 SWE (O. Lestander,

No.	Year	Country	Site	15 km		30 km		50 km		Relay, 4 × 10 km
										J. Halvarsson,
										I. Sandström,
										L. G. Åslund)
										4 NOR
										(O. Martinsen,
										H. Grönningen,
										P. Tyldum,
										E. Steinelde)
										5 SUI (W. Geeser,
										A. Giger, A. Kälin,
										E. Hauser)
										6 ITA (F. Nones,
										R. Primus,
										G. Stella,
										U. Kostner)
29	1972	JPN	Sapporo OWG XI	1 S.-A. Lundbäck	SWE	1 V. Vedenin	SOV	1 P. Tyldum	NOR	1 SOV
				2 F. Simaschov	SOV	2 P. Tyldum	NOR	2 M. Myrmo	NOR	(V. Voronkov,
				3 I. Formo	NOR	3 J. Harviken	NOR	3 V. Vedenin	SOV	Y. Skobov,
				4 J. Mieto	FIN	4 G. Larsson	SWE	4 R. Hjermstad	NOR	F. Simaschov,
				5 Y. Skobov	SOV	5 W. Demel	BRD	5 W. Demel	BRD	V. Vedenin)
				6 A. Lesser	DDR	6 F. Simaschov	SOV	6 W. Geeser	SUI	2 NOR (O. Braa,
										P. Tyldum,
										I. Formo,
										J. Harviken)
										3 SUI (A. Kälin,
										A. Giger, A. Kälin,
										E. Hauser)
										4 SWE
										(T. Magnusson,
										L.-G. Åslund,
										G. Larsson,
										S.-Å. Lundbäck)
										5 FIN (H. Taipale,
										J. Mieto, J. Repo,
										O. Karjalainen)
										6 DDR (G. Hessler,
										A. Lesser,
										G. Grimmer,
										G.-D. Klause)
30	1974	SWE	Falun	1 M. Myrmo	NOR	1 T. Magnusson	SWE	1 G. Grimmer	DDR	1 DDR (G. Hessler,
				2 G. Grimmer	DDR	2 J. Meito	FIN	2 S. Henych	TCH	D. Meinel,
				3 V. Rochev	SOV	3 J. Staszel	POL	3 T. Magnusson	SWE	G. Grimmer,
				4 J. Mieto	FIN	4 I. Garanin	SOV	4 S.-Å Lundbäck	SWE	G.-D. Klause)
				5 O. Braa	NOR	5 L.-G. Aslund	SWE	5 V. Rochev	SOV	2 SOV (I. Garanin,
				6 I. Formo	NOR	6 G. Grimmer	DDR	6 A. Biriukov	SOV	F. Simashev,
										V. Rochev,
										Y. Skobov)
										3 NOR (M. Myrmo,
										O. Martinsen,
										I. Formo, O. Braa)
										4 FIN (R. Lehtiner,
										K. Laurila,
										O. Karjalainen,

No. Year Country Site	15 km	30 km	50 km	Relay, 4 × 10 km
				J. Mieto)
				5 TCH (F. Simon,
				J. Beran,
				J. Fajstavr,
				S. Henych)
				6 SUI (A. Kälin,
				A. Giger,
				E. Hauser,
				W. Geeser)
31 1976 AUT Innsbruck OWG XII	1 N. Bajukov SOV	1 S. Saveliev SOV	1 I. Formo NOR	1 FIN (M. Pitkaenen,
	2 E. Beliaev SOV	2 W. Koch USA	2 G-D Klause DDR	J. Mieto,
	3 A. Koivisto FIN	3 I. Garanin SOV	3 B. Sodergren SWE	P. Teurajavri,
	4 I. Garanin SOV	4 J. Mieto FIN	4 I. Garanin SOV	A. Koivisto)
	5 I. Formo NOR	5 N. Bajukov SOV	5 G. Grimmer DDR	2 NOR (P. Tyldum,
	6 W. Koch USA	6 G-D Klause DDR	6 P-K Aaland NOR	E. Sagstuen,
				I. Formo,
				O. Martinsen)
				3 SOV (E. Beliaev,
				N. Bajukov,
				S. Saveliev,
				I. Garanin)
				4 SWE (B. Sodergren,
				C. Johansson,
				T. Wassberg,
				S-A Lundback)
				5 SUI (F. Renggli,
				E. Hauser,
				H. Gaehler,
				A. Kaelin)
				6 USA (D. Peterson,
				T. Caldwell,
				W. Koch,
				R. Yeager)
32 1978 FIN Lahti	1 J. Luszczek POL	1 S. Saveljev SOV	1 S-A Lundback SWE	1 SWE (S-A Lundback,
	2 J. Beljajev SOV	2 N. Zimjatov SOV	2 J. Beljajev SOV	C. Johansson,
	3 J. Mieto FIN	3 J. Luszczek POL	3 J-P Pierrat FRA	T. Limby,
	4 M. Pitkanen FIN	4 M. Pitkanen FIN	4 M. Pitkanen FIN	T. Magnusson)
	5 N. Zimjatov SOV	5 J. Beljajev SOV	5 L-E Eriksen NOR	2 FIN (E. Lahtevanoja,
	6 S-A Lundback SWE	6 S-A Lundback SWE	6 J. Beran TCH	J. Mieto,
				P. Teurajarvi,
				M. Pitkanen)
				3 NOR (L-E Eriksen,
				O. Aunli,
				I. Formo, O. Braa)
				4 SOV (J. Beljajev, N. Zimjatov,
				S. Saveljev,
				V. Rotshev)
				5 SUI (H. Kreuzer,

No.	Year	Country	Site	15 km	30 km	50 km	Relay, 4 × 10 km
							F. Renggli, E. Hauser, G. Ambuhl)
							6 BRD (P. Zipfel, G. Zipfel, W. Muller, D. Notz)
33	1980	USA	Lake Placid OWG XIII	1 T. Wassberg SWE	1 N. Zimjatov SOV	1 N. Zimjatov SOV	1 SOV (V. Rochev, N. Bazhukov, E. Beliaev, N. Zimjatov)
				2 J. Mieto FIN	2 V. Rochev SOV	2 J. Mieto FIN	2 NOR (L-E Eriksen, P-K Aaland, O. Aunli, O. Braa)
				3 O. Aunli NOR	3 I. Lebanov BUL	3 A. Zavjalov SOV	3 FIN (H. Kirvesniemi, P. Teurajarvi, M. Pitkanen, J. Mieto)
				4 N. Zimjatov SOV	4 T. Wassberg SWE	4 L-E Eriksen NOR	4 BRD (P. Zipfel, W. Muller, D. Notz, J. Behle)
				5 E. Beliaev SOV	5 J. Luszczek POL	5 S. Saveliev SOV	5 SWE (S-A Lundback, T. Eriksen, B. Kohlberg, T. Wassberg)
				6 J. Luszczek POL	6 M. Pitkanen FIN	6 E. Beliaev SOV	6 ITA (M. Dezolt, B. Carrara, G. Capitanio, G. Vanzetta)
34	1982	NOR	Oslo	1 O. Braa NOR	1 T. Eriksson SWE	1 T. Wassberg SWE	1 SOV (V. Nikitin, A. Batiuk, Y. Burlakov, A. Zavialov)
				2 A. Zavialov SOV	2 L-E Eriksen NOR	2 Y. Burlakov SOV	1 NOR (L-E Eriksen, O. Aunli, P-G Mikkelsplass, O. Braa)
				3 H. Kirvesniemi FIN	3 W. Koch USA	3 L-E Eriksen NOR	3 FIN (K. Haerkönen, A. Karvonen, H. Kirvesniemi, J. Mieto)
				4 Y. Burlakov SOV	4 O. Aunli NOR	4 A. Batiuk SOV	3 DDR (U. Bellmann, U. Wunsch, S. Schicker, F. Schröder)
				5 A. Batiuk SOV	5 J. Mieto FIN	5 A. Asko FIN	5 SWE (T. Wassberg,
				6 J. Mieto FIN	6 A. Zavialov SOV	6 A. Zavialov SOV	

No.	Year	Country	Site	15 km	30 km	50 km	Relay, 4 × 10 km
							J. Ottosson, S-E Danielsson, B. Kohlberg)
							6 BRD (J. Behle, S. Dotzler, F. Schoebel, J. Schneider)

No.	Year	Country	Site	5 km	10 km	Relay, 3 × 5 km
19	1952	NOR	Oslo OWG VI		1 L. Hideman — FIN 2 M. Hietamies — FIN 3 S. Rantanen — FIN 4 M. Norberg — SWE 5 S. Polkunen — FIN 6 R. Wahl — NOR	
20	1954	SWE	Falun		1 L. Kozyreva — SOV 2 S. Rantanen — FIN 3 M. Hietamies — FIN 4 M. Maslennikova — SOV 5 A. Leontjeva — SOV 6 S. Polkunen — FIN	1 SOV (L. Kozyreva, M. Maslennikova, V. Tsareva) 2 FIN (S. Polkunen, M. Hietamies, S. Rantanen) 3 SWE (A.-L. Eriksson, M. Norberg, S. Edström) 4 NOR (K. Gutubakken, M. Öiseth, R. Wahl) 5 TCH (O. Krasilová, M. Bartaková, E. Vasiková) 6 ITA (E. Mus, A. Parmesani, I. Taffra)
21	1956	ITA	Cortina d'Ampezzo OWG VII		1 L. Kozyreva — SOV 2 R. Eroshina — SOV 3 S. Edström — SWE 4 A. Koltjina — SOV 5 S. Rantanen — FIN 6 M. Hietamies — FIN	1 FIN (S. Polkunen, M. Hietamies, S. Rantanen) 2 SOV (L. Kozyreva, A. Koltjina, R. Eroshina) 3 SWE (I. Johansson, A.-L. Eriksson, S. Edström) 4 NOR (K. Brusveen, G. Regland, R. Wahl) 5 POL (M. Bukova-Gasienica, J. Peksa, Z. Krzeptowska) 6 TCH (E. Benesova, L. Patockova, E. Lauermannova)
22	1958	FIN	Lahti		1 A. Koltjina — SOV 2 L. Kozyreva — SOV	1 SOV (R. Eroshina, A. Koltjina,

No.	Year	Country	Site	5 km		10 km		Relay, 3 × 5 km	
						3 S. Rantanen	FIN	L. Kozyreva)	
						4 R. Eroshina	SOV	2 FIN (T. Mikkula-Pöysti,	
						5 E. Smirnova	SOV	P. Korkee, S. Rantanen)	
						6 M. Gusakova	SOV	3 SWE (M. Norberg,	
								I. Johansson,	
								S. Edström)	
								4 POL	
								(M. Bukowa-Kowalska,	
								S. Biegun,	
								J. Peksa-Konopka)	
								5 TCH (L. Patockova,	
								A. Finlova, E. Benesova)	
								6 DDR (Chr. Göhler,	
								E. Spiegelhauer,	
								S. Kallus)	
23	1960	USA	Squaw Valley OWG VIII			1 M. Gusakova	SOV	1 SWE (I. Johansson,	
						2 L. Baranova-Kozyreva	SOV	B. Strandberg,	
						3 R. Eroshina	SOV	S. Edström-Ruthström)	
						4 A. Koltjina	SOV	2 SOV (R. Eroshina,	
						5 S. Edström-Ruthström	SWE	M. Gusakova,	
						6 T. Pöysti	FIN	L. Baranova-Kozyreva)	
								3 FIN (S. Rantanen,	
								E. Ruoppa, T. Pöysti)	
								4 POL (S. Biegun,	
								H. Gasieniac-Daniel,	
								J. Peksa-Czerniawska)	
								5 DDR (R. Czech-Blasl,	
								R. Borges,	
								S. Kallus-Hausschild)	
24	1962	POL	Zakopane	1 A. Koltjina	SOV	1 A. Koltjina	SOV	1 SOV (L. Baranova,	
				2 L. Baranova	SOV	2 M. Gusakova	SOV	M. Gusakova,	
				3 M. Gusakova	SOV	3 R. Eroshina	SOV	A. Koltjina)	
				4 S. Rantanen	FIN	4 L. Baranova	SOV	2 SWE (B. Martinsson,	
				5 M. Lehtonen	FIN	5 M. Lehtonen	FIN	B. Strandberg,	
				6 E. Mekshilo	SOV	6 B. Martinsson	SWE	T. Gustafsson)	
								3 FIN (S. Rantanen,	
								R. Ruoppa,	
								M. Lehtenen)	
								4 POL (W. Stempak,	
								J. Czerniawska,	
								S. Biegun)	
								5 DDR (R. Dannhauer,	
								Chr. Herklotz,	
								S. Kallus)	
								6 TCH (V. Srnkova,	
								J. Skodova,	
								E. Paulusova)	
25	1964	AUT	Innsbruck OWG IX	1 C. Boyarskikh	SOV	1 C. Boyarskikh	SOV	1 SOV (A. Koltjina,	
				2 M. Lehtonen	FIN	2 E. Mekshilo	SOV	E. Mekshilo,	
				3 A. Koltjina	SOV	3 M. Gusakova	SOV	C. Boyarskikh)	
				4 E. Mekshilo	SOV	4 B. Strandberg	SWE	2 SWE (B. Martinsson,	

No.	Year	Country	Site	5 km		10 km		Relay, 3 × 5 km
				5 T. Pöysti	FIN	5 T. Pöysti	FIN	B. Strandberg,
				6 T. Gustafsson	SWE	6 S. Pusula	FIN	T. Gustafsson)
								3 FIN (S. Pusula,
								T. Pöysti,
								M. Lehtonen)
								4 DDR (C. Nestler,
								R. Czech-Blasl,
								R. Dannhauer)
								5 BUL (R. Dimova,
								N. Vassileva, K. Stoeva)
								6 TCH (J. Skodova,
								E. Brizova,
								E. Paulusova)
26	1966	NOR	Oslo	1 A. Koltjina	SOV	1 C. Boyarskikh	SOV	1 SOV (C. Boyarskikh,
				2 C. Boyarskikh	SOV	2 A. Koltjina	SOV	R. Achkina, A. Koltjina)
				3 R. Achkina	SOV	3 T. Gustafsson	SWE	2 NOR (I. Wigernaes,
				4 E. Mekshilo	SOV	4 E. Mekshilo	SOV	I. Aufles, B. Mördre)
				5 K. Stoeva	BUL	5 K. Stoeva	BUL	3 SWE (B. Martinsson,
				6 T. Gustafsson	SWE	6 B. Martinsson	SWE	B. Strandberg,
								T. Gustafsson)
								4 DDR (G. Nobis,
								A. Unger, Chr. Nestler)
								5 FIN (T. Pöysti,
								E. Ruoppa, S. Pusula)
								6 BUL (K. Stoeva,
								N. Vassileva,
								V. Pandeva)
27	1968	FRA	Grenoble	1 Toini Gustafsson	SWE	1 Toini Gustafsson	SWE	1 NOR (I. Aufles,
			OWG	2 Galina Kulakova	SOV	2 Berit Mördre	NOR	B. Enger-Damon,
			X	3 Alevtina Koltjina	SOV	3 Inger Aufles	NOR	B. Mördre)
				4 Barbro Martinsson	SWE	4 Barbro Martinsson	SWE	2 SWE (B. Strandberg,
				5 Marjatta Kajosmaa	FIN	5 Marjatta Kajosmaa	FIN	T. Gustafsson,
				6 Rita Achkina	SOV	6 Galina Kulakova	SOV	B. Martinsson)
								3 SOV (A. Koltjina,
								R. Achkina,
								G. Kulakova)
								4 FIN (S. Pusula,
								M. Olkkonen,
								M. Kajosmaa)
								5 POL (W. Budny,
								J. Czerniawska,
								S. Biegun)
								6 DDR (R. Kohler,
								G. Schmid,
								Chr. Nestler)
28	1970	TCH	Vysoké	1 G. Kulakova	SOV	1 A. Oljunina	SOV	1 SOV (N. Fjodorova,
			Tatry	2 G. Piljusenko	SOV	2 M. Kajosmaa	FIN	G. Kulakova,
				3 N. Fjodorova	SOV	3 G. Kulakova	SOV	A. Oljunina)
				4 M. Kajosmaa	FIN	4 H. Sikolova	CSF	2 DDR (G. Haupt,
				5 M. Endler	BRD	5 R. Fischer	DDR	R. Fischer, A. Unger)
				6 S. Pusula	FIN	6 G. Piljusenko	SOV	3 FIN (S. Pusula,
								H. Takalo, M. Kajosmaa)

								4 NOR (I. Aufles, A. Dahl, B. Mördre-Lammedal)
								5 TCH (M. Cillerova, H. Sikolova, M. Chlumova)
								6 BRD (M. Mrklas, I. Roth-Fuss, M. Endler)
29	1972	JPN	Sapporo OWG XI	1 G. Kulakova	SOV	1 G. Kulakova	SOV	1 SOV (L. Moukhatcheva, A. Oljunina, G. Kulakova)
				2 M. Kajosmaa	FIN	2 A. Oljunina	SOV	2 FIN (H. Takalo, H. Kuntola, M. Kajosmaa)
				3 H. Sikolova	TCH	3 M. Kajosmaa	FIN	
				4 A. Oljunina	SOV	4 L. Moukhatcheva	SOV	3 NOR (I. Aufles, A. Dahl, B. Mördre-Lammedal)
				5 H. Kuntola	FIN	5 H. Takalo	FIN	4 BRD (M. Mrklas, I. Roth-Fuss, M. Endler)
				6 L. Moukhatcheva	SOV	6 A. Dahl	NOR	5 DDR (G. Haupt, R. Fischer, A. Unger)
								6 TCH (A. Bartosova, H. Sikolova, M. Cillerova)

No.	Year	Country	Site	5 km		10 km		Relay, 4 × 5 km
30	1974	SWE	Falun	1 G. Kulakova	SOV	1 G. Kulakova	SOV	1 SOV (N. Baldicheva, N. Seljunina, R. Smetanina, G. Kulakova)
				2 B. Paulü	TCH	2 B. Petzold	DDR	2 DDR (S. Krause, P. Hinze, P. Petzold, V. Schmidt)
				3 R. Smetanina	SOV	3 H. Takalo	FIN	3 TCH (A. Bartosova, G. Sekajova, M. Jaskovska, B. Paulü)
				4 B. Petzold	DDR	4 B. Paulü	TCH	4 FIN (L. Suihkonen, H. Takalo, M. Kajosmaa, H. Kuntola)
				5 N. Baldycheva	SOV	5 V. Schmidt	DDR	5 SWE (L. Carlzon, G. Partapuoli, G. Fröjd, M. Bodelid)
				6 U. Fossen	NOR	6 B. M.-Lammedal	NOR	6 NOR (U. Fossen, K. Mo-Berge, A. Dahl, B. Mördre-Lammedal)

No.	Year	Country	Site	5 km		10 km		Relay, 4 × 5 km
31	1976	AUT	Innsbruck OWG XII	1 H. Takalo	FIN	1 R. Smetanina	SOV	1 SOV (N. Baldicheva, Z. Amosova, R. Smetanina, G. Kulakova.
				2 R. Smetanina	SOV	2 H. Takalo	FIN	2 FIN
				3 G. Kulakova	SOV	3 G. Kulakova	SOV	
				4 N. Baldicheva	SOV	4 N. Baldicheva	SOV	
				5 H. Kuntola	FIN	5 E. Olsson	SWE	
				6 E. Olsson	SWE	6 Z. Amosova	SOV	

No.	Year	Country	Site	5 km	10 km	Relay, 4 × 5 km
						(L. Suihkonen, M. Kajosmaa, H. Kuntola, H. Takalo)
						3 DDR (M. Debertshauser, S. Krause, B. Petzold, V. Schmidt)
						4 SWE (L. Carlzon, G. Partapuoli, M. Johansson, E. Olsson)
						5 NOR (B. Kvello, M. Myrmael, B. Johannessen, G. Kummen)
						6 TCH (H. Pasiarova, G. Sekajova, A. Bartosova, B. Paulü)

No.	Year	Country	Site	5 km		10 km		20 km		Relay, 4 × 5 km
32	1978	FIN	Lahti	1 H. Takalo	FIN	1 Z. Amosova	SOV	1 Z. Amosova	SOV	1 FIN (T. Impio, M-L Hamalainen, H. Riihivuori, H. Takalo)
				2 H. Riihivuori	FIN	2 R. Smetanina	SOV	2 G. Kulakova	SOV	2 DDR (M. Rostock, B. Schreiber, B. Petzold, C. Meinel)
				3 R. Smetanina	SOV	3 H. Riihivuori	FIN	3 H. Takalo	FIN	3 SOV (N. Rotscheva, Z. Amosova, R. Smetanina, G. Kulakova)
				4 G. Kulakova	SOV	4 G. Kulakova	SOV	4 H. Riihivuori	FIN	4 SWE (M. Johansson, E. Olsson, M. Bodelid, L. Carlzon-Lundback)
				5 C. Meinel	DDR	5 T. Impio	FIN	5 R. Smetanina	SOV	5 NOR (B. Johannessen, V. Ronning, M. Myrmael, B. Kvello)
				6 Z. Amosova	SOV	6 B. Kvello	NOR	6 B. Kvello	NOR	6 TCH (A. Pasiarova, B. Paulü, D. Paleckova, K. Jeriova)

No.	Year	Country	Site	5 km	10 km	20 km	Relay, 4 × 5 km
33	1980	USA	Lake Placid OWG XIII	1 R. Smetanina SOV 2 H. Riihivuori FIN 3 K. Jeriova TCH 4 B. Petzold DDR 5 N. Baldycheva SOV 6 G. Kulakova SOV	1 B. Petzold DDR 2 H. Riihivuori FIN 3 H. Takalo FIN 4 R. Smetanina SOV 5 G. Kulakova SOV 6 N. Baldycheva SOV		1 DDR (M. Rostock, C. Anding, V. Hesse, B. Petzold) 2 SOV (N. Baldycheva, N. Rocheva, G. Kulakova, R. Smetanina) 3 NOR (B. Pettersen, A. Boe, M. Myrmael, B. Aunli) 4 TCH (D. Paleckova, G. Svobodova, B. Paulü, K. Jeriova) 5 FIN (M. Auroma, M-L Hamalainen, H. Takalo, H. Riihivuori) 6 SWE (M. Johansson, K. Lamberg, E. Olsson, L. Carlzon-Lundback)
33	1980	SWE	Falun WSC in 20 km			1 V. Hesse DDR 2 G. Kulakova SOV 3 R. Smetanina SOV 4 M. Rostock DDR 5 N. Baldycheva SOV 6 Z. Amosova SOV	
34	1982	NOR	Oslo	1 B. Aunli NOR 2 H. Riihivuori FIN 3 B. Pettersen NOR 4 A. Böe NOR 5 K. Jeriova TCH 6 A. Pasiarova TCH	1 B. Aunli NOR 2 H. Riihivuori FIN 3 K. Jeriova TCH 4 B. Pettersen NOR 5 A. Böe NOR 6 M. Johansson SWE	1 R. Smetanina SOV 2 B. Aunli NOR 3 H. Riihivuori FIN 4 L. Liadova SOV 5 G. Kulakova SOV 6 M. Myrmael NOR	1 NOR (A. Böe, I-H Nybraaten, B. Aunli, B. Pettersen) 2 SOV (L Liadova, L. Zabolotskaya, R. Smetanina, G. Kulakova) 3 DDR (P. Sölter, C. Anding, V. Hesse, B. Petzold) 4 FIN (M-L Haemaelaeinen, H. Takalo, P. Maeaettae, H. Riihivuori)

No.	Year	Country	Site	5 km	10 km	20 km	Relay, 4 × 5 km
							5 TCH (A. Pasiarova, D. Svubova, G. Svobodova, K. Jeriova)
							6 SWE (M. Johansson, M. Thulin, K. Lamberg, L. Carlzon-Lundback)

THE BEST IN CROSS-COUNTRY WORLD CUP RACING

The World Cup in Cross-Country Ski Racing started with unofficial point compilations by European journalists for the 1973–74 season, and subsequently, on a trial basis sanctioned by the FIS, for the 1978–79 and 1980–81 seasons. World Cup points are awarded for a racer's best results in a specified maximum number of races of the pre-designated World Cup races for a season. First place earns 26 points, second 22 points, third 19 points, fourth 17 points, and fifth through 20th corresponding points at decreasing one-point differences. Both the maximum number of races counted and the number and location of World Cup races have varied through the years, so point totals from season to season are not always directly comparable.

In 1981 the FIS, the International Ski Federation, finally made the Cross-Country World Cup official. In summary, the FIS regulations now in effect call for nine World Cup races in even years, all in Europe, and ten in odd years, two of which are to be arranged outside of Europe. The best results from the three individual men's and three individual women's races during Winter Olympic Games and Nordic World Ski Championships will count in the final results, with points being totaled for a maximum of six of a racer's best results in the season's designated World Cup races.

Glossary

Cross-country skiing has its own special vocabulary. The following are the terms most used. Definitions not pertaining to cross-country skiing are not listed.

All trade names and trademarks are assumed to be registered.

ACRYLIC 1) A foam plastic, used in ski cores 2) Fibers or fabric, used in clothing.

AEROBIC Literally "with air," body processes requiring oxygen supply.

AEROBIC CAPACITY A measure of the ability to perform aerobic work over longer periods of time. Often expressed as maximum oxygen uptake.

AGILITY In skiing, the ability to use body flexibility efficiently.

ALPINE SKIING Recreational and competitive downhill skiing, originally developed in the Alps of Europe.

ANAEROBIC Literally "without air," body processes capable of functioning without an oxygen supply.

ANAEROBIC CAPACITY A measure of the body's capability to perform muscular work over and above the limit set by maximum oxygen uptake.

ANORAK Lightweight shell parka, usually with a hood.

ARM TRAINERS Various devices used in off-season training of arms in the diagonal stride or double-pole rhythms.

AVALANCHE Snow slide, usually on steep hillsides, often dangerous.

BACKSLIP Skis grip snow poorly and slide backward.

BAIL Clamp-down piece on toe binding; holds boot sole down with or against binding pins.

BASE 1) Running surface on ski bottom 2) Snow under surface snow.

BASE PREPARATION Compounds or process of their application, tars for wood ski bases, paraffin waxes for plastic ski bases.

BASE WAX Waxes used "under" final waxes to increase durability.

BASKET Disk attached near bottom of ski pole to prevent its sinking into the snow.

BIATHLON A competitive Nordic skiing event combining cross-country skiing and rifle marksmanship.

BIB KNICKERS Knickers with high bib front and shoulder straps.

BINDING Device, mounted on ski, to attach boot to ski.

BOWED Ski base convex instead of flat, center higher than edges; undesirable.

BOX Synthetic ski construction in which load-carrying material forms a box enclosing ski core on all four sides.

CABLE BINDING Binding with toepiece and cable or strap around boot heel, used on heavier wilderness skis.

CALORIE Unit used in physiology and nutrition, used to express the heat output of the body and the energy values of foods.

CAMBER Arching of the middle of a ski above its tip and tail.

CHRISTIE Short for Christiania, after the older name of Oslo, Norway; describes downhill turns using sideslipping.

CISM Conseil International Militaire du Sport—the International Military Sports Council—organizers of military skiing competition.

CITIZENS' RACE Cross-country ski race intended for recreational skiers, usually with a mass start.

CLO Unit used to express insulating value of clothing.

COLLAR 1) Part of jacket or shirt, around neck 2) Strip of material around top opening of a boot, often padded for comfort.

COMBINED In Nordic competitive skiing, an event combining 15-km cross-country ski racing and ski jumping on a 70-meter hill.

CORE Central part of a ski, between and/or encased by structural layers; gives ski shape.

CORK A block of material, originally natural cork, now usually foam plastic, used to rub and polish ski wax on ski bases.

CORN Large-grained snow, produced by settling, freezing, and thawing.

COURSE The route followed by a cross-country ski race.

CROSS-COUNTRY In common U.S. usage, the entirety of touring and cross-country skiing.

CROUCH High-speed downhill position allowing the body to rest naturally in a position of readiness.

CRUST Glazed snow surface, caused by freeze-thaw cycles.

CSA The Canadian Ski Association.

DIAGONAL STRIDE Stride in which opposite arm and leg move together, as in walking on foot.

DIN Abbreviation for Deutsche Industrienorm, the German national standards, often used for items of ski equipment made in Europe.

DISTANCE TRAINING Endurance training aimed at building aerobic capacity.

DOUBLE CAMBER Geometric interpretation of modern synthetic ski camber where center section is progressively stiffer as it flattens out.

DOUBLE POLING Both arms and both poles move in unison.

DYNAMIC In motion. Usually an adjective, such as *dynamic force.*

EDGE Bottom, outside edge of the ski base, or the use of these edges to control skis.

EGG Compact high-speed downhill position having the least wind resistance.

ENDURANCE The ability to perform prolonged work, such as distance cross-country, without fatigue.

EPOXY A resin, used as an adhesive and as a binder for various synthetic fibers in skis and poles. Also available as a glue for bonding.

ERGOMETER CYCLE A stationary cycle on which a subject pedals at a fixed speed against a fixed resistance. Used in measuring aerobic endurance.

FALL LINE The shortest line directly down a hill.

FARTSLEK From the Swedish; literally "speed game." A game form of training.

FIS Fédération Internationale de Ski—The International Ski Federation.

FISHSCALE Trademark for pattern-type waxless ski base having imbricated scales.

FLEX Bending properties of a ski or ski pole.

FLEXIBILITY 1) Flex 2) A measure of maximum physical movement such as how far in one direction you can bend.

GAITER Cloth covering around leg and boot at ankle; keeps snow out.

GLIDE Property of a ski base to slide on snow.

GLIDER Paraffin wax used on tip and tail section of synthetic ski bases for high-performance, maximum glide.

GORE-TEX Trademark for microporous film of expanded Teflon plastic, breathable and highly water repellent, used as laminate on fabrics.

GRIP 1) Skis' bite into underlying snow, gives traction 2) The handle of a ski pole.

GROOVE 1) Long, narrow indentation in ski base; aids tracking 2) Indentation, often V-shaped, in bottom surface of boot heel; mates with similarly shaped device on ski 3) Round indentation around outside of boot heel, to accept and hold cable of cable-type binding.

GRUNDVALLA Swedish for "base wax." Poorly defined. May mean base preparation or base wax, depending on the manufacturer.

HAIR BASE Waxless ski base; irregularities are natural or synthetic fur, usually inset in strips or rectangles, nap backward for ski grip.

HARD WAX Ski-touring wax for cold and dry to slightly wet snow.

HEEL PLATES Plates mounted under the heel on the ski, usually with features to keep heel from slipping sideways off the ski.

HERRINGBONE An uphill stride with ski tips spread to form a V, named for pattern skis make in snow.

HONEYCOMB Matrix of six-sided aluminum-foil cells resembling honeycomb made by bees, used in ski cores.

HYPOTHERMIA Subnormal body temperature that slows physiological processes; can result from prolonged exposure to cold; can be fatal.

HYTREL Trade name for type of polyamide plastic, used in thin, usually 7 mm (about ¼ inch) thick, ski boot soles.

IMBRICATED Overlapping in sequence like roof tiles or shingles; describes type of waxless ski base pattern.

IMITATION TRAINING Movements performed on foot to imitate and thus teach skiing movements.

IMPREGNATING Waterproofing process for wooden ski bases.

INJECTED BOOT Boot with soles formed on uppers by injecting plastic into a mold.

INJECTED SKI Ski in which core is formed by plastic injected into mold between structural top and bottom layers.

INTERVAL TRAINING A series of intense but relatively short exercise periods separated from one another by rest intervals.

IOC The International Olympic Committee.

KEVLAR Trademark for aramid fibers, used in ski structural layers.

KICK As in walking, a backward thrusting toe push-off and leg extension that propels the skier forward.

KICK TURN A stationary 180-degree turn performed by lifting and reversing direction of one ski, followed by the other ski.

KIDDIE PACK Frame-type backpack with seat designed to carry small child in sitting position.

KLISTER Tacky, fluid ski touring waxes for wet and/or settled snow. Wax comes in 2- to 4-ounce tubes.

KLISTER-WAX Ski-touring wax for conditions near freezing. Comes in round foil cans holding 1½ to 2 ounces of wax.

KNICKERS Breeches gathered at the knee, usually with elastic or buckle strap, most common pants for cross-country skiers.

LANGLAUF German for cross-country ski racing.

LIGHT TOURING Ski-touring equipment closely resembling cross-country racing equipment, but stronger and slightly heavier.

LIGHT TRACK Illuminated cross-country trail.

LIGNOSTONE (from the Latin *lignum,* meaning wood) Beech wood compressed to half its original volume, used for ski edges.

MOHAIR Originally, coat or fleece of Angora goat. In ski making, hair strips or rectangles inlaid in a waxless ski base, nap pointing backward.

MOUNTAIN Heaviest type of general-touring skis, intended for extensive mountain touring or polar exploration.

MUSCULAR FITNESS The ability of the skeletal muscles to perform movements.

NATURAL STANCE Natural erect body position. In downhill skiing, the easiest and most erect position to assume.

NORDIC Geographically defines Norway, Sweden, and Finland. In skiing, defines recreational ski touring, competitive cross-country ski racing, ski jumping, Nordic combined, and Biathlon events.

NORDIC NORM Standard stipulating boot and toe binding widths and sole side angles, and ski midpoint widths.

NORM 38 Design of racing boots and bindings, patented and developed by Adidas.

NORPINE Currently slang. A combination of Nordic and Alpine, describes downhill skiing on Nordic equipment.

NSPS National Ski Patrol System. U.S. and Canadian ski rescue and first-aid corps, originally for Alpine ski slopes, now with cross-country patrols.

ORIENTEERING A competitive event combining running on foot with map reading. Also done on skis; then correctly termed *ski orienteering.*

OWG Olympic Winter Games, held in leap years from 1924 on.

OXYGEN DEBT Anaerobic.

OXYGEN UPTAKE Measure of body's ability to supply oxygen to bodily processes.

PARALLEL TURN Downhill turn made with skis parallel throughout the turn.

PASSGANG Obsolete touring stride in which arm and leg on one side move in unison.

PATTERN BASE Waxless ski base where irregularities that grip comprise a regular pattern molded or machined into the base material.

PIN 1) Short peg projecting upward from base plate of toe binding; mates with corresponding recess in boot sole 2) Transverse spike that holds grip on ski pole.

PIN BINDING Toe binding comprising metal or plastic toepiece with pins projecting upward to mate recesses in boot sole.

POLE SET The act of planting a pole in the snow.

POLING Arm movements with poles that supply forward power.

POSITIVE BASE Pattern-type waxless ski base where waxless pattern protrudes beyond the level of the base.

POWDER Light, dry snow, usually new, at low temperatures.

P-TEX Trade name for polyethylene ski base material.

PULK Kayak-shaped sled, riding directly on snow as does toboggan, used by skiers to transport loads, small children, or injured.

PULLOVER SOCKS Rubber, rubberized nylon, or nylon-terrycloth socks pulled over cross-country boots for additional waterproofing and warmth.

RACING NORM Standard for racing boots and bindings, 50 mm wide at transverse line through pins of pin binding.

RAILED Ski base concave instead of flat, edges higher than center; undesirable.

RELAY A cross-country ski-racing team event: the international standards are a four-man event covering 40 kilometers or a four-woman event covering 20 kilometers. Shorter, or mixed men-women relays, are U.S. events.

RESILIENCE A component of muscular fitness.

ROLLER SKIS Wheeled platforms attached to the foot with standard cross-country bindings and boots. Used in imitation training.

RUCKSACK Knapsack with a frame, suitable for skiing.

SANDWICH SKI Wood or synthetic ski built up of several laminations bonded together in a sandwichlike fashion.

SCRAPER Metal or plastic rectangle or blade, used to remove old wax or flatten ski bases.

SHAFT Tubular, straight part of a ski pole.

SHOULDER Broadest part of a ski, at the shovel.

SHOVEL Upturned part of the ski tip.

SIA Ski Industries America.

SIDE CAMBER Sidecut.

SIDECUT Concave curve on side profile of a ski that gives it a slight hourglass shape; aids tracking and helps banked ski turn.

SIDESLIP A controlled sideways glide on skis.

SIDEWALLS Sides of a ski, usually of hard material to protect more fragile materials inside.

SIKLING Rectangular steel or plastic tool, similar to refinishing scraper used to hand-scrape paint and wood, but having one or more rounded or beveled corners for scraping ski bases and tracking grooves.

SKARE General term for hard and/or icy crust on snow.

SKATING TURN A flat terrain or downhill turn executed by one or more skating steps in the new direction.

SKI STRIDING A variation of walking or running done uphill on foot to imitate skiing movements.

SKI TOURING Recreational cross-country skiing.

SNOWMOBILE Tracked, motorized vehicle for travel on snow, usually with runners for steering, useful for supply transport, rescue, and pulling track-setting sleds. Recreational use curtailed or forbidden in most countries, but permitted in the USA and Canada outside of National Parks.

SNOWPLOW Downhill position for slowing down, stopping, and turning. Ski tips together, tails apart.

SNOWPLOW TURN Downhill turn executed in the snowplow position.

SOLE Boot bottom.

SPEED TRAINING Training aimed at attaining high speed.

SPLITS Intermediate times given to a cross-country racer during the course of a race, usually as "up on" (ahead of) or "down to" (behind) another racer.

STEM CHRISTIANIA Downhill turn initiated with a stem and finished with ski parallel and sideslipping through the fall line.

STEM TURN Downhill turn in which one ski is stemmed, or angled out pointing in the direction of turn, and weighted to perform the turn.

STEP 1) Stepped turn 2) Sawtoothlike pattern embossed in waxless ski base.

STEP TEST A test in which the subject steps up and down from a platform for a period of about 5 minutes, with pulse measured thereafter. Provides an indication of aerobic capacity.

STEP TURN A stationary or moving turn performed by stepping skis progressively around to the new direction.

STRENGTH A component of muscular fitness. The ability to lift, push, or pull against a resistance.

STRIDE In skiing, the walklike leg and arm movements that propel the skier forward.

TACKING TURN Uphill turn connecting two traverses, done in diagonal-stride rhythm.

TAIL The back end of a ski.

TAR General term for tarlike base-preparation compounds used on wood ski bases.

TELEMARK Region in south-central Norway. In skiing, a position with both knees bent, one leg trailing the other.

TELEMARK TURN A steered downhill ski turn, one of the oldest known, named for region in Norway. Characterized by little or no sideslip of the skis, body in Telemark position.

TEMPO TRAINING Running or skiing at racing speed for periods equalling 10 to 20 percent of a race's duration.

TIP The front end of a ski, or the bottom end of a ski pole.

TOE BINDING Ski bindings that attach the boot to the ski by clamping the front part of the boot welt to the binding.

TONKIN Bamboo cane, used for ski-pole shafts.

TORCH Usually a butane- or propane-fueled blowtorch equipped with a flame spreader and a waxing iron attachment. Intended for assisting base preparation, application and removal of waxes.

TOURING Recreational cross-country skiing.

TOURING NORM Standard for recreational cross-country boots and bindings, has profile of Racing Norm combined with boot-sole thickness of Nordic Norm.

TRACK 1) Depressions left by skis in snow 2) Depressions in snow, as if made by skis, but "set" by mechanical track setter 3) The course for a cross-country ski race 4) A warning shouted when overtaking another skier.

TRACKING Ability of a ski or pulk to follow a straight course.

TRACK SETTER Sled used to prepare ski trails and set tracks in snow, pulled by a snowmobile or other over-snow tracked vehicle.

TRAINING Any physical activity that maintains or improves physical ability.

TRANSITION SNOW Snow just at freezing, in transition zone between dry and wet.

TRANSPORT-TYPE UNDERWEAR Underwear of a synthetic fabric that keeps skin dry by transporting moisture out, away from the body.

TRAVERSING Skiing up or down a hill on a traverse at an angle to the fall line.

TUQUE Heavy stocking cap, usually wool, worn in Canada.

UIPMB Union Internationale de Pentathlon Moderne et Biathlon, the International Modern Pentathlon and Biathlon Association Organizers of biathlon skiing competition.

USSA The United States Ski Association.

USST United States Ski Team.

VELCRO Trade name for nylon closure tape, in pairs, one of which consists of loops, the other of pile; tapes lock to each other with slight pressure and are opened by a firm pull.

VULCANIZED BOOT Boot with soles formed on uppers by vulcanization of rubber or synthetic rubber.

WAXABLE SKIS Skis whose bases are waxed for grip and glide.

WAXING IRON Iron for waxing, may be heated by flame or electricity.

WAXING TORCH Small blowtorch, usually fueled by liquefied gas, used in waxing skis.

WAXLESS SKIS Skis with irregularities in the bases that both grip and glide on snow without the application of ski wax.

WAX REMOVER Solvent used to remove wax from ski bases.

WAX ZONE Marked areas on ski bases, for convenience in applying grip and glide waxes in high-performance waxing.

WEDGE Ski position in herringbone ascent and snowplow descent of hills.

WEIGHT SHIFT The transfer of weight from one ski to the other. The transfer always involves dynamic forces in addition to the static force of weight, and must be so understood in use.

WIDE-RANGE WAXING Wax systems for recreational skiers comprising two or three waxes, each matching a wide range of snow conditions.

WIDE-TRACK A stance in downhill skiing, skis parallel and 4 to 12 inches apart.

WIND CHILL Loss of insulating effect of air surrounding the body as wind increases.

WOOD SKIS Skis in which the structural layers are of wood.

WORLD CUP International cross-country racing competition for classified men and women racers, made official by the FIS in 1981. Points are awarded for a racer's best six results in nine (even years) or ten (odd years) preselected races each season: 26 points for first place, 22 for second, 19 for third, 17 for fourth, 16 for fifth, and so on, by one-point increments, down to one point for twentieth place. The skier with the most points at the end of the season is the World Cup winner. Theoretically the maximum is 156 points, corresponding to five first places.

WORLD LOPPET LEAGUE International citizens' race circuit comprising ten races, one in Canada, one in the USA, and eight in Europe. Points are awarded in the same manner as for the World Cup. To be eligible for winning, racers must compete in at least one race each in North America, Scandinavia, and Central Europe. All races must be at least Marathon distance, 42 kilometers or longer.

WRIST STRAP Strap fastened to ski pole grip; fits around wrist to facilite pole use and prevent pole loss.

WSC World Ski Championships, held in even-numbered years between leap years, sanctioned by and arranged by the FIS.

XC Common abbreviation for cross-country skiing.

For Your Information:
Addresses and Selected References

ADDRESSES

ASSOCIATIONS

U.S. Ski Association
1726 Champa Street, Suite 300
Denver, Colorado 80302
(303) 825-9183
The USSA is organized into
divisions: Alaska, Central, Eastern,
Intermountain, Northern, Pacific
Northwest, Rocky Mountain, and
Southern. Check with your local
club or shop, or contact USSA
headquarters for further
information.

Canadian Ski Association
333 River Road
Vanier, Ontario, Canada K1L 8B9
(613) 746-0060
The CSA has member associations,
by provinces. Check with
headquarters for addresses and
further information.

U.S. Biathlon Association
USOC
1750 East Boulder Street
Colorado Springs, Colorado 80909

U.S. Ski Coaches Association
P.O. Box 1747
Park City, Utah 84060
(801) 649-9090

MUSEUMS

United States Ski Hall of Fame
Ishpeming, Michigan 49849

Western American Skisport
Museum
Boreal Ridge
c/o Auburn Ski Club
839 N. Central Street
Reno, Nevada 89501

Canadian Ski Museum
457A Sussex Drive
Ottawa, Ontario K1N 6Z4

Wintersport Museum
Mürzzuschlag
Stadtegemeinde Mürzzuschlag
8680 Steiermark, Austria

Skimuseet
Holmenkollbakken
Oslo 3, Norway

Svenska Skidmuseet
Vasterbotens Museum
90244 Umea, Sweden

MAJOR MAGAZINES

Ski Magazine, Cross-Country Ski Magazine
380 Madison Avenue
New York, NY 10017

Skiing Magazine, XC Guide
One Park Avenue
New York, NY 10016

Cross-Country Skier
West River Road
West Brattleboro, Vermont 05301

Ski Racing
Box 70
Fair Haven, Vermont 05743

Ski Canada
425 University Avenue, 6th Floor
Toronto, Ontario, Canada M5G
1T6

SELECTED LITERATURE

For those who wish to delve further into the subject matter of this book, the following references are recommended. All are in English, and all are currently available in North America.

AVALANCHES

Dept. Agriculture, *Avalanche Handbook,* periodically updated and republished by the U.S. Government Printing Office.
One of the more complete publications available on the subject.

LaChapelle, E.R., *The ABC of Avalanche Safety.* Seattle: The Mountaineers, 1978.
A pocket-sized handbook, a must for all wilderness skiers.

BIOMECHANICS

Ekström, Hans, *Biomechanical Research Applied to Skiing* (monograph), Linköping Studies in Science and Technology, Dissertation no. 53, University of Linköping. Sweden: 1980.
A thorough, modern study, probably a future classic.

CROSS-COUNTRY SKIING

Brady, M., *Nordic Touring and Cross-Country Skiing.* Oslo: Dreyers Forlag (printed in Baltimore, Md.), 6th Edition, 1981.
A revised version of one of the two original standbys of the sport, first published in 1966.

Caldwell, J., *Cross-Country Skiing Today.* Brattleboro: Stephen Greene Press, 1977.
A revised version of one of the two original standbys of

MEDICINE

Ward, W., *Mountain Medicine.* London: Crosby Lockwood Staples, 1975.
A thorough text by a recognized authority; a storehouse of information.

Wilkerson, J.A. (editor), *Medicine for Mountaineering.* Seattle: The Mountaineers, 2nd edition, 1978.
Comprehensive, backpackable reference, a must for wilderness and expedition skiers.

PHYSIOLOGY

Astrand, P-O, and K. Rodahl, *Textbook of Work Physiology.* New York: McGraw-Hill, 2nd edition, 1977.
The acknowledged bible of the subject, an authoritative text.

Bergh, U., *The Physiology of Cross-Country Skiing,* translated from the Swedish by M. Brady and M. Hadler. Champaign, Illinois: Human Kinetics Publishers, under the auspices of the U.S. Ski Team: 1981.
A useful booklet, with interest beyond just racing.

Burke, E.J. (editor), *Toward an Understanding of Human Performance.* Ithaca: Mouvement Publications, 1978.
A compendium of information, of interest to coaches.

Hixon, E.G., *The Physicians and Sportsmedicine Guide to Cross-Country Skiing.* New York: McGraw-Hill, 1980.
A well-written, succinct overview of the sports medicine of cross-country skiing.

Karlsson, J. et al., *The Physiology of Alpine Skiing,* translated from the Swedish by W. Michael. U.S. Ski Coaches Association: 1978.
A booklet with information useful to ski mountaineers.

Tesch, J.C. et al., *Physiological Testing Manual, Laboratory and Field Tests for Cross-Country Skiers.* Research Unit, LaCrosse Exercise Program, University of Wisconsin: 1980. A publication of the U.S. Ski Team, 1980.
A how-to approach to a complicated subject.

RACING FOR CHILDREN

Lier, H. and H. Peterson (editors), *I Hope I Get a Purple Ribbon.* Official publication of the Bill Koch Ski League, Brattleboro, Vermont: United States Ski Association, 1980.
Spells out how to get them interested, and how to run races. All in straightforward language, this is a must book for parents with racing kids.

SKI EQUIPMENT

Brady, M.M., *Cross-Country Ski Gear.* Seattle: The Mountaineers, 1979.
A text on the subject, for interested skiers and ski industry persons alike.

SNOW

Bentley, W.A., and Humphreys, W.J., *Snow Crystals.* New York: McGraw-Hill, 1931, and Dover, 1962.
A classic by a self-educated Vermonter, who outdid the scientists of his day. Superb photos of snow crystals, an art as well as a ski book.

Mason, B.J., "The Growth of Snow Crystals," in *The Physics of Everyday Phenomena* (Readings from *Scientific American*). San Francisco: W.H. Freeman & Co., 1979, reprint from January 1961 *Scientific American,* 10 pages.
A lucid explanation of a complex subject.

TRAILS

Andersen, A., et al., *Nature Trails, Trim Trails.* Oslo: State Office for Youth and Sports, 1975.
Succinct and complete, a booklet reference on the Scandinavian approach to year-round recreational trail use.

Ontario Ski Council, *Cross-Country Ski Trail and Facility Design Manual.* Toronto: Ontario Ski Council, 1980.
A loose-leaf compendium handbook, the most complete and comprehensive available.

WAXING

Brady, M.M., and Skjemstad, L., *Waxing for Cross-Country Skiing.* Berkeley: Wilderness Press, 6th edition, 1981.
A pocket-sized, complete booklet on the subject.

WILDERNESS SKILLS

Ferber, P. (editor), *Mountaineering, The Freedom of the Hills.* Seattle: The Mountaineers, 3rd edition, 1979.
A source book for all who travel in wilderness.

Kjellstrom, B., *Be Expert with Map and Compass.* New York: Scribners, 1967.
A succinct paperback; none better.

Tejada-Flores, L., and Steck, A., *Wilderness Skiing.* San Francisco and New York: The Sierra Club, a "Totebook," 1972.
A standard reference, very readable and complete.

Index

Abdomen, and exercise, 113
ABS plastics, 165, 166
Accidents, 85, 86 (*See also* Falls; Injuries; Safety and
    survival techniques); slow down to avoid
    collisions, 84
Acrylic, defined, 255
Acute mountain sickness, 145–46
Addresses, 261
Adidas, 175
Adolescents, and sex differences, 127
Ads, for sports clothing, 17
Advanced skiers, and exercise level, 111, 113–14
Aerobic process, 114–15 ff., 118–20, 255
Aerobics (Cooper), 111
Age (*See also* Children): and exercise, 110; elderly
    racer, 99
Agility, defined, 255
Aircraft, no petroleum gas on, 220, 221
Airport, glider, 14
Alcohol, 87; hypothermia and, 144
Alpine skiing, 6–8, 46, 161, 217; and altitudes, 146;
    and avalanches, 151; closeness of races, 94–95;
    defined, 255; and hair bases, 166; wood skis
    and, 163
Alpine ski touring, 6
Alps, 6
Altitude, 145–47; elevations for racing, 93; and
    waxing, 213
Aluminum alloy poles, 180
American Alpine Journal, The, 145n
Amnesia, and hypothermia, 144
AMS, 145–46
Anaerobic process, 114, 117 ff., 255
Animals, and insulation, 191
Ankles, 30, 48, 54. *See also* specific maneuvers
Anorak, defined, 255
Apathy, hypothermia and, 144

Aramid-fiber skis, 163
Arctic region, 141. *See also* specific expeditions
Arm exercisers (trainers), 121, 255
Arms, 29, 113, 120, 121. *See also* Poles; Strides;
    specific maneuvers
Artificial snow, 213
Asia, and kick turns, 42
Associations, 261
Athletics, How to Become a Champion, 111
Athletic supporters, 191
Aunli, Berit, 92, 233
Auran Club, 230
Austria, 6
Automobiles. *See* Cars
Avalanches, 150–54; defined, 255; literature on, 262
Awls, 222

Back, exercise for, 113; lifts, 112, 114
Backache, 34
Backpacks. *See* Packs
Backslip (*See also* Slipping): defined, 255
Bail, defined, 255
Balaclava helmets, 193
Bandages, adhesive, 89
Band-Aids, 222
Barbed wire, 90
Bard, Alan, 13, 233
Base (*See also* Skis): defined, 157, 255
Base flatness, 169
Base preparations, 201, 266
Base waxes (binders), 201, 208, 211, 214, 217
Baskets (*See also* Poles): defined, 255
Bears, grizzly, 191
"Beats," 40
Beech-wood bases, 165
Be Expert with Map and Compass, 140

265

Beginners (*See also* Learning and instruction): and
    exercise level, 111, 113
Belly button, 15–16
Biafo Glacier, 7
Biathlon, defined, 255
Bib knickers, 255. *See also* Knickers
"Bicycle bumps," 70
Bicycling. *See* Cycling
Binders. *See* Base waxes
Bindings, 174–75, 176–77, 178, 179; defined, 255;
    for kids, 133–34; four categories of, 158, 159;
    and race-day preparations, 100
Biomechanics, 262
Birch bases, 165
Birkebeiner citizens' races, 3, 97
Bivouacs, 143, 148–49
Blackout, epoxy and, 225
Blisters, frostbite and, 142
Blood, blood pressure, and fluid loss, 145
Bobbing, 47
Body building. *See* Weight lifting and body building
Body heat. *See* Clothing; Safety and survival
    techniques
Books, 262–63
Boots, 164, 174–78, 179, 195; for bivouacs, 148;
    four categories of, 158, 159; height related to
    ski width, 160; kids', 133; and race-day
    preparations, 100
Bowed bases, 169, 255
Bower, John, 232
Box, defined, 157, 255
Boys. *See* Sexes
Bra, sports, 191
Braa, Oddva, 95
Brain (cerebral) edema (CE), 145, 146
Breath (*See also* Lungs): altitude and shortness of,
    146; exhalation and moisture loss 83
Briefs, 191, 196
Brooks, 89–90
Brushes, paint, 222
Bumps and dips, 68–70
Butane gas, 220, 221

Cable, Wisconsin, 97
Cable binding (*See also* Bindings): defined, 255
Caldwell, Hep, 127
Caldwell, John, 127, 200
Caldwell, Tim, 231
Calories, 186, 189, 255
Camber and stiffness, 157, 170–74, 256
Camels, 16
Camel walk, 31
Canadians, and gloveless racing, 193

Canadian Ski Association (CSA), 92, 100, 261
Canadian Ski Museum, 261
Candles: base-repair, 222, 224; for bivouac, 149
Canoeing, 121
Caps, 86, 88, 192–93, 195, 196; and avalanche
    danger, 153; for children, 134
Carbohydrates, 114
Carbon-fiber equipment, 163, 180, 214
Caribou, 191
Cars (autos; driving), 212–13; engines, 115; learning
    to drive, 18; and weather, 24
Carter, Tom, 233
"Catalog-syndrome skier," 87
Cerebral edema (CE), 145, 146
Cerutty, Percy Wells, 111
Cheeks, and frostbite, 141
Children, 10, 11, 125–34, 161, 183 (*See also* Juniors);
    book on racing for, 262; equipment and clothing
    for, 132–34; and family skiing, 127–28; and
    learning by doing, 128–32; start easy for, keep
    it simple, 126; who and how soon?, 127
"Children's skis," 132, 133
Chill. *See* Clothing; Cold; Safety and survival
    techniques; Wind chill
China, 134
Chop, 31
Christiania turn (christie), 66, 256. *See also* Stem
    christies
Chronology, 228–34
Chutes, 74–75, 90; and avalanches, 151
CISM, 256
Citizens' races, 3, 92, 95–96, 97 (*See also* Fitness and
    training); hours of training for, 124; how to
    start, 100; skill and, 100
Clamps. *See* Ski testers
Classified races, 91, 92–95, 100. *See also* Racing
Cleaners: hand, 220; solvents, 201, 206–8, 219,
    220–23
Clo, 191; defined, 256
Clothing, 87–88, 164, 185–96; basics, 190; for
    bivouac, 149; children's, 132, 134; four
    categories, 158, 159; and frostbite, 142; hands,
    193; head, 192–93; and hypothermia, 144; legs
    and feet, 193–95; models, 13, 17; practical
    outfits, 195–96; race-day, 100, 101; selecting,
    191–92; skin outward, 190–91; in starting to
    learn, 23
Clouds, and waxing, 214
"Coaching," 11
Cold, 140–47 (*See also* Safety and survival
    techniques); clothing and, 186–89 (*See also*
    Clothing)
Collar, defined, 256
Collisions, slowing down to avoid, 84

Coma, altitude and, 146
"Combined," defined, 256
Compasses, 81, 88, 140, 143
Conditioning. *See* Fitness and training
Conduction heat loss, 142
Confusion, hypothermia and, 144
Contact length, defined, 157
Convection heat loss, 142
Conway Saddle, 146
Cooper, Kenneth H., 111
Coordination: altitude and, 146; hypothermia and, 144
Core, defined, 157, 256
Corks, 219 (*See also* Waxing); defined, 256; in race-day gear, 100
Corn (type of snow), 256
Cotton, 164, 190
Couloirs, and avalanches, 151
Course, defined, 256
Cramps, 34
Creeks, 89–90
Crimean War, 193
"Cross-country," defined, 256
Cross-country downhilling. *See* Telemarking
Cross-Country Skier, 261
Cross-Country Ski Gear, 157
Cross-Country Skiing, 200
Cross-Country Skiing Today, 200
Cross-Country Ski Magazine, 261
"Cross-country ski racing," 6
Cross-country waxing, 201–2. *See also* Waxing
Crouch, 54
Crust, 76–77; defined, 256
CSA. *See* Canadian Ski Association
Curves, slowing down at, 84
Cycle ergometer, 114, 115, 256
Cycling (bicycling), 12, 114, 118, 120; and calories, 189

Day tours, 79–90 (*See also* Tours): clothing and equipment for, 87–89; know where you go, 80–81; obstacles and the unexpected, 89–90; on-trail nourishment, 83–87; picking a tour, 80; and skiing weather, 81–83
Dehydration, 144–45; altitude and, 145; and hypothermia, 143
Delamination, 69, 224
Diagonal stride, 14–19, 22, 25–34, 102–3; changing from, 38–39; defined, 23, 256; knee drive and hip block, 39; in racing efficiency, 107; troubles with, 29–34; uphill, 46, 47–49; and washboard, 69
DIN, 256

Dips (exercises), 112
Dips and bumps, 68–70
Dirt, 76, 89, 161, 211
Disorientation, hypothermia and, 144
Distance training, 118, 124, 256
Dizziness, epoxy and, 225
Dogs, 84; and pulks, 183
Double camber, defined, 256
Double poling and double-pole stride, 35–38, 70, 72, 73, 104–5; changing to and from, 38–39; defined, 23, 256; and icing, 75; troubles with, 36–38; and washboard, 69
Downhill, 4, 6, 11, 51–56 (*See also* Alpine skiing; Chutes; Tracks; specific maneuvers); and snow difficulties, 76; and stability, 52–54; straight, 54–56; and tip flex, 170; and tracks ending, 73; turns, 52, 56–66 (*See also* Turns); and washboard, 69, 70
Drinks (liquids), 83 (*See also* Dehydration); in bivouac, 149; in race-day preparations, 101; on trips, 83–87
Drowsiness, and hypothermia, 144
Dynafit, 175
"Dynamic," defined, 256
Dynamic forces, 16

Ears, and frostbite, 141
East, the: and avalanches, 150; and chutes, 74
Edema, altitude and, 145, 146
Edge, defined, 256
Edging, 58, 76
Eggen, Gjermund, 93, 232
Egg position, 54–55, 256
Elevation. *See* Altitude
Ellesmere Island, 4, 183
Emergencies. *See* Safety and survival techniques
Encyclopaedia Britannica, 3
Endurance, 113, 118, 121; defined, 256
Energy, 188 (*See also* Fitness and training; Safety and survival techniques); joules to measure, 186; and various activities, 189
Epoxy, 222, 224, 225; defined, 256
Equipment (gear), 155–83 (*See also* specific items); and avalanche danger, 153; best is best for you, 157–58; book on, 262; checking on, 84; for children, 132–34; race-day, 100, 101; start big, end small, 156–57; starting with good, 23; start with the obvious, 158–60; for trips, 87–89; types four, 158–59
Erect stance, 54
ERG, 83, 101
Ergometers, cycle, 114, 115; defined, 256
Erratic behavior, hypothermia and, 144

Groin, 191
Grönningen, Harald, 95
Groove, defined, 157, 256
Group lessons, 11
Groups, skiing in, 80, 143
Grundvalla, defined, 257

Hair bases, 166; defined, 257
Hair dryers, 211
Hallucinations (visions), 12; altitude and, 146
Hands, 193 (*See also* Gloves; Mittens; Poles); and
   downhill, 53
HAPE, 145, 146
Hard pack snow (*See also* Tracks; specific equipment;
   maneuvers): and downhill difficulties, 76
Hard waxes, 200, 204, 207, 218; defined, 257
Hare and hounds game, 131–32
head, 192–93 (*See also* Frostbite; specific coverings);
   and skiing cramps, 34
Headache, altitude and, 145, 146
Headbands, 88, 193
Headlamps, 88
Health (*See also* Fitness and training): and racing,
   98–99
Heart, 110, 114. *See also* Endurance
Heat. *See* Clothing; Energy; Safety and survival
   techniques; Sun
Heel plates, 176–77; defined, 257
Height (*See also* specific equipment): of course, and
   race regulations, 93; ski, defined, 157; weight in
   relation to, 114
Herringbone, 46, 49–50; defined, 257; and uphill
   chutes, 74
Heterogeneous bases, 167
Hickory bases, 165
Hide-and-seek, 130
High-altitude pulmonary edema (HAPE), 145, 146
High-performance skis (*See also* Racing; Racing skis;
   specific materials); waxing, 214–17
Hiking, 89, 117; and hypothermia, 142; and
   speed, 4
Hills, 45–66 (*See also* Racing; Safety and survival
   techniques; Tracks); chutes, 74–75; downhill,
   46, 51–66 (*See also* Downhill); uphill, 46–51 (*See
   also* Uphill); and washboard, 69–70
Hip block, 39
History of Lapland, The, 1, 227
Holmenkollen race, 95, 231, 232, 234, 235
Honeycomb, defined, 257
Hoods, 192, 193
Horse, waxing, 216
Houston, Charles, 145n
Humidity, 214

Huttunan, Miina, 229
Hypothermia, 87, 140, 142–44; defined, 257; and
   dehydration, 145
Hytrel, defined, 257

Ice (*See also* Icing): in chutes, 90; and downhill
   difficulties, 76; hair bases and, 166
Icing, 75–76, 161
Igloos, 148
Imbricated, defined, 257
Imitation (imitation training; mimicking), 10, 12, 23,
   257
Impregnating, defined, 257
Injected boot, 257
Injected ski, 157, 257
Injuries, 85 (*See also* Safety and survival techniques);
   and first aid, evacuation, 147; and heel
   restraints, 177; and pain, 117
Ink, polyethylene skis and, 216
Inside swing kick, 42–43
Instruction. *See* Learning and instruction
Insulation, 187–88 ff. (*See also* Clothing); measuring,
   191
Intermediates, and exercise level, 111, 113
International Ski Federation, 84 (*See also* World Ski
   Championships); regulations, 93
Intersections, slow down at, 84
Interval training, 118–19, 120, 124, 257
In-track skiing. *See* Tracks
IOC, 257
Irons, waxing, 210, 211, 216, 219, 222, 260
Irrational behavior, hypothermia and, 144
Italy, 6

Jackets, 134, 196. *See also* Parkas
Jack Rabbit, 208
Jargon. *See* Vocabulary
Jeans, 142, 186
Jernberg, Sixten, 98
Jogging, 113–14, 116; on conditioning table, 112; to
   correct camel walk, 31; and race-day
   preparation, 101; in sand, 17; and speed, 4; on
   wet tracks, 72
Joules, 186
Jumping, 12, 66; jump turns on crust, 77; and
   Telemark turns, 64; wood skis and, 163
Juniors, 95, 231; race regulations for, 93
Junior skis, 132, 133

Karakorums, the, 7, 146
Kayak paddling, 121

Kevlar fiber, 214, 257
Kiandra, Australia, 228
Kicks, 14, 25–26 (*See also* Skis; Strides; specific
   maneuvers); defined, 23, 257; late, 32, 33;
   "scooter," 33; and washboard, 69
Kick turns, 42–43, 51, 257; for crust, 77; over
   fences, 90; in tracks, 70
Kiddie pack, defined, 257
Killy, Jean-Claude, 94, 95
Kilojoules, 186
Kits, wax, 222, 223
Kjellstrom, B., 140
Klister, 76, 172, 200, 206, 207, 210, 211, 218;
   defined, 257; in race-day gear, 100; for skare,
   76; Vaseline to remove from hands, 220
Klister-wax, 201, 206, 211; defined, 257
Knee drive, 39
Knees, 30, 47, 48 (*See also* specific maneuvers);
   exercise with arms and, 29
Knee socks, 186, 191, 193, 195; for kids, 134
Knickers, 186, 191, 192, 195; defined, 257; for kids,
   134
Knives, 88, 147, 222
Koch, Bill, 4, 234
Kofix, 166
Koltjina, Alevtina, 230
Korean War, 140
Kruckenhauser, Stefan, 126
Kulakova, Galina, 92, 98
Kumpulainen, Elsa, 229

Lactic acid (lactate), 115, 117
Lake Placid, New York, 92–93, 94, 193, 218
Lakes, and icing, 75
Lamination, 164; delamination, 69, 224
Langlauf, 6; defined, 257
Lapps, the, 1, 2
"Leading," 11
Learning and instruction, 9–19. *See also* Children;
   Terrain; specific maneuvers
Leather, for boots, 164, 176, 195
Legs (*See also* Kicks; Strides; specific maneuvers): and
   clothing, 193–95 (*See also* specific items);
   extension stride exercise, 112; and warm
   dressing in starting to learn, 23
Lessons. *See* Children; Learning and instruction
Lifts, 6
Lighter fluid, 206–8
Lighters, spark, 222
Light-touring equipment, 158–59, 160, 257
Light track, defined, 257
Lignostone, 165; defined, 257

Lips, hypothermia and blue, 144
Liquids. *See* Dehydration; Drinks
Literature, 262–63; magazines, 261
Littering, 86
Locals, listening to, 143
Long johns, for children, 134
Long run, 6
Lungs, 110, 114 (*See also* Endurance); altitude and
   edema, 146

Mackinaws, 190
McKinley, Mount, 13, 150
Magazines, 261
Mahre, Phil, 94
Males. *See* Racing; Sexes
Mantyranta, Eero, 95
Maps, 81, 88, 139–40, 143
Marathon runners, 12
Marlborough Pond, 4
Mate and closure, 169
Maximum strength, 121
Medical history, exercise and, 110
Medicine. *See* First aid
Medicine for Mountaineering, 147
Men. *See* Racing; Sexes
Mental pictures, 17
Midwest, the, and chutes, 74
Mieto, Juha, 95
Minerals, in snow, 213
Minnesota, 6
Mirror, use of, 15
Mitchell, Dick, 147
Mittens, 88, 180, 193, 195 (*See also* Poles); and
   avalanche danger, 153; for children, 134; to
   prevent frostbite, 142
Models, clothing, 13, 17
Mohair, 166; defined, 257
Money, 89
Mosesen, Ole, 218
Mountaineering downhill equipment (mountain
   skis), 159, 160, 257
Mountaineering First Aid, 147
Mountaineering: The Freedom of the Hills, 140
Mountains. *See* Alpine skiing; Safety and survival
   techniques
"Multiple-beat diagonal" ("multi-step diagonal"), 40
Murstad, Tomm, 130, 131
Muscle stiffening, hypothermia and, 144
Muscular fitness (*See also* Fitness and training):
   defined, 257
Muscular strength. *See* Strength
Museums, 261

Naltene, 166
Nansen, Fridtjof, 200
Napoleon, 140
Natural interval training, 118–19
Natural stance, 54, 257
Nausea: altitude and, 145; epoxy and, 225
New Jersey, lost skiers in, 138
New snow (*See also* Powder snow; specific equipment, maneuvers): and icing, 75; and wobbly tracks, 72
New Zealand, 136, 233
Noise, waxless skis and, 162
"Nordic," defined, 257
Nordic Norm, 174, 175, 178, 179; defined, 257; children's equipment, 133, 134
"Nordic skiing," 6
Nordic World Ski Championships. *See* World Ski Championships
Norheim, Sondre, 66
Norm 38, 174–75, 178, 179; defined, 257
Norpine skiing. *See* Telemarking
Norway, 3, 16, 66 (*See also* World Ski Championships); ancient pictograph, 2; instruction in, 18, 130–31
Nose, and frostbite, 141
Notebooks, 222
Notifying others of route, 86, 143
NSPS, 258
Nylon, 191, 192, 195, 196; overboots, 193

Oilstone, 222
Olav V, King, 232
Ole's Special wax, 218
Olympics (*See also* Winter Olympics): motto of, 111
Orange slices, as race-day food, 101
Orientation, 81
Orienteering, 81, 258
Oslo, Norway, 66, 92; children's ski school in, 130–31
Out-of-track skiing, 13 (*See also* Tours); equipment, 159; and flex, 170; and slipping on hills, 49; wobbly tracks and, 73
Outrigger obsession, 29–30
Outside swing kick, 42–43
Overboots, 193–95
Overdistance training, 118
Owen, Allison, 231, 234
OWG, defined, 258
Oxidation, 216
Oxygen (*See also* Aerobic process): altitude and, 145–46; debt, 115, 258; uptake, 258

Pacific Northwest, avalanches in, 150
Packs, 82–83, 181–82; and avalanche danger, 153; for bivouac, 148; imagine wearing, to cure backache, 34
Pain, 117
Painter, Hal, 200
Panties, 196
Pants, 134. *See also* Jeans; Suits
Paper test, for camber, 173
Paraffin wax, 201, 215–16, 217, 225
Parallel turns, 61–64, 258; in chutes, 75; for crust, 77
Parkas, 188, 190, 192, 193
Park maps, 139
Passgang, 16; defined, 258
Passing other skiers, 84–85
Pattern bases, 161, 166–67; defined, 258
Performance waxing, 202
Perrialt, Guy, 95
Perspiration (sweat), 83, 88, 189 ff.; and dehydration, 144–45; feet and, 195; hands and, 193
Petroleum gas, 220, 221
Petroleum waxes, 207
Pets, leaving at home, 84
Physiology, literature on, 262
Pickup game, 132
Pictograph, ancient, 2
Pictorial relief maps, 81
Pin, defined, 258
Pin binding (*See also* Bindings): defined, 258
Pine trees, 73
Pioneers on Skis, 200
Plastic bags: to melt snow, 145; for race-day warm-up, 101–2; for skis, 214
Plastics. *See* Synthetics; specific equipment, materials
Playboy, 200
Pole plant (pole set), 23, 258
Poles (poling), 25, 28–29, 31, 178–81 (*See also* Strides; Terrain specific maneuvers); and avalanche danger, 153; for bivouac, 148; for children, 134; and children's training in Norway, 131; definition of poling, 23, 258; double poling (*See* Double poling and double-pole stride); extra baskets, 222; four categories, 158, 159; keep in close, 85; and outrigger obsession, 29–30; tired poling, 32–33; Tonkin, 164, 180, 259
Pole set (pole plant), 23, 258
Pole stop, 36–37
Pole straps. *See* Straps
Polyethylene, 165, 166, 210, 215 (*See also* Waxless skis); "candles," 222, 224

Polypropylene bases, 165
Polypropylene tricot, 190
PolySport, 190
Poplin, 191, 192, 195, 196; mitten shells of, 193; overboots of, 193
Positive base, defined, 258
Powder snow, 211–12, 258 (*See also* New snow); and downhill difficulties, 76; hair and pattern bases and, 166; in hard, cold tracks, 72; and waxing, 218
Propane gas, 220, 221
Property, respecting, 86
P-Tex, 166, 258
Pulks, 126, 128, 181 ff.; defined, 258
Pullover socks, defined, 258
Pulmonary edema. *See* HAPE
Pulse, 115, 118; hypothermia and, 144
Push-ups, 112, 114
Putney, Vermont, 4

"Racer-image skier," 87–88
Racing (racers), 6, 91–107; book for children, 262; and Calories, 189; and camber stiffness, 171, 172; closeness of cross-country, 94–95; clothing for, 195–96; equipment for, 158 (*See also* specific equipment); fitness and training, 116–22, 124; hand protection, 193; how to start, 100; instruction by racers, 12; international regulations, 93; major race results, 236–53; race day, 100; spectrum of, 92–97; speeds, 4; and suits, 192; think ahead, judge yourself regarding, 98–99; and tip flex, 170; various strides shown, 102–3, 104–5; wherewithal for, 102–7
Racing Norm, 174–75, 178, 179; defined, 258
Racing poles, 180, 181
Racing skis, 160 (*See also* High-performance skis); and sidecut, 168
Radiation of heat, 142
Railed bases, 169, 258
Rain, and hypothermia, 142
Raratonga, 19
Red Cross, 147
Relays, 93, 258; race regulations, 93
Repetition, 24
Repetitive strength, 121
Reporting situations, 86
Resilience, defined, 258
Reynolds, Jan, 136
Right side, keeping to, 85
Road crossings, 90
Robson Channel, 183
Rockwell, Martha, 231

Rocky chutes, 90
Rocky Mountains, 6; and avalanches, 150
Roller skiing, 121–22, 124; defined, 258
Route and destination: knowing, 80–81, 84; notifying others of, 86, 143
Rubber overboots, 193
Rucksacks, 181; defined, 258
Rules of conduct, 84–86
"Runner's drinks," 83, 101
Running, 17, 113–14, 118–19; marathon, 12; and speeds, 4
Russia and Russians, 93 (*See also* specific skiers); and gloveless racing, 193; and hip block, 39; and Napoleon's campaign, 140
Ruth Glacier, 13, 150

Safety and survival techniques, 11, 84, 137–54; avalanches, 150–54; avoid, but expect, emergencies, 138; bivouacs, 148–49; cold: friend and potential foe, 140–47; first aid and evacuation, 147–48; know where you are, 138–40; literature on wilderness skills, 263
Salomon System, 175, 179
Salt, 90, 145, 213; and saltwater, 214
Sanctioned races. *See* Classified races
Sand, 17, 19, 90
Sandpaper, 222
Sandwich, ski, 157, 258
Scale, and weighting, 17
Scalp, 192
Scandinavia, 3, 6n (*See also* specific locations); and ideal weight, 114; pulks in, 183; and wilderness safety, 143
Scheffer, Johan, 1, 2, 227
Scooter kick, 33
Scouring pads, 222
Scrapers (and scraper-corks), 88, 206, 207, 219, 222 (*See also* Waxing); and icing, 75–76; in race-day gear, 100
Scratches, 224
Screws and screwdrivers, 88, 222, 224
Sears Tower, 110
Second World War, 140
Seefeld, Austria, 234
Selected waxing, 202
Sexes (*See also* Racing): and Calorie consumption, 189; and children's abilities, 127
Shaft, defined, 258
Sheehan, George, 111
Sheep, Dall, 191
Shirts, 191, 195, 196
Shivering, and hypothermia, 144
Shoulder, ski, defined, 157, 258

Shovel (ski part), defined, 258
Showering, post-race, 102
SIA, 258
Side camber. *See* Sidecut
Sidecut, 157, 167–68; defined, 258
Sideslip, 58; defined, 258
Sidestep, 46, 50
Side-sway, 47
Sidewalls, 157; defined, 258
Sierras, the, and avalanches, 150
Signs, obeying, 86
Sikling, defined, 258
Silicone sprays, 166, 195
Simulation, 15
Sit, the (sitting), 36, 37, 48; and herringbone, 50
Sit-ups, 112
Skare, 76–77; defined, 258
Skaters and skating, 12, 22
Skating steps, to change tracks, 72
Skating turns, 41, 59, 70; defined, 258
Sketch maps, 81, 139–40
Ski Canada, 261
Skiing (souvenir book), 200
Skiing Magazine, 261
Skill, and racing, 99
Skilled skiers, 23; and clothing, 195–96; and speed, 4; various strides shown, 102–3, 104–5
Ski Magazine, 261
Skin (*See also* Frostbite): and epoxy, 225
Ski News, 53
Skimuseet, 261
Ski Racing, 261
Skis, 160–74 (*See also* Racing; Terrain Tours; specific maneuvers,); and avalanche danger, 153; bagging, 214; bases: waxless and waxable, 134–37, 160–67; for bivouac, 148; camber and stiffness, 170–74; care and repair, 223–24; for children, 132–33; common defects, 169; and continual slip, 33, 34; and dirt, 76, 89, 161, 211; finding center zone, 215; and first aid, evacuation, 147; flex and stiffness, 168–70; four categories, 158, 159; and icing, 75–76, 161; length of, 168; mounting bindings (*See* Bindings); prepping bases, 215–16; and race-day preparations, 100; roller, 121–22, 124, 258; side shape, 167–68; starting with good equipment, 23; storing, 224–25; structure: wood versus fiberglass, 163–65; and washboard, 69; waxing and care of, 199–203 (*See also* Waxing)
Ski striding, defined, 258
Ski testers, 172–73
Ski tips. *See* Tips
Ski touring. *See* Touring; Tours
Slab avalanches, 152

Slap, ski, 30–31, 37–38
Sleds (*See also* Pulks): improvised, for evacuation, 147
Slipping, 33–34, 48–49. *See also* Skis; Uphill; specific strides
Slush, pattern bases for, 167
Smetanina, Raisa, 91
Smoking (tobacco): and exercise, 110; and hypothermia, 144
Snow, 67–77 (*See also* Safety and survival techniques; Skis; Tracks; specific maneuvers, equipment); avalanches, 150–54, 255, 262; and camber stiffness, 171–72; and chutes, 74–75; don't apply to frostbite, 141; downhill difficulties with, 76; impossible conditions and slipping, 34; literature on, 263; melting, to prevent dehydration, 145; temperature ranges, 217–18; unruly, 75–76; and waxing, 200–2, 203 (*See also* Waxing); what's coming?, 68; wind-drifted snow and skare, 76–77
Snowmobiles, 15, 259
Snowplow, 55–56, 259; in chutes, 74–75; in tracks, 70
Snowplow turns, 56–58, 60, 259
Snowshoe baskets, 180
Soccer, ski, 132
Socks, 88, 176, 195, 196 (*See also* Knee socks); for bivouac, 148
Soldering irons, 210, 219
Sole, defined, 259
Solvents. *See under* Cleaners
Southern Cross Expedition, 233
Spades, snow, 148
Speech, hypothermia and slurred, 144
Speed, 4, 17 (*See also* Downhill; Racing; Tracks); slow down at certain points, 84
Speed training, defined, 259
Speed waxes. *See* Glide waxes
Splay, 169
Splits, defined, 259
Spring, 214 (*See also* Fitness and training); and sun on tracks, 73
Squat, 31, 54
Staggering, altitude and, 146
Stanley Tools, 219
Star turns, 40, 41
Steel poles, 180
Stem christies (christianias), 60, 259; in chutes, 75; and parallel turns, 63
Stem turns (*See also* Stem christies): defined, 259
Stenmark, Ingemar, 94
Step, defined, 259
Step test, defined, 259
Step turns, 41, 59, 70; defined, 259
Stilt step, 30

Transport-type underwear, 191, 195, 196; part of race-day gear, 100
Traversing, 46, 51, 259; for crust, 77
Treadmills, 114
Treasure hunt, 130
Trees (woods): and icing, 75; pine, 73; and winds, 82
Trips (tours), 79–90, 128, 134 (*See also* Fitness and training; Safety and survival techniques); clothes and equipment, 87–89; know where you go, 80–81; obstacles and the unexpected, 89–90; on-trail nourishment, 83–87; picking a tour, 80; and skiing weather, 81–83
Trolls, 199
Trunk, the, 113, 121
T-shirts, 196
Tuque, defined, 259
Turns, 40–41, 56–65, 70, 76 (*See also* specific types); and bumps, 69–70; on crust, 77; edging and, 58; and flex, 170; and heel plates, 176–77; in tracks, 70
Turpentine, 208
Turtlenecks, 195
Twist, in skis, 169
"Two-beat diagonal" ("two-step diagonal"), 40
Two-wax system, 162, 202, 208–9

UIPMB, 259
Unconsciousness, hypothermia and, 144
Underwear, 100, 191, 195, 196
United States Biathlon Association, 261
United States Eastern Amateur Ski Association, 53
United States Ski Association (USSA), 4, 92, 100, 261
United States Ski Coaches Association, 261
United States Ski Hall of Fame, 261
Uphill, 46–51, 120; in chutes, 74; racing training, 121; and troubles, 48–49; and washboard, 69, 70
Uphill diagonal stride. *See* Uphill
USSA. *See* United States Ski Association
USST, 260

Vaseline, 89, 142, 220
Velcro, defined, 260
Videotape, 17
Vises, waxing, 223
Visions (hallucinations), 12; altitude and, 146
Vocabulary, 23, 157, 255–60
Vomiting, altitude and, 146
Vulcanized boot, defined, 260

Waist, ski, defined, 157
Waivers, for racing, 100
Walking, 15, 16, 18, 25, 26–27, 98, 110, 113 (*See also* Hiking); and Calories, 155, 189; conditioning table, 112; and picking skiing tour, 80; in ski boots, 177–78; and speed, 4
Warm-up and -down, 122; plastic bags for race-day warm-up, 101–2
Warm-up suits, 192
Warning, shouting, 84–85
Warp, 169
Washouts, trail, 89–90
Washboard, 68–70
Wassberg, Thomas, 94, 95, 218
Water: for frostbite, 142; saltwater, 214; and skis, 75
Waterproofing. *See* Base preparations; specific equipment
Waterskiing, 46
Waxable skis (*See also* Skis): defined, 260
Waxing, 163, 199–223 (*See also* Racing; Skis; specific equipment, maneuvers, terrain); aids, 219–23; book on, 263; and continual slip, 33, 34; and dirt, 76; high-performance skis, 214–17; leap into the art, 209–11; look at snow first, 203–4; putting it on, 204–6; taking it off, 206–8; thoughts on, 200; three ways to go, 202; tricks for connoisseurs, 217–18; tricks of the trade, 211–14; two waxes are first resort, 208–9; types of waxable bases, 165–66; what's in wax, 207; "why" of, 200–2
Waxless skis, 160–65, 166–67 (*See also* Racing; specific materials); for children, 132, 161; and continual slip, 33; defined, 260; and dirt, 76; and slipping on hills, 49; and starting on flat, 23
Wax remover (*See also* Cleaners): defined, 260
Wax zone, defined, 260
Weakness: altitude and, 145–46; dehydration and, 145–46
Weasels, 191
Weather, 81–83 (*See also* Safety and survival techniques; Snow; Tours); forecasts, 143
Wedge, defined, 260
Weight (*See also* Weight shift): benefits of light equipment, 156; and camber, stiffness, 171; and exercise, 110; in relation to height, 114; versus strength, 113
Weight shift (weighting), 16–17, 76 (*See also* Strides; specific maneuvers); defined, 23, 260
Weight lifting and body building, 113, 121
Wenzel, Hanni, 94
West, the: and avalanches, 150; and chutes, 74
Western American Skisport Museum, 261

Wet clothing. *See* Clothing; Safety and survival techniques
Wet snow (*See also* Skis; Waxing): and icing, 75; in tracks, 72
Whiteouts, 82
Wide-range waxing, defined, 260
Wide-track skiing, 52, 260
Wiens, Doug, 13, 183
Wiggling, 34
Wilderness. *See* Safety and survival techniques
Wilkerson, James, 147
Wind, 82, 86 (*See also* Clothing; Wind chill); and avalanches, 150–51, 152; resistance, and downhill, 54; and waxing, 214
Wind chill, 188, 194, 260
Wind-drifted snow, 76–77
Winter (*See also* Racing; Safety and survival techniques; Tours): sun and direction-finding, 81; and sun on tracks, 73
Winter Olympics, 71, 73, 92–93, 94, 95, 98, 193, 218, 234; best in, 231–53
Wintersport Museum, 261
Wobbly tracks, 72–73
Wolves, 191
Women. *See* Racing; Sexes
Woods. *See* Trees

Wood skis, 162, 164, 260 (*See also* Skis); versus fiberglass, 163–65; and washboard, 69; waxable bases, 134–35
Wool, 164, 190, 195. *See also* specific items
World Cup, 253–54, 260
World Loppet League, 94, 260
World Ski Championships (WSC), 92, 93, 98, 230 ff., 260 (*See also* Winter Olympics); Children's Day, 135
World Trade Center, 110
Wrist straps, 222, 260 (*See also* Poles); and race-day preparations, 100
WSC. *See* World Ski Championships
Wu Ming Su, 134

XC, defined, 260

Yangshou, China, 134
Yawing, 169

Zigzagging, 46, 51
Zimjatov, Nikolai, 92–93